Praise for *While Canada Slept*

"Relentlessly chronicles just how far this country has fallen from global grace." – *Ottawa Citizen*

"A serious critique. . . . In well-crafted prose and on a foundation of extensive knowledge of our diplomatic history, Cohen recounts a tale of how we have created . . . a make-believe foreign policy."
– Richard Gwyn, *Toronto Star*

"Cohen is an erudite man. . . . A damning and timely indictment. Paul Martin should read Cohen's book and wince."
– Graham Fraser, *Toronto Star*

"A trenchant critique of modern Canadian foreign policy."
– *Time Magazine*

"Cohen's contribution is invaluable. A book full of . . . rich detail, written with passion and engaging prose. . . . A must read for all of those who wish to understand the roots of Canada's global outlook."
– Jennifer Welsh, *The Globe and Mail*

"Mr. Cohen . . . has hit the bull's-eye."
– Jeffrey Simpson, *The Globe and Mail*

"There could hardly be a better time for *While Canada Slept*, Andrew Cohen's cogent and sobering survey of this country's long slide into the margins of global importance. . . . A powerful indictment of how we've neglected our role in the world." – *Victoria Times-Colonist*

"Provocative and persuasive. . . . [Cohen's] arguments are persuasive and ably defended in a book that is brisk, on the mark and wonderfully readable." – *London Free Press*

"Persuasive and compelling. . . . A long-awaited wake-up call to Canadians who have for years been blinded in a glare of self-satisfaction about their own international importance." – *Halifax Chronicle-Herald*

ALSO BY ANDREW COHEN

While Canada Slept: How We Lost
Our Place in the World (2003)

Trudeau's Shadow: The Life and Legacy of Pierre
Elliott Trudeau (with J.L. Granatstein, 1998)

A Deal Undone: The Making and Breaking of
the Meech Lake Accord (1990)

THE UNFINISHED CANADIAN

THE PEOPLE WE ARE

ANDREW COHEN

McCLELLAND & STEWART

971
C678v
2007

Library and Archives Canada Cataloguing in Publication

Cohen, Andrew, 1955-
The unfinished Canadian : the people we are / Andrew Cohen.

ISBN-: 978-0-7710-2181-7

1. National characteristics, Canadian. I. Title.

FC97.C59 2007   971   C2006-904296-9

We acknowledge the financial support of the Government of Canada through the Book Publishing Industry Development Program and that of the Government of Ontario through the Ontario Media Development Corporation's Ontario Book Initiative. We further acknowledge the support of the Canada Council for the Arts and the Ontario Arts Council for our publishing program.

"W.L.M.K." on page 223 is from *F.R. Scott: Selected Poems*. Used by permission.

Typeset in Janson by M&S, Toronto
Printed and bound in Canada

McClelland & Stewart Ltd.
75 Sherbourne Street
Toronto, Ontario
M5A 2P9
www.mcclelland.com

2   3   4   5   11   10   09   08   07

For my father, Edgar Horace Cohen,
from whom I learned much.

CONTENTS

Introduction

At the 2006 Winter Olympics in Turin, the Canadian women's hockey team did not lose a game. They did not defeat their opponents; they *destroyed* them. They beat Italy 16–0, Russia 12–0, Sweden 8–1. When they dispatched Finland by a score of 6–0, it seemed like a squeaker. But instead of bringing a chorus of congratulations from home, their string of triumphs brought hissing and hand wringing. Don Cherry, whose redneck ramblings on *Hockey Night in Canada* enjoy a large following, accused the team of "running up the score. It is not the Canadian way." Father Raymond J. de Souza, a columnist with the *National Post*, said it was "unsporting" to win by humiliating margins and proposed abolishing women's hockey because other countries could not compete with teams like Canada's. Success had made the critics uncomfortable, suggesting that the only thing worse than losing in Canada is winning. Rather than taking pride in excellence, you see, Canadians should feel shame. Winning – or winning this big – simply isn't the Canadian Way.

Between 1924 and 1952, Canada's men's hockey teams dominated the game, too. Their reign ended when other countries iced better teams and began to beat the Canadians year after year.

Instead of our falling to their level, they rose to ours. Yet in women's hockey in 2006, it was un-Canadian to do your best. Winning was like stealing third base, feeling guilty, and going back. Cassie Campbell, the gifted team captain, wondered: "Why is women's hockey the only sport that gets put down for excellence? Why should we stop, and not get better?" It was a distinctly Canadian question, unimaginable in other countries.

Then again, this is Canada. We always have questions about ourselves. "How Canadian are you?" asked the banner headline over an article on second-generation immigrants in *The Globe and Mail* on January 12, 2007. On almost any day, you can find articles, books, or lectures plumbing the depths of the national soul. *What is a Canadian? Whither Canada? Why Canada? Whose Canada?* If we are not explaining ourselves, we are excusing ourselves. These are not only fundamental questions, they are existential. Most of all, they are questions of character. They tell us what we are about.

As central Canada basked in the balmiest January in memory, the Canadian Press pondered what Canada would do if winter were a casualty of global warming. Bad enough that our northern dominion would lose polar bears, glaciers, and skiing; worse, we might lose our very identity. Perhaps that was why the prime minister created a new sub-cabinet portfolio that month called Multiculturalism and National Identity, as if he thought it necessary to put identity under ministerial protection.

Character, character. In December 2006, Stéphane Dion, the new leader of the Liberal Party of Canada, was asked whether he would renounce his dual citizenship if he became prime minister. Critics wondered where Dion's loyalty would lie – with Canada or with France. Also in December, the seventy-fifth anniversary of the Statute of Westminster, a British law which made Canada a sovereign nation, passed unnoticed, like so many historic anniversaries. In November, Parliament declared the Québécois "a nation" within Canada. It unleashed a tempest. A minister resigned, backbenchers dissented. It would be the end of Canada; it would be the renewal of Canada. The previous spring, after less than a day of debate, Parliament narrowly voted to extend Canada's military commitment in Afghanistan, Canada's first shooting war since Korea. And so it goes.

In the first decade of the twenty-first century, which no one dared claim would belong to Canada (as Sir Wilfrid Laurier famously declared in different words of the twentieth century), we could see our national character in that cascade of events – every day, every week, every month – as they tumbled down upon us.

Pondering ourselves is the occupational hazard of being Canadian. The Canadian Identity, as it has come to be known, is as elusive as the Sasquatch and Ogopogo. It has animated – and frustrated – generations of statesmen, historians, writers, artists, philosophers, and the National Film Board. Still, we try. "How could we assemble a collection of stories that would truly represent everything that Canada is – and everyone who lives there?" asked the earnest editors of *Chicken Soup for the Canadian Soul.* "At some point it became apparent that we simply could not." Instead, they published the reflections of Canadians about themselves and called it Canada. Some are saccharine, some are deeply affecting. But ultimately their chicken soup is thin gruel; it never really hits the spot. Canada resists easy definition.

In 2000, Canadians saw themselves in "The Rant," a popular beer commercial. "I have a prime minister, not a president . . ." Joe Canadian fumes. "I speak English and French, not American. I believe in peacekeeping, not policing; diversity, not assimilation." Well, it was a point of view, as they say, and characteristically, it was largely cast in the form of what we are *not.* At other times, we have seen ourselves in the novels of Margaret Atwood, Margaret Laurence, and Robertson Davies, the plays of Michel Tremblay, or the stories of Roch Carrier. Or the humour of Stephen Leacock or the history of Donald Creighton. Pierre Berton famously described the quintessential Canadian as having a capacity to make love in a canoe, proving that Canadians are both amorous and amphibious.

"I suppose that a Canadian is someone who has a logical reason to think he is one," writes Mavis Gallant, the expatriate Canadian, in an introduction to a collection of her short stories in 1981. "My logical reason is that I have never been anything else, nor has it occurred to me that I might be." From the beginning, we have looked for that reason, logical or visceral, so much so that we may think that we are unique in our search for ourselves. We aren't alone. In recent years, China, Taiwan, Denmark, Syria, Mexico, and other nations have questioned their identity. Samuel P. Huntington, the prominent American political scientist, says the United States is now among them. "America is not unique in having an identity problem," he says in *Who Are We?: The Challenges to America's National Identity*. "Debates over national identity are a pervasive characteristic of our time. Almost everywhere people have questioned, reconsidered, and redefined what they have in common and what distinguishes them from other people: Who are we? Where do we belong?"

The Unfinished Canadian looks for the answers in our experience – our past, our politics, our practices, our leaders, our institutions. All shed light on our shadowy selves. Rudyard Griffiths, the imaginative co-founder and executive director of the Dominion Institute, which promotes the study of the history of Canada, notes that it was "institutions and not the free play of ideas that Canadians came to rely upon in entrenching a common civic culture. From the exploits of the Royal Canadian Mounted Police to the driving of the Last Spike on the CPR, the country's history is filled with larger-than-life stories of how founding institutions tamed a continent and defined Canada's national character in the process."

Some of our characteristics as a people are clear. Some are contradictory. As much as this is a self-portrait, it is painted in broad brush rather than short strokes. Of little interest are the hoary shibboleths, the soothing mythologies, and the old saws that dominate our conversation. If we can find it, a little irreverence, unencumbered by our proverbial politeness and suffocating political correctness, would be refreshing.

There is so much that we are, in so many shades and hues. A study like this, which makes no claims to be comprehensive, is limited by its very nature. How to assign elements of character to a diverse, eclectic country of almost 33 million souls? How to decide which to include? Is our character not to have a character, as some suggest? The approach here is to draw on contemporary examples from our political and civic life, as well as our history. A disclaimer: this book is unscientific, selective and subjective. In offering examples, it makes no claim to regional, linguistic, or ethnic balance. It has commissioned no surveys, though it occasionally draws on them. Nor does it present a statistical portrait of Canada, much as statistics are sometimes useful, too.

This is a mix of reportage and reflection. If the tone is more critical than congratulatory, blame a journalist's natural skepticism. But to look critically at Canada in 2007 isn't to endorse the high priests of pessimism who always see darkness. In our worst times, such as the referendum of 1995, they believe that Canada is a failure and bet on it. In their world Quebec is always leaving, the dollar is always falling, crime is always rising, and the future is always fading. It is a view of the country that has inspired books called *The End of Canada* and *Breakup*. Then again, how many other nations have spent their lives asking themselves: Will we survive?

Today, on the 140th anniversary of Confederation, our challenge is to be frank about our country and our prospects. Too often we avoid what is uncomfortable or unattractive about ourselves.

We revere home truths and avoid hot buttons that could help us understand one another, preferring to dine on our warm purée of platitudes and consommé of clichés.

This study of national character begins with others. It looks first to the British, the French, and the Americans, identifying some of the attributes and impulses commonly associated with them. The hope is to understand how others define themselves, or are defined by others. We then turn to Canada. We examine character in history, recalling what visitors have said of Canadians, as a people, over the last century or so.

We examine memory and how we have forgotten our past; our enduring uneasiness with and misperception of Americans; and the nature of our citizenship, which is one of the easiest in the world to obtain. We look at our sleepy national capital, and how it reflects our national personality – or doesn't. Lastly, we turn to prominent elements of national character: envy, resentment, and pettiness; ambiguity and vagueness; moderation and compromise; and generosity and incivility. We find our character in the debate over the divergence of values between Canada and the United States; the winner of *The Greatest Canadian*; the state of our national museums and historic sites; the absence of national heroes; the pillorying of Adrienne Clarkson and the ascent of Michaëlle Jean; the other side of multiculturalism; the meaning of the national election of 2006; the vagueness of the Clarity Act; the flowering of the tall poppy syndrome, a byword for the dangers of becoming too successful.

Along the way, we try to answer some other questions. Why don't we teach our history? Why do we disparage politicians? Why do we begrudge leaders a proper place to live? Why does Ottawa look like a Prairie outpost? Why was Mackenzie King a shrewd leader? Why don't our wealthy give more to charity? Ultimately, we return to national character and ask whether we can be a more united, ambitious people and, more fundamentally, if we have what it takes to carry us through the next hundred years and beyond.

At root, the purpose of this little enterprise is to answer that imperishable question asked by Samuel Huntington, and so many others, in different places, at different times:

"Who are we? Where do we belong?"

Chapter 1

The Hybrid Canadian

On May 23, 1951, *The Love of Four Colonels* made its debut at Wyndham's Theatre in London. Written by Peter Ustinov, the play is a parody of four colonels administering a territory in Occupied Germany. Each of the colonels represents one of the great powers – and a few national stereotypes, too. The Briton is Desmond de S. Rinder-Sparrow; the Frenchman is Aimé Frappot; the Russian is Alexander Ikonenko; the American is Wesley Breitenspiegel. Each reflects his country as we imagine it. The Briton puffs on his pipe, "his eyes glazed in the manner of an Empire-builder hypnotized by his greatest enemy, the horizon." He refers with melancholy to the Charge of the Light Brigade, which he would like to have led. He likes dogs. The American is direct and impatient. He refers with resignation to Custer's Last Stand, a calamity for the army; he muses breezily about his psychiatrist. Desmond observes that Britons cannot afford psychiatrists (not that these people of the Stiff Upper Lip would understand them, anyway).

The Love of Four Colonels was Ustinov's first success. It played for two years in London, as well as in Paris and New York. Cosmopolitan that he was, Ustinov presents a witty but penetrating meditation on national character. Aimé is a resolute realist who laments that "my wife has always seemed to me to be so embarrassingly un-French." He likes "laughing at others but not at myself." Wesley is a confirmed romantic but surprisingly laconic. Alexander is a tribune of the people, who are "the legitimate owners" of everything. Desmond proposes "some good sound British common sense."

Later in this burlesque, our four horsemen find themselves in a vine-clad, eighteenth-century castle where they discover Sleeping Beauty. Driven by lust, they try to wake her and conquer her. All see in her his national ideal. To the American Wesley she has "red hair, like a flame"; to Desmond she is "a lovely, fair-haired English rose"; to Aimé she is "the dark Mediterranean beauty one finds in Marseilles"; to Alexander she is flaxen, like the "stout farm girls of the Ukraine."

As the colonels struggle to woo her, each drapes her in national history and wraps her in national mythology. When Aimé places her in pre-revolutionary France, Alexander muses about the working class. Desmond's ideal is "fair, lovely and desperately Elizabethan." Wesley's idealized woman, Rory, sits in a smoky after-hours speak-easy in a great metropolis. She calls herself "a working girl" and rails against guys who "try to smash the little things, and the beautiful deep things, and the U.S. Constitution." As for Alexander, his freckle-faced beauty with strong arms and child-bearing body sits in a Chekhovian garden in 1900. He, too, fails to stir her.

Ultimately, none will succeed. Each will surrender his ideal – but not before showing romance, idealism, practicality and resignation. The Russian and Englishman choose reality, and go home to their wives; the American and the Frenchman continue their romantic quest. Each tells us something about national character. As one theatre critic said, all nationalities have a great capacity to appreciate the foibles of others but only some of their own. Ustinov captured that.

What is national character? Hans J. Morgenthau, the great German political scientist, suggests national character is one of the elements of national power. In *Politics Among Nations: The Struggle for Power and Peace*, his classic textbook on international relations published in 1948 and revised many times since, he examines character alongside geography, natural resources, population, industrial capacity, and military preparedness. He cites national character and national morale for their "permanent and often decisive influence upon the weight a nation is able to put into the scales of international politics." In his view of world affairs, "certain qualities of intellect and character occur more frequently and are more highly valued in one nation than in another. These qualities set one nation apart from others, and they show a high degree of resiliency to change." In history and statecraft, he finds clear examples of French logic, British individualism, German authoritarianism. In Americans, he sees tension between pragmatism and idealism. In Russians, he sees a thread of "elementary force and persistence," words used first by Otto von Bismarck, the nineteenth-century German statesman. To Morgenthau, national character inevitably shapes national power. The reason? Those who make policies, represent the government abroad, and shape public opinion "all bear to a greater or lesser degree the imprint of those intellectual and moral qualities that make up the national character." In other words, common sense, inventiveness, initiative, discipline, and thoroughness – all ascribed to people – will ultimately manifest themselves in the actions of a nation.

One of the more unorthodox assessments of national character comes from Martin J. Gannon, a professor of business at the University of Maryland. He finds character – he calls it "cultural metaphor" – in any "activity, phenomenon, or institution" that represents a people's values. Gannon examines almost two dozen countries, identifying in each a single element that reflects a way of life. His book, *Understanding Global Cultures: Metaphorical Journeys*

Through 23 Nations, is a quirky if illuminating *tour d'horizon* of the peoples of the world.

He says, for example, that the most distinctive symbol of Japan is the spare, landscaped garden. In the garden he finds form and order. In Turkey, the symbol is the coffeehouse, which mixes elements of the religious and the secular. In Brazil, it is the Samba, which suggests passion. In Germany, it is the symphony, reflecting a society handling complexity in harmony. In Sweden, it is the *stuga*, or summer home, demonstrating a love of nature. In Ireland, it is conversation, the staff of life for a gregarious people in thrall to the melody and meaning of language. In Korea, it is *kimchi*, the country's most popular dish, cabbage preserved through immersion in salt and vinegar, which represents national self-preservation. In Israel, it is the kibbutz, or the collective farm, a deep-seated association with the land. In the United States, it is football, incorporating speed, competition, aggressiveness, and specialization. In Britain, the traditional house, "the three-bedroom semi-detached," is so standard that people know what to expect anywhere – as they know what to expect of each other.

Other countries, other metaphors. In the Italian opera, we see pageantry, beauty, and spectacle, an expression of emotion, the importance of chorus and soloists. In the Mexican fiesta, we see diversity, conviviality, piety, and history. In the Russian ballet, we see unpredictability, mystery, spirituality. In the Spanish bullfight, we see a fascination with the tragic, as well as pride, individualism, passion, and devotion to spectacle.

These are the varied and arresting musings of one cultural observer, not necessarily consistent or complete. Generally speaking, though, Gannon's canon addresses some of what explains a people. As for Canada, he says almost nothing at all.

Others tend to think of national character in terms of stereotypes and cliché. The Americans are aggressive, friendly, bombastic, bossy, parochial, vulgar, innovative, generous. The French are arrogant, sophisticated, refined, prejudiced; they eat well and dress well. The British are stuffy, aloof, detached, practical; they eat badly and dress badly. The Russians are rude, pushy, sentimental, determined. The Italians are amorous, charming, passionate, better lovers than soldiers. The Chinese are inscrutable. The Indians are spiritual. The Norwegians are humourless. The Japanese are docile. The Germans are formal.

In Canada, in the early years, there were no Japanese, Norwegians, Russians, and Chinese. Beyond native peoples, there were only the English, the French and, later, the Americans. Here are three of the world's great peoples who, by example and experience, have made us much of what we are. The country was explored, conquered, and colonized by the French and the English. The Americans exerted the same kind of influence, in more subtle ways, especially since the mid-twentieth century.

Bill Bryson, the American writer who lived in Britain from the early 1970s to the early 1990s, offers a wry, unsparing view of the British. In *Notes from a Small Island*, he writes of a visit to the fading glory of Bournemouth, a Victorian seaside resort. On a winter's day he sees a man and a woman on the porch of a tiny beach hut, sitting in lawn chairs, wrapped in coats and lap blankets against a relentless wind. They own the hut along the beach and are determined to use it, looking "as if this were the Seychelles and they were drinking gin fizzes under nodding palms, rather than sitting half-perished in a stiff English gale." They are happy to have what they have, and are cheered by the prospect that, maybe, if they were really cold, they could go inside and make a cup of tea and have a chocolate digestive biscuit.

From this, Bryson rhapsodizes about this "island race," as Winston Churchill called it. "One of the charms of the British is that they have so little idea of their own virtues," Bryson writes, "and nowhere is this more true than with their happiness. You will laugh to hear me say it, but they are the happiest people on earth. Honestly." Well, maybe. Bryson finds that the British are happy with small pleasures. It reflects a sense of restraint, a practicality in a small, crowded country defined by limits of class and space. Offer a Briton a choice of a chocolate or a piece of strawberry *gâteau* and he "will nearly always hesitate and begin to worry that it's unwarranted and excessive, as if any pleasure beyond a very modest threshold is vaguely unseemly." This kind of moderation, Bryson notes, is absolutely alien in America: "To an American the whole purpose of living, the one constant confirmation of continued existence, is to cram as much sensual pleasure as possible into one's mouth more or less continuously. Gratification, instant and lavish, is a birthright."

Of course, Bryson's Britain is changing. It is wealthier than it was in the 1970s and 1980s. A growing middle class that remembers little of the post-war privations is spending more and demanding more – dining out, buying holiday homes in France and Spain, acquiring all kinds of baubles. This has tested that much-heralded self-control. Fewer Britons are content with small pleasures any more, and it is unlikely their aristocracy ever was. Churchill was famous for his love of champagne, wine, caviar, cheese, silk sheets, and the finer things of life, some of which he took with him into the trenches of France in 1917. "My father was easily satisfied with the very best of everything," says his daughter, Lady Mary Soames, and so he was. But Bryson is on to something here regarding national character, both British and American. He recalls with relish a televised academic competition between teams of American and British students. The Britons won overwhelmingly, leaving them "wretched with embarrassment, since nothing causes the British deeper unease than to be seen to do exceptionally well at something." That hasn't changed.

Nor has Britain's exquisite eccentricity. "Nothing gives the English more pleasure, in a quiet but determined sort of way, than to do things oddly," Bryson writes of a nation that drives on the left side of the road, gives peculiar names to its villages and hamlets, navigates an impenetrable web of lanes, ways, and closes, and confers ancient titles on its patricians, real or imagined. When *As It Happens* on CBC Radio wants to find someone odd, you know who it will be: the dotty aunt with the house of cats in the Fens; the nutty publican building a boat of toothpicks in Conwy; the unhinged ornithologist in the Orkneys. No one does eccentric like the British.

What is particularly striking to Bryson as he rambles about the island is how deep, how old, and how varied the country is. "That is its glory, you see – that it manages at once to be intimate and small scale, and at the same time packed to bursting with incident and interest. I am constantly filled with admiration at this – at the way you can wander through a town like Oxford and in the space of a few hundred yards pass the home of Christopher Wren, the buildings where Halley found his comet and Boyle his first law, the track where Roger Bannister ran the first sub-four-minute mile, the meadow where Lewis Carroll strolled; or how you can stand on Snow's Hill at Windsor and see, in a single sweep, Windsor Castle, the playing fields of Eton, the churchyard where Gray wrote his 'Elegy,' the site where *The Merry Wives of Windsor* was first performed. Can there anywhere on earth be, in such a modest span, a landscape more packed with centuries of busy, productive attainment?"

Here we see a national character shaped by centuries of history. Bryson doesn't speak of the British endurance and resolve, but well he could. It was a theme Churchill sounded as he was rallying his people in the early days of the Second World War, when all Europe had fallen and England (and its dominions) stood alone against the Nazis. "The peoples of the British Empire may love peace," he told the House of Commons in Ottawa on December 30, 1941. "They do not seek the lands or wealth of any country, but they are a tough and hardy lot. We have not journeyed all this way across the centuries, across the oceans, across the mountains, across the prairies, because we are made of sugar candy." Later, he famously reminded his rapt audience of how the French had seriously underestimated the British. "In three weeks England will have her neck wrung like a chicken," he declared with scorn, referring to the mistaken prediction the French generals made to their prime minister. Then, with a theatrical pause, he added: "Some chicken! Some neck!"

A few days earlier, Sir Winston had asked the United States Congress: "What kind of people do they think we are?" In other words, what sane, prudent adversary could attack Britain and think they could come out ahead? "Is it possible that they do not realize that we shall never cease to persevere against them until they have been taught a lesson which they and the world will never forget?" Here was Churchill speaking of Britain at war, facing the greatest crisis of its history and asking that ageless question, *What kind of people do they think we are?*

Jeremy Paxman, Britain's popular television presenter, thinks things were clearer in the past. "Being English used to be so easy," he writes in *The English: A Portrait of a People*. "They were one of the most easily identified peoples on earth, recognized by their language, their manners, their clothes and the fact that they drank tea by the bucketload." The tweedy manner and sensible shoes are passé, no longer able to define a people as they once did. For one thing, English is less synonymous with British than it was two generations ago; the Scots and Welsh are quick to point out the differences, however small they may be. The appeal of Europe and the advance of commerce also pose a threat to British distinctiveness.

And yet. Whatever the argument of a changed Britain, it was their unflagging will that made the British a lousy target on July 7, 2005, when Islamic terrorists detonated bombs on buses and in subway cars in London. They killed fifty-two people. There was no great public panic, no renting of clothes or pulling of hair. No one said it was the end of the world. The next day, in an article headlined "With characteristic fortitude, Britons carry on," the *International Herald Tribune* reported: ". . . many people returned to work with a display of the renowned British stiff upper lip – a bit anxious, they acknowledged, but grimly determined not to let the bombers get the better of them." Things were slower, of course, and service disrupted because of "the incidents." For those not directly affected by the attacks, the newspaper said, "'getting on with it' carried an important symbolic meaning." Londoners thought it important for things to continue as usual.

Did the bombers really think that they would unnerve these survivors of the London Blitz, the Battle of Britain, and the Irish Republican Army? Who else in the West were so temperamentally prepared for this kind of thing, and so thoroughly nonplussed by it? Had those bombs exploded in New London, Connecticut, or London, Ontario, the response from Americans and Canadians would surely have been less muted. The British are unexcitable. "D'you think we would have acquired our Empire if we had kept asking the whys and wherefores of things?" asks Mabel, the wife of the Briton in *The Love of Four Colonels*. "And d'you think my husband would be the first-class administrator he is if he bothered to find out what other people thought?"

"Ask the travelled inhabitant of any nation in what country on earth would you rather live?" asked Thomas Jefferson, the celebrated American polymath who lived in Paris as an envoy of his government before he was president. After America, it was France, the country that gave the world Monet and Manet, Vimy and Vichy, Racine, Molière, Balzac, Zola, Dumas, Descartes, Rousseau and Voltaire, Louis XIV, Napoleon Bonaparte, Charles de Gaulle, Henri Cartier-Bresson, Provence for a year and Paris for a lifetime. Is there a country that inspires greater reflection and greater rhapsody than France? Listen to the late Julia Child, the enthusiastic American cook who lived in France and became infatuated with all things French, in her book *My Life in France*. "The sweetness and generosity and politeness and gentleness and humanity of the French have shown me how lovely life can be if one takes time to be friendly," she writes, later adding: "How I *adored* sweet and natural France, with its human warmth, wonderful smells, graciousness, coziness and freedom of spirit."

As Winston Churchill was an observer of America, he was also an observer of France, where he fought in the fields and sunbathed on the beaches. On June 25, 1937, as their government was falling, Churchill offered these reassuring words about the French: "Many countries, not excluding our own, are apt to regard the French as a vain, volatile, fanciful, hysterical nation. As a matter of fact, they are one of the most grim, sober, unsentimental, calculating and tenacious races in the world." He was confident, he added, that the French would hold fast against the forces of tyranny: "France is not going to be the country to betray the cause of democracy. Nor will she be false to the inspiration of freedom and individualism which was the message – however falsified in practice – of the French revolution. The 'will to live' is strong in the French people. They will not fail mankind in these years . . ." They did fail, of course, and an agonized Churchill was forced to destroy the French fleet in 1940 lest it fall into German hands.

Churchill knew the resonance of *liberté, egalité, fraternité*, but he also knew the swelling currents of dictatorship, fascism, racism, and anti-Semitism in France. In other words, he knew the country's contradictions. Stanley Karnow, the American journalist who lived in France from 1947 to 1957, was daunted by what he called "the intricacies" of the French. Though they proclaimed themselves *une et indivisible*, he sees inconsistencies everywhere. "The French were simultaneously sophisticated and parochial, methodical and anarchistic, individualistic and conformist, flexible and stubborn, liberal and antediluvian, prudent and rash, puritanical and wanton, logical and wildly irrational," Karnow says in *Paris in the Fifties*, his chronicle of post-war France. "While espousing the principles of the Revolution . . . they recoiled from performing the most elementary civic duties. They combined tolerance with bigotry, kindness with malice, elegant taste with appalling vulgarity. Politeness ranked high on their list of virtues, yet they could be uncommonly rude, not only to foreigners but to each other." He found that despite their reputation for gaiety – Paris as the City of Light – they were often gloomy.

Karnow sees in the French "the contrast between their contempt for government and their veneration for the state." The state was what ensured the continuity of the French experiment, which is why it is famously said that France is "administered rather than governed." Churchill noted that in Britain, governments change their policies without changing men; in France, they change their men without changing policies. France is seen by its leaders as sweet, beautiful, generous, glorious, first among nations. The superiority of the French, trumpeted in the last generation by leaders from Valéry Giscard d'Estaing to Jacques Chirac, is rooted in their past. The French are canonized by Gustave Flaubert (*"le premier peuple de l'univers"*) and Victor Hugo (*"France, France, sans toi le monde serait seul"*). "Inculcated from infancy with such chauvinism," says Karnow, "the French were convinced that every aspect of France, from its culture to the contours of its landscape, was unique; if they went abroad, which they seldom did, it was only to find other countries barbaric." Unsurprisingly, "chauvinism" – which means excessive, zealous, belligerent patriotism or blind enthusiasm for military glory – was inspired by Nicholas Chauvin, a soldier in Napoleon's army. How fitting.

If Americans are obsessive about July 4, the French are as patriotic on July 14. Here, the Revolution is glorified in windy speeches from politicians. Music blares, wreaths are laid, veterans parade. *La gloire* comes naturally to the French, who know all about royalty. When John F. Kennedy visited Paris in 1961, he was struck by the ceremony with which he was saluted by the French in honour guards and processions, and he thought of importing some of it to elevate the presidency. The office may be the most powerful in the world, but in folksy, informal America, it didn't always look that way. Kennedy thought it should be more formal and looked for inspiration to the French. Not only did he wear a cutaway coat and a black silk top hat to his inauguration, he brought some of the elegance of France with him. His wife, Jacqueline, had studied in Paris, spoke French, and loved French design, food, and fashion. After hosting a glittering state dinner at Mount Vernon in 1961, the Kennedys were accused of creating "the grandeur of the French court at Versailles."

For the French, of course, there is no one but the French. "France occupies an exclusive place in the world, and could accept nothing less," writes journalist Jonathan Fenby in *France on the Brink: A Great Civilization Faces the New Century*. "It is, its President declares, a beacon for the human race. The nation and its people may be loved or hated, but they can never be ignored." Since 1958, when Charles de Gaulle assumed power, France has developed a self-confidence that is not always becoming, Fenby says, but which leaves little doubt that it offers the rest of the world something out of the ordinary. That is an understatement. French leaders have cast themselves as exemplars of everything bright and beautiful.

De Gaulle, among the most influential of Frenchmen, famously said: "I have a particular idea of France." He did, and so does every Frenchman. Their idea of it may have meant France as a unique nation, in its way of thinking and acting, from its government to its economy to its politics. Or, as journalist Richard Bernstein writes: "It is to represent something beyond themselves, to light up the world, to glow with the torch of civilization itself."

National character reveals itself in different ways. In divining the American character, let us consider a weathered opera house on a hill above Stonington, Maine, a fishing village on the Atlantic Ocean. The opera house was built in 1893, when Stonington was prosperous and had a population five times what it is today. It burned down in 1910, was rebuilt in 1912, fell into disuse in the 1980s, and was restored in 2003 by four ambitious women from New York City. For much of its life, it has been an unlikely venue of the arts in a working man's town – presenting opera, theatre, vaudeville, music, film. It was a refuge for the granite stonecutters, many of them Scotsmen and Italians, who came for the work. They mined, cut, shaped, and polished the pink-flecked granite from local quarries for the bridges, banks, libraries, cathedrals, and skyscrapers of America's cities. Recognizing its importance, the National Register of Historic Places listed the Stonington Opera House in 1991. A blue-and-white placard on a low wall of the building recalls its history and celebrates its contribution to the community. It says that the building is important "in order to give a sense of orientation to the American people."

A lovely phrase, that. Used in the preamble to the National Historic Preservation Act, passed by Congress in 1966, it reminds us that "the spirit and direction of the nation are founded upon and reflected in its historic heritage." It suggests that a people are what they create and how they remember it. It may be little more than a shingled, three-storey opera house on the seacoast, or the Jefferson Memorial in Washington or the Empire State Building in New York. Designating an opera house historic suggests that this kind of enterprise, for this kind of a purpose, means something. It situates people somewhere, gives them that "sense of orientation." It conveys a sense of place and a sense of self.

More than most, Americans know who they are. They have never suffered much from a lack of self-confidence. Even as they have prospered, multiplied and settled North America, they have remained fundamentally the ambitious, optimistic, idealistic, sentimental people that they are today. They spring from the bosom of the British and owe much of their success to their forebears, but their national character is different. This has as much to do with geography as history. The *leitmotif* of the United States is freedom, physical and psychological. It flows from a country as big as a continent, rich in everything. It is the appeal of the frontier. America has always beckoned the adventurous. Unchecked by the constraints of class and space that have confined Britain, America has offered land, money, acceptance, opportunity. Not every American has benefited – blacks were most painfully excluded, as well as the Hispanics, the Irish, the Jews, and other minorities. Many of those immigrants who thought America's streets were paved with gold were the ones who paved them. But the promise has remained: people have looked to the United States for a better life, and for the most part they have found it there. This is why there are some 11 to 15 million illegal immigrants in the country.

Where to start in assaying the Americans? Perhaps the most enduring view is that of Alexis de Tocqueville, the French aristocrat who made a long visit to the United States in 1831 and published his seminal two-volume study, *Democracy in America*, in 1835 and 1840. He saw and wrote of many things in America, but it is de Tocqueville's view of the country's character, through observations of its politics, government, and the economy, that is of interest here. In Jacksonian America, de Tocqueville notes the American disposition to treat "business in clear, plain language, devoid of all ornament" but laments "the pomposity" when the subject turns to politics, as if he were speaking of the modern-day election campaign. He understands, implicitly, the meaning of freedom, equality, and individualism, however qualified and shaded. He understands class in America, though it is less stratified than in Europe: "In the United States, the more opulent citizens take great care not to stand aloof from the people; on the contrary, they constantly keep on easy terms with the lower classes: they listen to them, they speak to them every day." He understands, as well, American initiative and enterprise: "It would seem as if every imagination in the United States were upon the stretch to invent means of increasing the wealth and satisfying the wants of the public."

As if he were laying this pioneer society on his couch, de Tocqueville makes pointed observations. On religious fundamentalism: "Here and there, in the midst of American society, you meet with men, full of a fanatical and almost wild enthusiasm, which hardly exists in Europe. . . . Religious insanity is very common in the United States." On freedom: "The inhabitants of the United States alternately display so strong and similar a passion for their own welfare and for their freedom, that it may be supposed that these passions are united and mingled in some part of their character." On national pride: "The Americans in their intercourse with strangers appear impatient of the smallest censure and insatiable of praise. . . . It would seem as if, doubting their own merit, they wished to have it constantly exhibited before their eyes."

A generation after de Tocqueville, James Bryce, a British historian and politician, made five visits of his own to America. In his three-volume study published in 1888, *The American Commonwealth*, he says the sheer bounty of the place has shaped the mind and manner of Americans. Like de Tocqueville, Bryce is dazzled by the diversity and wealth of the land. Blessed with a moderate climate, much sunshine and rich soil, separated from Asia and Europe by vast oceans, endowed with weak or friendly neighbours, the United States is uniquely positioned to fulfill its destiny: "Thus is it left to itself as no great State has ever yet been in the world; thus its citizens enjoy an opportunity never before granted to a nation, of making their country what they will have it," Bryce declares.

"Making their country what they will" is the telling epigram of America. That instinct is at the heart of the American character. It wasn't just geography that allowed the United States to succeed; it was history – or the lack of it. Free of the prejudices of the past, open to ideas, America did not carry the baggage of older societies, at least not by the end of the nineteenth century. So it appeared to a young Winston Churchill, visiting a few years after the publication of Bryce's book. "This is a very great country," Churchill wrote to his brother. "Not pretty or romantic but great and utilitarian. There seems to be no such thing as reverence or tradition. Everything is eminently practical and things are judged from a matter of fact standpoint." In observing a trial, Churchill was struck by the absence of wigs, robes, and uniformed ushers. He found instead men in black coats who "manage to hang a man all the same . . ." Here was the early informality of America. It also meant a frankness, often called rudeness, which is less admirable today. The American was "a great lusty youth," Churchill observed on the same trip, "who treads on all your sensibilities, perpetrates every possible horror of ill manners – whom neither age nor just tradition inspire with reverence – but who moves about his affairs with a good-hearted freshness which may well be the envy of older nations of the earth."

Another Englishman with a strong sense of the American character was Alistair Cooke, the patrician author and journalist whom columnist William Safire said "interprets America better than any foreign correspondent since [de] Tocqueville." Cooke spent some sixty years living in the United States, writing books and recording a weekly radio commentary called *Letter from America*. More than de Tocqueville and Bryce, Cooke understood that the success of America isn't just that it has land and wealth; after all, countries such as Russia have that, too. He learned early on that much has to do with the people themselves, one of Morgenthau's elements of national power. "The enviable richness of America's natural resources is a theme that Europeans like to dwell on whenever they are feeling peevish about some new American achievement like a moon shot. . . . While the Europeans attribute America's bounty to the luck of her resources, Americans on the other hand like to ascribe it to nothing but character. It usually required a combination of both."

Curiously, none of these three Englishmen who crossed the Atlantic to discover America – Bryce, Churchill, and Cooke – brought with them the condescension common among Europeans. To the European, the American is often coarse, vulgar, materialistic. "What's the difference between yogurt and America?" asks the lower-classman at Oxford. "In two hundred years," he answers, "yogurt grew a culture!" The American in history is seen as pampered, weak, and soft. He is no soldier, declared Adolf Hitler, who so believed this that he declared war on the United States after Congress had declared war only on Japan. His folly sealed his fate. The Japanese made the same mistake at Pearl Harbor. As Morgenthau says, both made judgments on the state of the American military and the isolationist sentiment, underestimating a people's ability to improvise and innovate. Today, the depiction of the American is too much the soldier, the bully, the swaggering global policeman.

To less critical observers, the Americans are about money and bigness, which is an American obsession. The length of the Brooklyn Bridge, the heat of Death Valley, the breadth of the Grand Canyon, the speed of Nolan Ryan's fastball, the size of the Pentagon. Or about a people's affinity for technology: the electric light bulb, the phonograph, the jet engine, the space rocket, the Internet. Or about an overworked society that often leaves its weakest vulnerable. Or one that doesn't take holidays. "In observance of Labor Day," read a sign posted in a shop window in Rockville, Maryland, "we will close at six o'clock today."

A biting, contemporary view of America that confirms the Old World's worst prejudices comes from the pen of another Frenchman, philosopher Bernard-Henri Lévy. In *American Vertigo: Traveling America in the Footsteps of Tocqueville*, Lévy knocks around the United States, much like his nineteenth-century compatriot.

But Lévy prefers to ruminate less on institutions, laws, or custom than to dwell on the seamier side of American society: strip clubs, swingers clubs, trade fairs, gun shops, national political conventions. Everything is grist for his intellectual mill, where much cake is made of dust, which isn't unusual for the archetypal woolly-minded French intellectual. For Lévy, everything is a metaphor. It is not that America isn't contradictory – it is – but that it isn't as complicated as he would like to think. Of Lévy's tome, humorist Garrison Keillor writes: "It is the classic Freaks, Fatties, Fanatics & Faux Culture Excursion beloved of European Journalists for the past 50 years. . . . But there's nobody here whom you recognize. In more than 300 pages, nobody tells a joke. Nobody does much work. Nobody sits and eats and enjoys their food. You've lived all your life in America, never attended a megachurch or a brothel, don't own guns, are non-Amish. . . . There's no reason for it [the book] to exist in English, except as evidence that travel need not be broadening and one should be wary of books with Tocqueville in the title."

Keillor looking at Lévy looking at America reminds us of the dangers of being too certain about national character in the United States, or anywhere else. This isn't to say that Lévy's findings are invalid; he has something to say to us in 2007 as de Tocqueville did in 1840. Both try to get at the heart of the American character. Both try to understand the texture of democracy. Which brings us back to the opera house in Maine and its sense of orientation. When *The New York Times* visited Stonington and learned of the building's history, it asked Linda Nelson why she and three other women from New York would buy and restore a crumbling opera house in a village of a thousand souls. She replied: "This is not about money or property for us. It's about living a good life, doing what you think is important and giving something to the community. That's how democracy works. Democracy is participation."

So what does a modest survey of national character tell us? In a general sense, it is that the British, the French, and the Americans are great peoples, rich in history, culture, and achievement, and they have bequeathed much to us. Institutionally, we draw on all three. Some are obvious reflections of our forefathers: our system of democratic government, our commitment to capitalism tempered by social democracy, our rule of law, our liberalism, our internationalism. Canadians are an echo. We have both civil and common law, which are French and British; a constitutional monarchy and a Charter of Rights and Freedoms, which are British and American; the rule of Parliament and the power of the courts, which are also British and American. We have an economy of both public and private ownership, mixing capitalism (American) and socialism (British and French). We have social programs that are not as broad as those in Britain and France nor as limited as those in America. We have French and English languages, and a good deal of American in our vocabulary, too. And that's just government, language, and law.

Temperamentally and intellectually, we are the products of the French and the British who created us and the Americans, whose influence has grown as that of the others has faded. We play baseball and football, not soccer and cricket. We take vacations of two and three weeks (American), not five and six weeks (British and French). We have universal health care but no jobs for life. We like peacekeeping and multilateralism and oppose capital punishment, like the Europeans, but have the frontier and sense of distance and space of the Americans. There is a greater percentage of Canadians in labour unions than in the United States but fewer than in Britain and France. Our income taxes are higher than in the United States and Britain but lower than those of France. Our approach to immigration is more American and British; it is certainly not French. And so it goes. Ultimately, we are hybrids: British Canadians, French Canadians, American Canadians, and that is before we consider the influence of aboriginals and those from the many other countries that make up the Canadian mosaic.

There is no Canadian among Ustinov's quartet of quarrelsome colonels. If there had been, we might wonder what vision he would evoke, what ideal he would pursue, what dream he would imagine. Unlike the American, the Briton, the Frenchman, and the Russian, he would have to think about it. He could not have dipped into a reservoir of imagination. A country without empire or revolution or civil war, a country without heroes or conquest or colonies, Canada does not offer the same kind of tableau. Of course, were he to look he would find something to celebrate, for there is a romance in the discovery and development of Canada. Indeed, were he looking for a woman, he might have found his ideal in the courageous Laura Secord, the tragic Evangeline, the freckled Anne of Green Gables, the graceful Cindy Klassen, or the sultry Diana Krall. But even if he did find his ideal, our Canadian colonel would be reluctant to trumpet it. That's not us.

Rather, we are the product of memory, geography, complexity, uncertainty. This is the character we seek to explore and understand. It is not British, French, or American. It is Canadian, and these are the people we are.

Chapter 2

The Observed Canadian

In 1963, Time-Life Books published *Canada*, one in a multi-volume series on the countries of the world called *Life World Library*. The idea was to commission a novelist or journalist of renown to paint a portrait of the place. Readers would open the book to find a country map and an introduction written by a former ambassador of the United States or the secretary of state, presumably to confer a sense of authority. The books were the size of an atlas with a bright white spine and a broad white border across the top stamped with the cheerful red *LIFE* logo in the upper left corner. Illustrated with maps, charts, and photographs, they had enough gravity to carry them from the coffee table to the bedside table. You could find the books in American and Canadian homes, libraries, and schools in the 1960s under titles such as *Tropical Africa*, *The Arab World*, or *The River Plate Republics: Argentina, Paraguay, Uruguay*. Subscribers would order them by mail and display them as they would back issues of *National Geographic*. Today, long out of print, the books turn up in used-book shops, garage sales, and small-town libraries, smelling of the basement, the attic, and another time.

To write *Canada*, the editors of Time-Life approached Brian Moore, the gifted writer who had come to Canada from Belfast in 1948. He had lived in Toronto and then Montreal, where he began as a proofreader and became a reporter for the Montreal *Gazette*. By the mid-1950s, he had turned to fiction. Moore wasn't just another luckless Irishman looking for a bolt-hole in Canada after the war; he was a stylish wordsmith of international stature whose novels included *The Lonely Passion of Judith Hearne* and *The Luck of Ginger Coffey*, which won the Governor General's Literary Award for Fiction in 1960. In Moore, the editors engaged a perceptive, elegant interpreter. His was the personal view of a restless soul who had come to Canada, found success here, and then moved on to America.

Why he wrote *Canada* in 1962 and 1963, when he was immersed in fiction in New York, is uncertain; probably it was for the money. At *The Gazette*, Moore had been very fast and it may be that he was able to toss off this book as if he were reporting a double homicide. Unlike other commentators, his tone is more detached, though thoughtful and respectful. "Writing *Canada* is turning out bitter indeed. . . . The more I read, the less I admire your countrymen," he wrote his friend Mordecai Richler in early 1963, "the English Canadian ones anyway." It isn't clear what he meant here, or if his fondness for Canada had waned, or whether he missed the place at all. But that winter he sold his house in Montreal and never returned to the city. His *Canada* reflects his desire for an open, diverse society, which it became. In a personal sense, though, he appeared to resent Canada.

Published in 1963 and revised in 1968, *Canada* reflects a jaunty country turning one hundred years old. In 1967, Canada's centenary was celebrated in song, books, festivals, galas, exhibitions, projects and pageants in villages, towns, and cities. In its tenth decade, Canada was congratulating itself. At home, the country was prosperous, safe, orderly, compassionate, and ambitious. It had established universal health care and a pension scheme, embraced official bilingualism, and adopted a new flag. Abroad, Canada was the honest broker in the world's councils and the ubiquitous peacekeeper on the world's battlefields.

This was before things soured in the late 1960s. It was before separation, stagflation, western alienation. It was before the expansion of professional hockey; the Toronto Maple Leafs and the Montreal Canadiens fought for the Stanley Cup in 1967, a storied rivalry that has never been the same since. Expo 67, the international exhibition that ran for six months in Montreal, drew 50 million visitors. Three decades later, Pierre Berton would call 1967 "Canada's last good year."

"He doesn't want to talk about Canada . . ." says a character in Moore's *The Luck of Ginger Coffey*. "There you have the Canadian dilemma in a sentence. Nobody wants to talk about Canada, not even us Canadians. You're right, Paddy. Canada is a bore." But Moore *did* want to talk about Canada, exciting or not. His Time-Life book is a portrait in sepia, a finely etched period piece of reportage and observation. Moore opens his story on a transcontinental jet flying from Vancouver to London. As the plane takes off, the stewardess speaks in "American accents" and "strangely accented French." The passengers seem "a little odd." Although they look and dress "like Americans," there is "a European touch in their orderly manners, durable overshoes and sensible woolly scarves." They "obediently" accept magazines and are "placidly engrossed" by the *Saturday Evening Post* and *Maclean's*. Below them is the forbidding, empty land, so large that no one has ever seen all of it, so big that it is "invisible."

Moore is not yet over the Okanagan Valley before he has informed his readers in Kansas and Ohio of the fundamentals of their northern neighbour: Canadians are both American and European. They speak English and French. They are orderly, durable, and sensible, and not only in manner and dress. They are odd. They are deferential. They are serene. Their land is big, they are small, and they are the first of their kind to see it in one day – not that these latter-day Argonauts will know it any better than the Indians, the explorers, the voyageurs, or the settlers who have roamed those bottomlands, scaled those mountains, paddled those rivers, and farmed that loamy soil below.

Moore sizes up Canada with a journalist's eye and a novelist's pen. "Canadians are not chauvinistic about their country's size and are sometimes apologetic about its past," he writes. He notes the country's history is without wars of independence or great political crises, declaring that "their enemy is climate and geography: their battle is not yet won." In a country sprawling some 3,300 miles over six time zones, size and nature are paramount. So is regional isolation. "Walls, both physical and political, have always partitioned this enormous land, turning its citizens' gaze inward, fixing their minds on local loyalties, and local faiths," he writes.

A sense of national belonging is missing. Moore mentions a distillery that wanted to sell liquor to Canadians by appealing to their sense of patriotism. The pitch: *The only ism for Canadians is Canadianism.* It flopped. "Canadians simply ignored the advice," Moore says. "For, unlike Americans, they have rarely been indoctrinated with official appeals for patriotism, nor has the country made any real effort to become 'a melting pot' or a haven for Europe's poor and dispossessed." At the time, five of six Canadians were born in Canada, most of them of British and French ancestry. "Canadians, if asked to define Canadianism, usually do so in negative terms. It is not Americanism, they say. And equally, they insist, they are not British or French."

Moore, the Irish-Canadian-American observer, says that possibly the only definition of Canadians that some citizens would accept is that "a Canadian is someone who has turned down a chance to go and live in the United States." He identifies other elements of the Canadian character as he saw them forty or more years ago. For example, he finds a distaste for heroes or men of real achievement other than hockey players. He thinks the reason is the land and climate. "There are no heroes in the wilderness. Only fools take risks." Perceptively, he sees "a weak revolutionary, or radical, strain, and a strong counter-revolutionary, or conservative one," a theme addressed by historians. In William Lyon Mackenzie King, who was Canada's longest-serving prime minister and canniest politician, he sees the self-effacing but practical Canadian – dull, colourless, and plodding but highly successful and eminently pragmatic. "In his combination of shrewd practicality and hidden uncertainty, he is perhaps the most startling example of that dichotomy which governs the Canadian character," Moore says.

The country's cities, he observes, are practical and utilitarian. "There is something makeshift in their composition, and the Canadian dislike of show results in a drab absence of civic gaiety." The exterior of homes is often neglected, he finds, which reflects "a frontier attitude, an ingrained sense of impermanence reinforced by the brutal truths of geography." More broadly, Moore finds Canadians without pomposity, genuine and engaging. "For they are neither so reserved as to seem cold, nor so ebullient as to appear tiresome. In a real way, the Canadian seems the North American Everyman, open and unaffected, at home with people wherever he meets them." For their gentility, affability, and good manners, he called them "the quiet Americans" who, in the eyes of the world, are "dependable and just." Their absence of flamboyance he attributes to caution; "they seem to lack dash and a nationalistic fervour" necessary for survival.

Moore takes his readers across the country with a running historical, cultural, and psychological commentary. The arts, immigrants, Quebec, the North – all suggest to him an idea of what it means to be a Canadian. He recalls that 1967 is not only the hundredth anniversary of Canada, but also the fiftieth anniversary of the Russian Revolution. To him, Russia was more nationalist than ever while Canada remained "unsure of its national character and most national differences between Canadians and Americans have withered away." Whatever the display of pride in the Centennial Year, Moore believes that Canada's biggest problem is national identity. If it was no longer British, and was wary of the United States, what was it? Curiously, if Moore were to return to Canada in 2007, he could ask the same question.

Canada is perceptive. "They [Canadians] have been lectured, advised, warned and dismissed by a stream of professors, novelists, poets and pundits, many of them American or Britons, whose ignorance of Canada's problems has only been matched by their sublime condescension," Moore writes sharply. Much of what he sees in Canadians, through their land, institutions, and government, has resonance today. That many of our cities are ugly, that we do not take risks, that we are supremely practical, that we are allergic to heroes, that we are loath to display – are all very much *us*.

We have always cared what others thought; in the nineteenth century, newspapers in Canada republished reports of what the Americans or the British had to say about Canada. We still do care; when *The Economist* called Paul Martin "Mr. Dithers" in 2005, it was front-page news in Canada and repeated in Parliament, with more impact than if a Canadian had said it. (As a matter of fact, the writer was a Canadian.) When Clifford Krauss, the Canadian correspondent for *The New York Times*, wondered if Canada was just a little too "virtuous," his comments were highly publicized in Canada. Criticism is good for us, said essayist B.K. Sandwell in an article in *Queen's Quarterly* in 1930. Sandwell thought that to grow "in mental and moral stature," nations should have as clear and true a picture of themselves as possible. Smart, self-aware nations benefit from what others say: "Complete insensitiveness to this external criticism . . . is a sign of decay, a sort of hardening of the national arteries . . ."

Foreigners bring a critical eye and an open ear. They have a unique view. Some are deliciously and shallowly tart in their assessment of Canadians. Enid Bagnold, the English playwright and novelist who wrote *National Velvet* in 1935, spent an unhappy four weeks crossing Canada by rail in 1919. She described Canada as "naïve, touchy, longing to be praised, young." She was constantly asked "what do you think of us?" and she wanted to reply: "I think you're a bore." John Dos Passos, the American novelist, was uninterested in Toronto in 1917. "So you've been to Toronto – don't you think it's a beastly place?" He spoke of "utter middle-class gracelessness" and allowed that "I loathe it." His contemporary Ernest Hemingway, who worked for the *Toronto Star*, spent longer in Canada and didn't always like it, either. He famously called Canada "the fistulated asshole of the father of seven among Nations."

Rupert Brooke, the English poet and patriot who made a cross-country visit in 1913, found Canadians "churlish," "horribly individualistic," "vastly vulgar," and "very stiff." He was happy to leave. But Rudyard Kipling, the bard of Empire, visited Canada seven times between 1889 and 1930 and was smitten. "I have realized here the existence of an assured nationhood," he says of the country in 1907. "The spirit of a people contented not to be another people or the imitators of any other people – contented to be themselves." He finds these differences in the character of Canadians and Americans: "Always a marvel – to which Canadians seem insensible – was that on one side of an imaginary line should be Safety, Law, Honour, and Obedience, and on the other, frank, brutal decivilization; and that despite this, Canada should be impressed by any aspect whatever of the United States."

Kipling and Brooke were just two of the company of observers who have, over the years, taken the measure of the Canadian character in letters, journals, newspapers, and travelogues. Some loved the country, some hated it, some were indifferent. Three illuminating reflections on Canada, in full-length books, come from a Frenchman, an Englishman, and an American. Written in different periods, all offer a foreigner's pointed perspective.

André Siegfried was one of the more informed and least known of Canada's intellectual explorers. A Frenchman who would become one of his country's most distinguished scholars, he made his first visit to Canada in 1898, followed by three more. He published his first book, *The Race Question in Canada*, in 1906. He called it a "psychological analysis." Forty years later, after trips to Canada in 1914, 1919, and 1935, he published *Canada* in 1937. He revised and republished the book in 1949 as *Canada: An International Power*.

Of Siegfried's two books, the second is of more interest here; it offers a more tangible sense of his view of the Canadian character. "At the beginning, in the middle, and at the end of any study of Canada, one must reiterate that Canada is American," he declares. "History occasionally loses sight of this fact, but at every step geography imperiously recalls it. And yet a political bond does exist with the old world, and herein lies the novelty and uniqueness of the Canadian problem." Character begins with geography, and this defines Canada, because it is forever challenged by its very existence. Siegfried understands that geography, especially the north-south axis of North America, is undeniable, and it pulls Canada into the American orbit. Historically, it is the east-west axis that matters, though he argues that this is "artificial." As the two collide, they define the country. "Which axis will prevail in the end? Will geography finally efface the play of history? If so, the American nations will gradually become more alike, more pan-Americanism will prevail, and, possibly, there will be no Canada." If Canada can resist "a gravitation which seems irresistible, Canada will fall back on her east-west axis, and will maintain a separate existence and a personality of her own."

That personality, particularly the country's political personality, is a result of this duality: the balance between the United States and Europe. If this were upset, Canada's existence would be in danger, he warns. That Canada is distinct from the United States is "a mere accident of history, in fact a political paradox." While nature is central to Canada, he argues that this alone doesn't make Canada distinctive. "Nature has not conferred upon Canada any particular personality of her own. There is no geographic difference to separate her from her great neighbour to the south." The great geographical features of Canada – the Prairies and the Rockies – are actually a continuation of the United States.

To Siegfried, the political centre of gravity is in Britain and the geographical centre is in the United States. Here is the importance of space in shaping character. Because Canada has so much land but so little of it is populated – a thin band of people clinging to the American border – "she is tempted to seek a centre of gravity outside her own borders." Looking north, Siegfried sees Canada as "an Arctic nation," a doctrine that "expresses an essential aspiration of the Canadian nation." (That notion was embraced enthusiastically by Adrienne Clarkson as governor general.) Ultimately, geography is both a weakness and a strength. Canada is "a country which is hybrid and divided, and which is not sure of itself. It cannot choose between the United States and England without destroying itself in the process."

This gives rise to "the uncertainty of a heterogeneous people – British, French and American – who are not sure they want the degree of cultural unity that would be necessary for the definite achievement of their personality." At the same time, though, this weakness, caused by the country's "complexity," has advantages. Canada has retained its link with Europe, and is compelled to be international in its thinking. In this, it rises above itself.

With great acuity, Siegfried sees the ethnic diversity of Canadian society, its impact on the national character and the threat it poses to national unity. He sees a French-Canadian "civilization" maintaining its individuality, "a British civilization enjoying the prestige of England," and "an American civilization" seeking "its basis and its very being" in the United States. The challenge for Canada, he writes in the 1940s, is developing a Canadian nationality: "It exists, but if it is to persist it is essential that all Canadians, whatever their tradition, must be first and foremost Canadians."

Siegfried compares the nature of French Canadians and English Canadians and Americans. He sees the character of French Canada as a reflection of a certain attitude to life shaped by the "moral discipline" of the church. "It believes in hard work, commends thrift and self-discipline, accepts the doctrine of large families as a Christian duty, and restricts ambition to sensible proportions. Such thoughtful asceticism is the very negation of Americanism. Its principles are contrary to the underlying inspiration of the American civilization. . . ." He argues that it is impossible for French Canadians to compromise, that to assimilate would be to abandon their traditions. They will survive only if they refuse to become Americans.

In Siegfried's Canada, the English are "the conquering class." English is the most widely spoken language but that actually undermines Canada's prospects because "through it Americanism is insinuating itself everywhere without let or hindrance." For the English Canadian, he finds, America is irresistible. Siegfried is dazzled by the impact of America on the Canadian imagination. "The north-south current is always present, silently, anonymously, persistently, irresistibly, and fatally turning men's minds towards the United States." It is the universal law of gravitation that governs Canadians, too. "In times of prosperity, or even when there is not an acute depression, American prestige shines like a sun," he says. "In the neighbouring country which is more modest, people feel that in this theatre, which is vaster and more brilliantly lit up, there must be more chances of success, and so there are."

The great republic is a strong draw for those ambitious people who find Canada too small. In America, they are assimilated immediately, he finds. He sees what is now called the brain drain as "a fatal attraction," not to be confused with infidelity, revenge, and rabbits boiling in pots.

In speaking of relations between French and English, Siegfried discovers the two solitudes, around the same time as Hugh MacLennan, the perceptive novelist from Montreal, was describing them. He says it is like external relations, "a modus vivendi without cordiality." Encountering a French Canadian in Montreal and an English Canadian in Toronto on the same day is "like experiencing different pressures in a diving bell." But the modus vivendi works, and each recognizes the importance of the other in his enterprise. Alas, the conciliatory genius of Canadians.

Patriotism? What patriotism? For the French Canadian, "French Canada . . . is the only reality," Siegfried says. He feels no sentiment toward the Confederation. Canada is a cold, legal entity to which he has no loyalty. The man from Quebec "feels as much a foreigner in Toronto as he does in New York!" Siegfried concludes that Canada is precarious but will carry on indefinitely. "She has been in existence long enough and has been sufficiently active to have acquired a political personality of her own which she will not give up," he says.

Alistair Horne, a British author and journalist, was introduced to Canada as a seventeen-year-old air force trainee during the Second World War. He became better acquainted in long sojourns in the country in 1956 and 1958. Out of this came *Canada and the Canadians: Profile of a Modern Nation*, published in 1961. It is another of those obscure post-war period pieces. Its jacket copy describes the book as "a chance to see ourselves objectively," even as it cautions that the author isn't writing "to flatter Canadians." Actually, he does.

In the late 1950s, Horne found a country that had grown to a population of 17 million from 3 million in 1860. It had recently welcomed its two millionth immigrant since the end of the Second World War, and was becoming "a great sovereign nation." Like all of those looking for the big picture – which makes their observations useful a generation later – Horne wants to know what all of this means. "And what of 'the average Canadian' himself?" he asks. "What has he become in the two centuries since the British burst so rudely in upon the bucolic serenity of New France? What manner of man is he now?"

Having asked the critical question, Horne answers with critical conciseness. "Like so much in modern Canada, he has become complicated. There are times when he does not even quite know what he is himself. No longer is it possible to point to any Canadian and reckon, with certainty of being right – as one might have done in 1860 – that his ancestors came from either France or Britain." "Complicated" is an adjective he uses more than once. As we know, today's Canada has become increasingly complicated. As John Ralston Saul declares in his magisterial study, *Reflections of a Siamese Twin: Canada at the End of the Twentieth Century*, "the central characteristic of the Canadian state is its complexity." Horne, who doesn't play on the same intellectual plane as Saul, is still on to something, if in a somewhat more narrow way. He was writing in the shadow of the Hungarian Revolution, which brought forty-two thousand refugees to Canada, the largest number accepted by any country. After a restrictive immigration policy before and during the war (under which Canada admitted fewer European Jews than any other country but Bolivia), he could see that Canada was changing. Horne was present at the re-creation of Canada, so to speak. "Thus there is no such thing – if there ever was – as 'a typical Canadian'; a fact that deters the generaliser," he writes. "Yet it is difficult to discover what kind of people the Canadians really are, in a mass, without casting forth a few broadly true, but vulnerable, generalisations; and perhaps it is safest to begin by generalising on what Canadians are *not*." Then he issues the disclaimer, if qualified, beloved by foreigners: "The Canadian is *not* an American – at least, not entirely, not yet."

How to describe the Canadian in the 1950s? Horne draws a picture. He suggests that the most obvious quality of Canadians is the "quietness" of their speech, which points to a general dislike of noise, to a distrust of ostentation, and to a tendency toward conservatism that is "distinctly more British than American." Call him the Quiet Canadian. "He wears quieter suits, less spectacular ties than his southern cousins; builds his cities of sober grey stone instead of coloured glass and bronze. He may be a little slower to take a newcomer to his bosom than an American, but when he does his friendship may be less fickle." To our visitor, in the 1950s, Canadian quietness is manifest as well in business and politics, reflecting "an underlying leisureliness in Canadian affairs" less prominent in the United States. Yes, the rat race exists, but Canadians have an ability to keep it "to a healthier mean." It is important that more Canadians die of the flu than ulcers. He thinks the Montrealer or Torontonian is "more contented and more in harmony with the world than the New Yorker."

In contrast to the Briton, whom Horne knows best, the Canadian "is more self-reliant and better able to stand on his own feet; in the not-too-distant pioneer past he had to do so to survive." In politics, Horne sees moderation. He finds "the charivari and hurly-burly" of American political conventions unknown in Canada and sees "no soberer or more reflective electorate in the whole world."

In contrast to the United States, Horne finds Canada more disciplined, deferential, and dull. Canadians are less parochial, better informed, and more interested in international affairs, reflecting a country that depends heavily on trade and which is engaged in international institutions. Horne says Canadians have never been allowed the luxury of "absolute intellectual isolation, of not caring what happens in the rest of the world." Although Horne forgets that Canada was isolationist in the 1930s, living in its "fireproof house," his views reflect post-war Canada, basking in the glow of Pearsonian internationalism and the golden age of Canadian diplomacy. He marvels that Canada entered both world wars in Europe as quickly as it did, because it didn't share the anxiety, greed, and passions of Europe nor the obligations of leadership imposed on the United States.

Horne has other unorthodox observations. He finds in Canadians an affinity for gardens, more so than among Americans. He calls this instinct to fill a window box with nasturtiums or garnish a house with a patch of tended flowers "one of Canada's great prides." (Here, Horne disagrees with Brian Moore, who notes an absence of the aesthetic in Canada, reflected in the indifferent towns and villages of Quebec and Ontario. They pale beside the genteel whitewashed churches and village greens of New England or the Norman or Tudor villages of France and England.) Another area of divergence, says Horne, is self-criticism. The Canadian, he says, "can be remarkably rude about the shortcomings of his fellow nationals, and he will never ask you for your opinion of the Canadians." Yet he says Canada itself is "sacred; criticise any aspect of it if you dare." Like Enid Bagnold, Horne suggests that Canadians need praise, that a neutral response to the question "what do you think of Canada?" will not be appreciated. "To a Canadian – like all North Americans – no praise, or restrained praise, equals dispraise." Canadians are touchy. Says Horne: "No people in the Western World are more fiercely proud of their country than the Canadians; nor is there any place that is more entitled to this pride."

Like other observers, Horne comes to realize the importance of space in Canada. "Next to her people, her size is the principal conditioning factor of Canada," he says. As the Royal Commission on Canada's Economic Prospects put it in 1957, "space enters the bloodstream." The psychological impact of this is that Canada can think and act bigger than it is. Moreover, the frontier is not far away, as is the challenge it presents. Horne advises Britons contemplating immigration that living in Canada is not like living on their immensely crowded island. In a nation more rural than it would become, he finds living in Canada a physical challenge requiring "a toughness of mind."

Writing when he did, Horne makes much of the connection between Canada and Britain, understanding that Canadians were becoming less British and more American, particularly in their ethnic diversity. But that reality didn't prevent Horne from finding, a half century ago, a country still attached to the monarchy. "At its lowest common denominator, to the average Canadian – whether of British, French or Ukrainian extraction – the Crown is the one thing he has that the rich and mighty Americans have not got. It makes him feel a little superior." He talks about the monarchy's "mystic symbolism" and the affection most Canadians hold for it, while acknowledging the growing doubts about its necessity, especially in Quebec. As he points out, for many Canadians the Crown evokes "that persistent image of Britain as a superior, slightly condescending, and sometimes still faintly bossy mother figure."

He calls this "the colonial taint," which we have come to see as a colonial mentality. Canadians interpret "British diffidence as arrogance," he says, "restrained enthusiasm as disguised disparagement." He quotes a Canadian, the head of a publishing empire, a cultured man: "I so often feel frankly uncomfortable in the presence of the British, an unaccountable sense of inferiority." Here is the Canadian inferiority complex. Horne's analysis: "Canada is in a state of psychological flux at the moment, trying to establish a character for herself that is neither British nor entirely American. When she succeeds, her people will be more sure of themselves and altogether less sensitive to what others think of Canada.

Already the rising generation in Canada shows a sureness that its elders lack."

Like all visitors of the post-war era, Horne is struck by Canada's openness to immigrants. (In the 1950s, one in nine Canadians was an immigrant, a percentage that has sharply increased.) With some foresight, he sees this instinct – which we might call practical, generous, and moderate – as one of the hallmarks of Canadians. It prompts him to make one of his boldest declarations: "History may well record the way in which Canada has assimilated, and adjusted herself to, this huge influx as one of the outstanding manifestations of the intrinsic greatness of her people. . . . No nation, not even the United States, with its famed hospitality and vastly greater powers of assimilation, has ever welcomed immigrants with such open arms as Canada in the post-war era." Horne is right, though immigration would have its fluctuations. While crises in Hungary and Suez had brought 280,000 immigrants to Canada in 1957, the greatest influx since 1913, the numbers fell to 124,851 in 1958, when Canada went into recession. With generosity, practicality.

What particularly strikes Horne, as a Briton visiting Canada, is the sense of freedom. He calls this "an intangible quality of Canada" among the most important. Once again, to a Briton, it is a different kind of freedom than that sought by the refugee from oppression. "In its simplest forms it is freedom from the wastefulness of petty snobberies and antique prejudices; freedom to stand and rise on one's own merit; and . . . freedom from the tyranny of the State and the Trade Union caucus. At its highest level, there is a sublime freedom that a country of the vastness of Canada alone can offer . . ."

In his coda, Horne says Canada's greatest asset is the qualities of Canadians. Like Morgenthau and Cooke, he understands it isn't necessarily in the land, its riches, its position; it is the character of its people. It isn't just their "kindness and hospitality," which not even the Americans can outdo. It is something deeper. "There is a fundamental goodness and good sense that belong particularly to Canada," he concludes. "These people will never produce a Hitler or a Stalin; nor, very probably, will they produce even a McCarthy or an Alger Hiss, or a Huey Long. These Canadians, one feels, know both where they are going and what is right. If it is to Canada that the future belongs, a neurotic and uncertain world should indeed have cause to rejoice that the Canadians are the people they are."

Twenty-five years later, in a different world, Andrew H. Malcolm published *The Canadians*, "a probing yet affectionate look at the land and the people." Malcolm, whose parents were Canadian, lived and worked in Canada as the Toronto bureau chief of *The New York Times*. As Horne offers the Canadian character from the perspective of a Briton in the 1950s, Malcolm offers it from an American perspective in the 1980s. Malcolm's modus operandi in Canada was similar to Horne's – impression through immersion – and he asks the same fundamental question: "Who are these people?"

Those people making love in a canoe are a metaphor for a country that had to develop "a most keen sense of balance and propriety just to survive." After all, Canada has faced a harsh climate, political division, and geographical obstacles with one-tenth as many people as its neighbour and one-tenth more space. That it did all this peacefully reflects "a certain amount of skill and grace."

Once again, geography shapes character. Malcolm says "the shared hardship of their geography is one of the few national bonds" within the country. "If the frontier-taming experience convinced Americans that anything was possible, the geography of Canada taught its captives true skepticism, that everything, especially themselves, has its limits." Geography creates or accentuates division among Canadians. In disparate Canada, Malcolm finds "these varied, sprawling, separate kingdoms have few things in common with each other save their dogged determination to remain separate and their abiding suspicion of each other." Instead of a homogeneous nation with a common identity, he finds Canada "a conservative collection of regional solitudes separated from each other by formidable natural barriers and from their natural American neighbors by artificial political boundaries." Distance and size, then, are a defining reality for Canadians, but for all that, Malcolm finds, there is not much sense among Canadians of "their geographic whole." Indeed, Northrop Frye, the esteemed literary critic, argued that "the fundamental question in English Canada is not, 'Who am I?' but 'Where is here?'"

Like other foreigners, Malcolm believes that Canadians suffer from an identity crisis. They are no more certain of themselves in 1985 than they were in 1960. "Statistics can show where Canadians come from, where they live now, where they marry and give birth and divorce and die, how they earn a living and spend their time and money. But after 360 years of settlement and after nearly one and a quarter centuries of independence, no one – least of all, Canadians themselves – has been able to tell Canadians who they are." Here, again, in a country that had patriated its Constitution and entrenched a Charter of Rights and Freedoms, routed the separatists in the referendum in Quebec, and established a national energy policy, there is anguish over identity. Indeed, Malcolm concludes that for "many Canadians perhaps their unfortunate identity was to search forever for an identity. . . . If they ever sat down and relaxed and pretended not to care about it for a moment, they would suddenly find that elusive sense of self-comfort lurking just out of the corners of their eyes. . . ."

When the British left in 1867, Malcolm says, they "instilled magnificently in Canadians an inferiority mindset from the start." He finds that whatever their achievements – that Alexander Graham Bell invented the telephone, that Banting and Best discovered insulin, that Raymond Massey played Abraham Lincoln

– Canadians feel uncertain of their accomplishments. They "desperately would like their due recognition yet feel an equal distress when they get it," he says. Their inclination is never to praise themselves or each other. When a Canadian wants to show how successful one of his compatriots is, he will say that the person turned down offers from the United States. "Oh, he must be good then! The American offers confirm his quality; his rejection of them makes everyone feel better, especially those who never get such offers." Malcolm notes what everyone knows: that success at home can make friends and associates "maliciously envious."

With a fear of success comes a comfort with failure. Canadians seem to expect the worst in any situation. "If failure came," Malcolm says, "they knew it all along. If it didn't come, that proved no one paid any attention to Canada. And if somehow success erupted, there must be something wrong somewhere – perhaps it was a bogus victory or the victor wasn't very Canadian anymore." Malcolm allows that when he was reporting on Canada "Canadians were not consumed by any drive for originality or excellence. Many still aren't. Adequate has been fine, thank you very much. Try too hard, and you might turn into one of those pushy Yanks. You also might, God forbid, fail."

Like Horne, Malcolm ponders the impact of immigration on a country with "virtually no national bonds of significance" and argues that it has played a large role in shaping the country's modern personality. He notes that the largest influx to Canada came during and after the American Revolution, as Loyalists fled forces of change they could not embrace. "They came not because that land was a challenging new frontier or because it offered a new promise for tomorrow, with spices and riches and golden opportunities beyond anyone's imagination. They came simply because Canada was less awful than where they were, a key conditioner to Canada's generally conservative personality that puzzles its friends." In Canada, Malcolm finds, it is quite acceptable – indeed, in some circles, encouraged – to live apart, speaking a different language, living a different life from other Canadians. "You see, being Canadian usually means also maintaining a simultaneous strong emotional tie to another country," he writes, himself a descendant of Scots who arrived in Canada in the early nineteenth century. "You may not intend to go back, but you don't have to forsake the old country to embrace the new one if it's Canada." This is one reason, he says, that Canada could accept draft dodgers and deserters, who commemorated the anniversary of their arrival in Canada with a weekend colloquy in southern British Columbia in July 2006. The meeting was condemned by veterans in the United States but ignored by Canadians.

Order or happiness? Malcolm cannot resist here. He notes that the American Constitution promises "life, liberty and the pursuit of happiness," while the Canadian promises "life, liberty and security of the person." He argues that the law matters. "The emphasis is on orderliness. Police can stop cars without probable cause. Pedestrians generally obey traffic lights."

Self-deprecation is as Canadian as the Shield. Praise is met with skepticism; Malcolm finds that when a visitor rhapsodized over the cleanest air, the most abundant fresh water, the largest woods, the most reliable city services, the most imaginative museums and parks, he was met with a chorus of qualification, as if nothing of the sort could be true. "It is instinctive," he says. "The only way to get a Canadian to praise his or her country is to announce that you are American and then to criticize Canada unmercifully." He recalls the number of times Canadians asked him why he came to Canada, and what his reaction was when his boss informed him he had to move there, as if it were a sentence. When he would tell Canadians they had a great country, they would listen quietly and politely and incredulously. "Canadians, it seemed, did not think much of their country, of each other, of their future together, or, thus, of themselves."

For this American, it went beyond self-deprecation. He is too polite to call it self-loathing, though it sounds like it. "Nobody in Canada bragged about Canada . . . few Canadians publicly and openly appreciated Canada either, not until someone attacked or mocked it. Praising the country was rarely done. Canadians always seemed to be apologizing for something. It was so ingrained." He finds a people simply happy to endure against the odds, survival being a touchstone. Be happy with what you have. "Canadians were content to settle. To survive comfortably was enough for many. Canadians were not in a hurry for anything."

Looking at Canadians through the eyes of foreigners, we get a sense of how they see us. They say so much about us: that we are nice, hospitable, modest, blind to our achievements. That we are obedient, conservative, deferential, colonial, and complex, particularly so. That we are fractious, envious, geographically impossible, and politically improbable. That we will make it. That we may not. Some of this was written one hundred years ago, some twenty years ago. As we look at the character of Canadians today, we see echoes of what others have seen in the past. There are traits that endure, such as self-doubt and the negative self-definition, and ones that appear and disappear, such as complacency.

We can learn something in the people who took the measure of Canada, as well as the response to their impressions. Often it says as much about us as about them. In writing his famous poem "Our Lady of the Snows," for example, Rudyard Kipling thought that he was paying homage to Canada and the Canadian Preferential Tariff of 1897.

A Nation spoke to a Nation,
    A Queen sent word to a Throne:
"Daughter I am in my mother's house,
    But Mistress in my own.

The gates are mine to open.
As the gates are mine to close,
And I set my house in order,"
Said our Lady of the Snows.

He was truly dazzled by snow. But his writings were greeted badly by Canadians, who thought he was making too much of the white stuff; some thought it would discourage immigration. "Snow has much to do with the formation of our national character," said B.K. Sandwell in 1930. "So far as I am aware, no high-latitude country has ever shown a disposition to be ashamed of snow, until Canada early in the present century decided to masquerade before the world as a sub-tropical nation, and found Mr. Kipling's poem an obstacle to that ambition."

When André Siegfried wrote his first book about Canada in 1907, it was published in Britain, not Canada. After all, the publisher seemed to think, why would Canadians be interested in reading about themselves? When the book did make the voyage across the Atlantic, it was welcomed, and then quickly forgotten, as if his observations were less de Tocqueville than *Tatler*. It wasn't republished until 1966. Today Siegfried is virtually unknown; he has no entry in *The Canadian Encyclopedia* and is scarcely mentioned in national histories.

When Andrew Malcolm's book came out in 1985, a review in *The Globe and Mail* was delightfully telling. The reviewer, columnist Jeffrey Simpson, praises Malcolm's tireless reportage and gentle findings, suggesting that Malcolm has more confidence in Canada than Canadians do in themselves. Simpson's opening observation is as true as it is ironic: "Andrew Malcolm will perhaps find it typically and irritatingly Canadian to observe that his portrait of us is probably too kind," he says. "Seldom, if ever, have we been so generously treated by a foreigner . . ."

As for Brian Moore, although his novels were critically acclaimed, they didn't sell well in Canada. When he won the

Governor General's Literary Award for Fiction again in 1975 for *The Great Victorian Collection*, *The Globe and Mail* complained that he should not be eligible because he no longer lived in Canada. "I'm irritated when I'm not treated as a Canadian," Moore said in an interview in 1979. "Canadians tend to ignore the fact that I use Canada and Canadian characters in my novels. I'm dependent on Canada for at least half my literary terrain. I feel at home here, in the social sense." By then he had been gone two decades. He did summer in Nova Scotia and late in life he built a house down east, but his association wasn't what it was. He died in 1999 in the United States, where he had gone to live forty years before. Always the exile, he may have liked Canada, but at the end of the day, he couldn't live there.

Chapter 3

The Unconscious Canadian

In the spring of 1998, J.L. Granatstein published *Who Killed Canadian History?* For admirers of the country's most prolific historian, this might have seemed like yet another in a stream of books on immigration, military history, and foreign policy he seems to produce at a rate of one or more a year. This one, though, was different. This was a polemic. This was passionate. This was personal.

Granatstein wonders why a history as rich and varied as Canada's has become virtually irrelevant. He convenes his own forensic inquiry and acts as chief coroner. Granatstein has spent his life thinking and writing about Canada, learning, interpreting, and imparting its lessons in the classroom and on public platforms. He studied history as a graduate student in Canada and the United States and spent almost thirty years teaching at York University in Toronto until his retirement in 1995, when he was named professor emeritus. He has written, co-written, edited, and co-edited seventy-one books and pamphlets, many of them bestsellers, and served as director of the Canadian War Museum in Ottawa from 1998 to 2000. The recipient of six honorary degrees, he is a Member of the Order of Canada.

His argument is that we no longer teach our history. It is unimportant to us. In some parts of the country, we simply ignore it; in other parts, we diminish it. Equally harmful, we distort it, deny it, and dismiss it, largely by concentrating on the wrong ideas and themes. Our mistreatment of history is self-destructive. "Canada must be one of the few nations in the world, certainly one of the few Western industrialized states, that does not make an effort to teach its history positively and thoroughly to its young people," he writes. "It must be one of the few political entities to overlook its own cultural traditions – the European civilization on which our nation is founded – on the grounds that they would systematically discriminate against those who come from other cultures. The effects of these policies on a generation of students are all around us as the twentieth century draws to a close."

As only an historian of his eminence can, Granatstein shows how Canada has neglected its history. He blames politicians for failing to establish national standards; bureaucrats for failing to set rigid curricula and yielding to political correctness; historians for writing about the frivolous, the anxious and the aggrieved; the media for trivializing history; ethnic interest groups for whitewashing history. Who killed Canadian history? In a sense, we all did.

This is no small matter in a nation uncertain of what it is and where it is going. "The nation is fragile indeed," Granatstein writes in 1997, two years after Quebec came within a half a per cent of leaving Canada, "and one reason for this lamentable state of affairs might well be the lack of a history that binds Canadians together. It is not that we do not have such a history. It is simply that we have chosen not to remember it."

How was Granatstein's critique of the teaching of Canadian history greeted? By the public, well. His book sold some twenty thousand copies and was received warmly. And his colleagues? Those who had long shared his thesis – fellow travellers such as Desmond Morton, David Bercuson, Robert Bothwell – applauded.

Michael Bliss had made some of the same arguments in a provocative essay in 1991 called "Privatizing the Mind: The Sundering of Canadian History, the Sundering of Canada." Other professional historians were critical. In a lengthy essay in the *Canadian Historical Review* in 1999, A.B. McKillop accused Granatstein of being on the side of virtue and blind to other realities. "Canadians need to be aware that there is another view of Canada's national past," he says. "They need to know that in the interests of polemic, Granatstein miscasts the role of the scholar as citizen, misrepresents the purpose of scholarship and distorts the nature and quality of academic historical writing. In doing so, he puts forward a conception of Canada's 'national' history that is no better suited to serve national self-understanding than the scholarship he dismisses. Canadian history, in short, is vastly more complex and more interesting than the one he would like Canadians to write about and Canadian students to learn." McKillop argues that there is nothing wrong with studying the history of maids in Belleville in the 1890s, Granatstein's scornful example of narrow, particularist history. Studying social history of this nature is important because it tells us something about people lower in the hierarchy, McKillop says.

A year later, Robert Wright, another historian, responded to Granatstein, as well as McKillop, in the *Canadian Historical Review*. He accepted Granatstein's view that Canadians know little about their past but said the reason is not because of political correctness or bureaucratic folly, as Granatstein argues. The reason is far deeper. History is irrelevant to most Canadians because they do not live "historical" lives. "I take the view that if Canadians actually still lived within a historical paradigm – that is, if history provided the social, cultural, economic, and political architecture within which they contextualized their lived experience – then surely high school history would be the robust and exciting program that Granatstein imagines it ought to be." Wright seems to be arguing, if you can wade through his contextualizing, that the collapse of history is part of the new socio-economic order that ignores the past, if not denies its value. The real problem? It's the zeitgeist, stupid. Wright would like to see history become "the organizing principle of Canadians' lived experience" but there is too much in the way.

The point remains that history is essential to our process of self-discovery as a people. The Unconscious Canadian is an ignorant Canadian. He has detached himself from his past, a touchstone of identity in a world of accelerating scientific advance, technological innovation, and the free movement of people and ideas. History guides us, explains us, inspires us, anchors us – even if we may not always agree on what happened, where, why, and to whom. It is what we are because it is what we were. In 1941, Samuel Bronfman, of the House of Seagram, made this argument in his introduction to *Canada: The Foundations of Its Future*, a chronicle of the country the distillery commissioned from Stephen Leacock, the essayist, political economist, and humorist. "The history of Canada is the sum total of the biographies of all its citizens," he said. "In its unfolding, all have a share; from its narrative, all derive that pride that comes of participation. Written in national terms, it is yet, in so far as every Canadian is concerned, a deeply personal record; for here, fashioned into a composite picture are the activities, in peace and war, of industry and commerce, of labour and capital, of the great and the humble. Other departments of letters may perhaps have a special appeal; history belongs to all."

It belongs to all of us because history is us. We didn't just arrive here yesterday, *deus ex machina*. We came from somewhere. We did things together. We survived. Astonishing as it may seem, though, we choose not to remember this, and it has consequences for us as a people. Almost ten years after Granatstein's warning, we are no smarter. As older Canadians die, taking their repository of memory with them, our collective sense of the past dims. It makes us an ignorant people. We stumble about in a kind of poetic fog, with little idea of where we were and what we did. Because we do not know our past, we cannot teach it to our children or to our compatriots who have come here from abroad. Behold Canada, a nation of amnesiacs.

How little do Canadians know about their past? In 2006, pollsters commissioned by the Dominion Institute and CanWest Newspapers asked a broad sample of Canadians a series of questions about their country. The questions covered Canada's geography, its history, its arts and culture, its industry and commerce, and its role in the world. The questions tested a rudimentary knowledge of the country one would expect of an average citizen with a basic education. The answers were published on Canada Day in the *Ottawa Citizen* and other newspapers across the country.

On its birthday, barely two-thirds of those questioned knew Canada has ten provinces and three territories. Slightly fewer than that could name the three oceans bordering the country. Only 61 per cent could name the five Great Lakes. Tested on their history, Canadians knew even less. Barely half could name Canada's first prime minister, Sir John A. Macdonald. Just a tenth knew the Charlottetown Conference, at which Canada was founded in 1867; less than a third could identify Mackenzie King, Canada's longest serving prime minister. Only 42 per cent could name one of the wars (the American War of Independence, the War of 1812) in which Canada was invaded by the United States; only 23 per cent knew the United Empire Loyalists; only 46 per cent could name the United Nations as the body Canadians helped found after the Second World War: only 43 per cent could answer a similar question on Canada's role in creating NATO. It was an equally unhappy story in the number of respondents (21 per cent) who could identify Canada's role in the Universal Declaration of Human Rights (which was drafted by John Humphrey, a Canadian lawyer); Canada's historic opposition to apartheid in South Africa (50 per cent); and Canada's role in the creation of the International Criminal Court (10 per cent).

Who is Canada's head of state? Only 8 per cent knew it is Queen Elizabeth. When was the patriation of the British North America Act? Only 15 per cent knew it was 1982. What part of the Constitution guarantees "basic rights and freedoms"? Only 32 per cent could associate "rights and freedoms" with the Charter of Rights and Freedoms. When it came to identifying events related to the two world wars, the response was also dismal. Only 33 per cent knew why November 11 is called Remembrance Day (though 73 per cent knew the significance of wearing a poppy). Asked about the disastrous Canadian raid on the French port occupied by the Germans in 1942, only 27 per cent knew it was Dieppe. Some questions were particularly troublesome. Asked what great event ended in 1885 "with the hammering of the last spike," only 54 per cent answered the Canadian Pacific Railway, meaning that most could not match "spike" and "railway." When asked which minority was removed from the west coast of Canada during the Second World War, however, 61 per cent answered the Japanese.

More reason to wonder. Only 28 per cent knew what the conscription plebiscite in 1942 was about. Only 43 per cent knew that the Korean War, in which Canadians fought and died, was the first armed conflict of the Cold War. Only 50 per cent could identify "In Flanders Fields" as "Canada's most famous war poem." Just 46 per cent knew about the Halifax Explosion in 1917. Only 64 per cent could identify Vimy Ridge as Canada's great battle of the Great War, and only 44 per cent knew our fondness for "peace-keeping" began with the Suez Crisis of 1956. This was particularly telling. Here was Canada's great victory and vocation, celebrated in our pantheon, yet Canadians knew little of it. But don't despair. Almost all respondents (95 per cent) knew that *O Canada* is the country's national anthem – even if only 68 per cent could recite the first two lines.

The Dominion Institute, an independent, non-profit organi-zation founded in 1997 to promote the study of Canadian history, has commissioned these kinds of surveys regularly. The sad truth is that the results do not improve. Indeed, its findings in 2005 on Canada's economic history – for example, the National Energy Program or the name of the free trade agreement with Mexico and the United States – were the worst in seven years of surveys.

Other polls at other times have also reflected a widespread ignorance about Canada. In February 2006, Canadians failed a quiz on three of Canada's most famous prime ministers. Only 47 per cent knew that Sir John A. Macdonald was Canada's leading Father of Confederation; only 44 per cent knew that Pierre Elliott Trudeau invoked the War Measures Act; only 18 per cent knew that Sir Wilfrid Laurier was Canada's first francophone prime minister and had declared that the twentieth century belonged to Canada. These results were worse than those of a questionnaire in 2002.

Of course, these are just surveys. Some historians wonder what they prove. In a spirited exchange with Granatstein in a slender book called *Great Questions of Canada*, published by the Dominion Institute in 2000, Michael Ignatieff argued that many Canadians knew very little about Canada even as they fought for it in the trenches of Europe in the Great War. If you believe that historical knowledge is the *sine qua non* of citizenship, he said, "we can all too easily conclude that the country is going to hell in a handcart. We can surrender to the kind of nostalgic pessimism that is apt to seize anyone over 50 who surveys the apparently appalling ignorance of the younger generation. Historical ignorance is unattractive . . . but it is a *folie de grandeur* to believe the country is done for if our citizenry can't repeat the names of all our prime ministers back to Confederation, the major battles since 1759 and the key provisions of the BNA Act." The point made by Ignatieff, an historian turned politician, is that history is nice but not neces-sary for civic virtue.

Certainly one could question the value of some of these surveys. Is the country going to fall apart because 23 per cent of Canadians knew that Bricklin was the automaker that went bankrupt in the 1970s or because 43 per cent knew that the TD Financial Group (presumably one of the survey's sponsors) celebrated its 150th anniversary in 2005? These questions may have been asked for a reason, but it is unreasonable to expect ordinary people to know the answers. What is more worrisome, though, is the widespread ignorance of larger, more basic themes. One-third of respondents didn't know that the Hudson's Bay Company was built on the fur trade. Nine-tenths didn't know that the Pacific Scandal brought down Macdonald's government, and one-half didn't know the Great Depression was that dark decade of stagnation, unemployment, and despair in the 1930s.

Surveys are surveys, and no doubt some assistant professor of statistics with a doctorate from the College of the Contrary will parse every question and dissect every answer in search of a fatal inconsistency. But these polls reveal a pattern. It may be that far more than half of all Canadians actually know about Sir John A. Macdonald and his importance to Canada, and that a legion of his loyalists are holding clandestine meetings in the attic of his gabled home in Kingston, Ontario. It may be that there are secret societies studying the careers of Sir Charles Tupper, the notorious womanizer known as "the Ram of Cumberland," or Sir Mackenzie Bowell, the feckless Orangeman forced from office by his own party after sixteen troubled months. It may be that there are conspiracy theorists debating the assassination of D'Arcy McGee or high school students writing essays about George Brown. Or that there are midnight commemorations at the graves of our reformers and rebels or private celebrations on the anniversary of the passage of the Statute of Westminster. Possibly, Canadians may know more about their country than they admit. But it is unlikely. Surveys may not tell the whole truth, but they reveal a truth. They are one measure, however imperfect, of this country's amnesia.

How do we account for the Unconscious Canadian? We can examine the absence of history in the curricula of our schools. Or the deterioration of our historical sites. Or the content and presentation of our museums. Or the absence of biographies and memoirs about and by our leaders. Or the strange disappearance of Dominion Day. Sadly, we have many measures of our ebbing past.

Begin with the teaching of history in our high schools. Under the Constitution, education is a provincial jurisdiction; schools are run by the provinces, not the federal government. Edmonton, Victoria, and Halifax set the curriculum, not Ottawa. As Granatstein reminds us, the provinces decide what they will teach, when they will teach it, and what texts they will use. This is what happens when education is a provincial responsibility. Like so much else in this balkanized country, different practices apply in different places. In terms of history, the approach is inconsistent. On the whole, the fact is that most provinces do not teach Canadian history.

A decade ago, when Granatstein was writing his book, he found that four provinces required just one Canadian history course – sometimes only one term long – to graduate from high school. Two provinces required two courses. Four had no Canadian history requirement at all. More recently, the Dominion Institute has found that only three provinces require high school students to study Canadian history. "Incredible as it seems, there are provinces where you can go through high school and not be required to take a single course in Canadian history," Rudyard Griffiths told the *Toronto Star* in 2005.

It is sobering to survey the teaching of history in Canadian high schools. Province by province, according to the Dominion Institute, the pickings are slim. In British Columbia, there is no separate course for Canadian history; a Grade 11 social studies student will have had some exposure to twentieth-century Canadian history. In Alberta, there is no separate history course, though, as in B.C., students have some twentieth-century Canadian history as part of social studies. In Saskatchewan, Grade 12 students must take a course in Canadian studies in which they can select history, native studies, or social studies. In Manitoba, Grade 11 students must take a general survey course that includes twentieth-century Canadian history. In Ontario, there is a mandatory Canadian history course in Grade 10 that focuses on Canada after 1914. In Quebec, in Grade 11, there is a mandatory course on the history of Quebec in Canada. In New Brunswick, there is a compulsory course in Grade 11 on world history and an optional course in Canadian history. In Nova Scotia, the compulsory course in Canadian history allows students to choose to study Canadian history, African history, or Gaelic, African-Canadian, or Mi'kmaq studies. In Prince Edward Island, graduating students must have completed a history course with some elements of Canadian history. In Newfoundland and Labrador, there is no mandatory course; students can study Canadian history or world history.

What to make of this crazy quilt? Collectively, it suggests a country with no compulsion to tell its story to its children. In most provinces a student can receive a high school diploma – which may be all the formal education he or she receives in life – with little or no exposure to Canadian history in the upper grades. In New Brunswick, for example, it is fine to study the history of the world but not of Canada. In British Columbia, it is fine to take some history as part of something else. In Nova Scotia, other histories – those of blacks, Acadians, Africans, or aboriginals – are as important as Canada's. In Ontario, history is restricted to the twentieth century, and that seems to begin in 1914. A student in Tweed or Timmins can leave high school never knowing that Canada formally began in the nineteenth century, and although the twentieth century was said to be Canada's, it is fourteen years shorter than in other jurisdictions. Elsewhere, history is subsumed by "social studies," which may teach valuable lessons, though not necessarily those of history. Then there is Quebec. It is no surprise that history taught in secondary schools there is the history of Quebec, or perhaps Quebec within Canada. That has meant students learn the story of the tensions between French and English, often with the Québécois portrayed as victims. When the government of Jean Charest – perhaps Quebec's most federalist premier since Jean Lesage in the 1960s – proposed changes to the curriculum in the spring of 2006, it caused an uproar. The purpose was to play down linguistic and ethnic tensions. "It represents a departure from the traditional framework of history structured around conflict between francophones and anglophones to offer a more unifying history," explained historian Jean-François Cardin, who advised the government on the changes. But politicians, commentators, and unionists protested that the new approach would gloss over the Conquest of 1763, the patriation of the Constitution in 1982, and the collapse of the Meech Lake Accord in 1990. They called it an "ultra-federalist" view of the past that would represent Canada more than Quebec. They said it played down the sovereigntist movement, overlooking "essential elements of Quebec history."

This debate in Quebec is a lesson – indeed an inspiration – to the rest of Canada. Quebeckers think more about their history than English Canadians do about theirs. "History has always had a special status in the province," writes Kevin Kee, a history teacher who moved to Quebec from Ontario. As he quickly learned, it is largely because *"l'histoire est plus présente"* – Quebeckers are surrounded by their past in song, verse, places, names. They have a rich past, going back to the early explorers of the sixteenth century, and they cherish it. In 2008, they will mount a lavish celebration of the four hundredth anniversary of the founding of Quebec City by Samuel de Champlain; other cities in Canada barely observe their historic milestones.

It is true that English Canada is uncomfortable with *je me souviens* ("I remember"), the defiant slogan stamped on Quebec licence plates. Michael Ignatieff thinks that if it invites the Québécois to keep faith with old quarrels, injustices, hurts, and slights, "I'd prefer my licence plate to read 'I've forgotten.'" It's an example of history as controversy. When that declaration was originally adopted by the Parti Québécois in the 1970s, it suggested a sense of grievance. It may still, but not in the same way. What is important is that Quebeckers are *remembering*. It is the act itself, which reinforces their pride and self-awareness. The rest of Canada, take note.

As cities the age of Quebec know, history is not only found in classrooms and textbooks. History is written in the wood, stone, steel, tin, brick, and glass of houses, churches, legislatures, schools, libraries, statues, cemeteries, convents, bridges, factories, and other great public edifices. This is our physical history, which we are ignoring in our villages, towns, and cities. Neglecting our past is as dangerous as denying it. As Joseph Howe, one of the Fathers of Confederation, said in 1871: "A wise nation preserves its records, gathers up its muniments, decorates the tombs of its illustrious dead, repairs its great public structures, and fosters national pride and love of country by perpetual reference to the sacrifices and glories of the past."

So serious is the assault on our historic sites that Sheila Fraser, the Auditor General of Canada, devoted an entire chapter to it in her report to Parliament in 2004. Because she uncovered the improprieties of the sponsorship scandal in the same report, her warning went largely unnoticed. That was unfortunate. Fraser conducted what she called the first audit of cultural heritage anywhere in the world. She found that almost two-thirds of the historic properties then administered by Parks Canada (891 designated historic sites and 269 heritage buildings) were in "poor to fair condition" and in need of work in two to five years, without which they could be lost.

One of the worst was the Cave and Basin National Historic Site in Banff National Park – the first of Canada's national parks, established in 1885 – which draws thousands of visitors each year. Another is Fort Henry in Kingston, Ontario, an imposing stone redoubt that was built between 1832 and 1837; Fraser concludes the fort is "seriously impaired" and needs two years of work. A third is the National Library of Canada, the repository of millions of books and documents, where 90 per cent of the collection is housed in unacceptable conditions. "Once a piece of history is lost, it is lost forever," said Fraser. "And the situation is not improving. Our cultural heritage is continually growing and what we've got is already threatened."

Fraser's report has the antiseptic tone of the accountant she is. This is an audit, written in the numbered paragraphs of a legal brief, innocent of anxiety or anger, as dry as ancient timbers. But it carefully catalogues our inventory of things historic, traces why we have allowed this to happen (budgetary cutbacks), and proposes how to respond (money and administrative change). In a nutshell, the Auditor General describes the challenge facing Canada in protecting its heritage. Indeed, her *cri de cœur* on the loss of Canada's physical past may be more valuable than her findings of political scandal that overshadowed it. She told us what historians, archivists, curators, and others who tend the garden of the past have been warning for years: that we are in danger of losing a part of ourselves.

In February 2007, Fraser revisited these historic sites and found that Parks Canada had made "satisfactory progress" addressing problems at Fort Henry and the Carillon Canal on the Ottawa River (though she said the repairs were not quick enough or complete enough). The bad news, though, is that a whole order of buildings, battlegrounds, forts, and archeological sites is in danger of crumbling. Managed by other departments of government, these include the Halifax Armoury, the Citadelle and Cap-aux-Diamants Redoubt in Quebec City, the Admiral's Residence in Esquimalt, British Columbia, and the Royal Flying Corps Hangars at CFB Borden in Ontario. "When important parts of Canada's built heritage are lost, future generations are barred from access to key aspects of Canadian history," warned the auditor general. However unpoetic, her message was no less urgent than it was three years earlier. Examples of a past at risk, in one part of the country or another, in one form or another, are everywhere.

Consider how Canada remembers its prime ministers. Ours is a fitful approach to preserving and identifying their birthplaces, residences, and gravesites. We have an interest in some and not others. As national historic sites, we preserve the homes of Sir John A. Macdonald (Bellevue House in Kingston, Ontario); Sir Wilfrid Laurier (Sir Wilfrid Laurier House in Laurentides, Quebec), and William Lyon Mackenzie King (Woodside in Kitchener, Ontario). Both Laurier and King lived in Laurier House, the *grande dame* of prime ministerial residences, in Ottawa. (King left his leafy estate of cottages, gardens, and ruins at Kingsmere in the Gatineau Hills of Quebec to the people of Canada upon his death in 1950. It is not designated an historic site. The other designated residence belonged to Louis St. Laurent in Compton, Quebec.) The federal government does not maintain other residences. (Earnscliffe, where Macdonald lived and died, has been the residence of the British High Commissioner since 1930. A campaign to buy it back and turn it into a museum in 2007 foundered. Lester B. Pearson, the Nobel Laureate, is remembered on the second floor of Laurier House with a quirky reproduction of his study after he retired. That is the only place he is recognized, as if his desk and chair were an afterthought. His grave in MacLaren's Cemetery, overlooking the village of Wakefield in the Gatineau Hills, is marked with a flagpole and a plaque. These were not erected until 1992, twenty years after his death.

In his will, John G. Diefenbaker left his home in Rockcliffe Park in Ottawa to the government of Canada on the condition that it be made into an historical museum emphasizing "my lifetime devotion" to human rights. After his death in 1979, the government considered the offer and declined. The house was sold and the proceeds returned to the estate. But Diefenbaker, who had no small ego, saw to it that he would be remembered like no other prime minister. His career in public life is celebrated in the Diefenbaker Canada Centre, a library and archive on the campus of the University of Saskatchewan in Saskatoon. Although it eschews any notion of hagiography, it is a temple to Diefenbaker, a vainglorious, petty man who won the largest parliamentary majority in the country's history in 1958 and lost it all in 1963. His library is the only institution of its kind in Canada. Unlike the United States, which encourages and underwrites presidential libraries as repositories of artifacts and papers, Canada has no such practice. Diefenbaker's boyhood homestead, transplanted from the Prairie to Wascana Park in Regina, now sits in a pioneer village south of Moose Jaw.

For one reason or another, the homes of most other prime ministers are not designated historic sites. Some are identified by a plaque, however, as a kind of consolation prize. These include the homes of Alexander Mackenzie in Sarnia, Ontario; Sir John Abbott in Saint-André-Est, Quebec; Sir Charles Tupper in Warren, Nova Scotia; Sir Mackenzie Bowell in Belleville, Ontario; Sir Robert Borden in Grand Pré, Nova Scotia; and Arthur Meighen in Portage la Prairie, Manitoba. The others? Nothing. In fact, since Diefenbaker, Canada hasn't honoured any of his successors: Lester Pearson, Pierre Trudeau, Joe Clark, John Turner, Brian Mulroney, Kim Campbell, Jean Chrétien, or Paul Martin. While there was interest in acquiring Trudeau's art deco house on Pine Avenue in Montreal after his death in 2000 and turning it into a museum, it still hasn't happened.

On February 11, 1999, the federal government unveiled a program to commemorate the country's prime ministers. Andy Mitchell, then secretary of state (Parks), appeared at Laurier House to make the announcement. Parks Canada would establish a new webpage on the prime ministers. It would "continue" to recognize prime ministers "as persons of national historic significance" upon their deaths, waiving the twenty-five-year period required of other eminent Canadians to attain this exalted status. It would also continue "to preserve and protect" the five national prime ministerial historic sites. This was all very nice but not very new. What was noteworthy was the government's promise to maintain and mark the gravesites of the prime ministers. But even that came with a sheepish disclaimer in the last paragraph of a two-page explanatory note: "The current policy is that, with very rare exceptions, birthplaces and graves of prime ministers are not considered for designation as national historic sites." In other words, when it comes to honouring Canada's prime ministers, the government would promise all support short of commitment.

Since then, little has changed. A representative of the Historic Sites and Monuments Board of Canada – which, incidentally, calls itself the smallest unit in the government of Canada – confirms that we don't fuss over birthplaces and graves because "they are usually not very closely associated with these people or their accomplishments. A prime minister may have only lived in his birthplace residence for two years. . . . We can't commemorate a whole cemetery just because a prime minister is buried there." True, a prime minister may not have lived in a house very long but that wouldn't prevent Parks Canada from using the venue to create a museum or placing a plaque remembering a great Canadian. It doesn't stop other countries, which recognize almost every place their leaders have set foot.

It is encouraging that the government has now marked all the graves of the prime ministers except Pierre Trudeau and Sir John Abbott. And it isn't as if this is all we do. We raise statues to them, and we name colleges, schools, foundations, scholarships, streets, ships, bridges, and lakes after them. We put them on postage stamps and the backs of paper bills. Louis St. Laurent has an icebreaker bearing his name. Diefenbaker, Pearson, and Trudeau have airports named after them. Honouring them, though, is not always easy. In 2001, when the federal government tried to rename Mount Logan in the Yukon in honour of Trudeau, who was a great outdoorsman, a chorus of protests forced its retreat. Mountaineers and natives opposed renaming the venerable peak, the highest in Canada. So did the descendants of Sir William Logan, the founder of the Geological Survey of Canada. Instead, the government renamed Montreal's Dorval Airport after Trudeau, a decision immediately denounced by a corporal's guard of noisy, unreconstructed sovereigntists.

If prime ministers fight for posthumous recognition in Canada, so do the Fathers of Confederation. According to an exhaustive investigation by Ian MacLeod of the *Ottawa Citizen*, most of the homes of the seventeen founding fathers who lived in Ottawa after 1867 have disappeared. Only six of the seventeen residences survive; the rest were destroyed by fire or demolished to make way for parking lots, office towers and apartment blocks. Of those that remain, five of the six have historical plaques associating them with their storied boarders or owners. When one of the plaques was stolen in 1999, a new one was made and placed on the wrong building, where it has remained. As for the other eleven historic sites, there is nothing to mark their significance. No one seems to care. Royal Galipeau, a member of Parliament from Ottawa, has appealed to the National Capital Commission and the City of Ottawa to put plaques on all those places where the buildings stood, lest we lose all memory of what was there. He has had no success. "Our Confederation has gone through a lot of turmoil and part of it is that we forget its birth," he told the *Ottawa Citizen* in 2006. "There's a lot of people who worked really hard to put this country together, and if it was any other country, they would all be honoured. Visiting Washington, D.C., you would find a plaque anywhere George Washington sneezed, but we're more modest."

Or, indifferent. After all, why spend public money to honour dead white males no one recognizes, anyway? Who really cares that Sir Alexander Tilloch Galt lived on Ottawa's Daly Street or that Sir George-Étienne Cartier lived on Princess Terrace? Today, in the Age of Ignorance, it isn't fashionable to care about the past, especially if you are twenty years old and know little about it. Most people, other than the passionate Royal Galipeau, only shrug. In other places, they don't shrug. History is celebrated. In Thomaston, Maine, a gracious colonial town on the state's mid-coast, a French expatriate had an inspired idea; he persuaded the city fathers to allow him to design plaques commemorating his adopted town's history and its eighteenth-century homes and organized a sequential walking tour. This is done in towns around New England. In Boston, the Freedom Trail takes visitors through the revolutionary events of late-eighteenth-century Beantown. There is some of this in Canada, to be sure, but not enough.

In the absence of a grand plan, Canada has still managed to preserve the homes of some great Canadians, such as Louis-Joseph Papineau, the lawyer, seigneur, and rebel whose manor house and gardens on the Ottawa River in Montebello, Quebec, are open to the public. In a unique example of binational collaboration, the U.S. National Parks Service and Parks Canada maintain the summer home of Franklin D. Roosevelt on Campobello Island in New Brunswick. The federal government preserves the home of

Alexander Graham Bell in Baddeck, Nova Scotia. In some places, such as Dawson City, Yukon, where Parks Canada administers an entire historic district, or in the nineteenth-century red-brick Distillery District in Toronto, which calls itself the best-preserved industrial architecture in North America, we make an exemplary effort to tell our story. In some places, we don't.

Generally, Canada remembers its luminaries reluctantly. Few governors general, soldiers, doctors, writers, musicians, scholars, inventors, scientists, artists, and athletes are celebrated as persons of stature in Canada, as they would be in other societies. Writers are revered in Ireland. Artists are venerated in Italy. Musicians are celebrated in Germany. Everyone is a star in America. Not in Canada. When a philanthropist proposed honouring Canada's military heroes with a succession of statues on Elgin Street in downtown Ottawa, there was opposition. It was said to be too "militarist." Eventually, the critics relented and fourteen statues and busts of military heroes from Canada's past were erected and dedicated by the governor general in 2006. They are called "the Valiants."

Apathy has a price. In Montreal, which was founded in 1642, lovely nineteenth-century homes and flats have been lost in the last generation. In the 1960s, when the Decarie Expressway was punched through the city, it destroyed buildings and neighbourhoods. The assault continued in the 1970s. One of the most bruising fights was over the demolition of the Prince of Wales Terrace at the corner of Sherbrooke and McTavish streets on the campus of McGill University. The preservationists lost and the glorious terrace was torn down to make way for the Samuel Bronfman Building, a monstrosity. Indeed, up and down Sherbrooke Street, the graceful thoroughfare known as the "Square Mile," captured in the photographs of nineteenth-century photographer William Notman, fine seats of the aristocracy have been torn down. It is still going on. In recent years, the city has lost the Queen's Hotel, the York Theatre, and the Montreal Hunt Club. Preservationists worry about losing the storied Redpath Mansion, one of the last examples of Queen Anne architecture in Montreal, as well as the Ste. Sulpice Library and the Montreal Public Library, both examples of the beaux arts style. They even worry about the Guaranteed Pure Milk Bottle, a riveted-steel confection ten metres high, which has been a landmark since 1932. The fight goes on. Activists were successful in saving a Carmelite convent that developers had hoped to convert to condominiums. The provincial government has declared it an historic site.

And that is just Montreal. Most cities in Canada have had to fight to save their past, some with more success than others. In Toronto, activists prevented the destruction of the Old City Hall in the 1960s. In 1971, in Ottawa, they successfully fought a scheme to turn King Edward Avenue into an expressway running through Sandy Hill, the shaded enclave near Parliament Hill where many of those unsung Fathers of Confederation once lived.

The loss of our past goes beyond schools that don't teach national history and governments that neglect historic places. Consider three cultural institutions in the national capital. One was built and evolves. One was begun and abandoned. One was imagined and never built. Together they show how we present and interpret our history – or don't.

On May 15, 2006, the Canadian Museum of Civilization marked its sesquicentennial with an open house that drew ten thousand visitors and some congratulatory notices. "Today Canada's national museum remains a place of philosophical discussion," wrote Val Ross in *The Globe and Mail*. "But its debates are no longer about utility, posed to elites by omnivorous scholar-entrepreneurs. Today, they are more public and fluid: Who are we?" Fundamentally, who we are is the *raison d'être* of the country's largest museum, which its president calls "one of the great public cultural institutions around the globe." For almost 151 years, the museum has been a showcase of the artifacts of Canada (now numbering some 2.95 million) drawn from history, archaeology, and philately. Its role is to gather, preserve, exhibit, and explain. It began in 1856 as the display hall of the Geological Survey of Canada and later became known as the National Museum of Man. In 1986, persuaded that "national" had been appropriated by Quebec and sensitive to the etymologically dubious view that "man" did not include "woman" – and was therefore sexist – the museum changed its name to "civilization." That seemed audacious for the national museum of a modest country, implying an older, more influential society. But the concern was that visitors might expect a "museum of civilization" to differentiate between "advanced" and "primitive" societies, and that was not the point – or the belief – within this institution.

In 1989, the museum moved from Ottawa to Hull (now Gatineau), Quebec, on the banks of the Ottawa River. Physically, the building is striking, the ochre, undulating vision of aboriginal architect Douglas Cardinal, who later helped design the National Museum of the American Indian in Washington, which looks remarkably similar. The reviews were enthusiastic. Critics loved the strength and daring of the design. They talked about it warmly, with reason, and still do. Some thought that the popular exhibitions were too "Disneyesque," reflecting the trend among museums to make themselves another form of entertainment competing with amusement parks, the theatre, cinema, and sports. But as the country changes, so have the museum's contents, and so has the *selling* of the contents. Once the museum's focus was aboriginal society and French Canada. "Now there's a much broader concern with what makes up multicultural Canada," says Victor Rabinovitch, the president and chief executive officer of the museum. "And it's no longer about beautiful objects from the lives of the wealthy. We're interested in all classes, all ways of life."

Commercially, the Canadian Museum of Civilization is a success. It drew almost 1.4 million visitors in 2005–6, the highest attendance of any museum in Canada, in spite of charging the highest admission (albeit matched by some other Canadian museums). No matter. Visitors keep coming. They are drawn immediately into the Grand Hall, celebrating the cultural heritage of the native peoples of the West Coast, distinguished by totem poles and representative houses. On the same level is the First Peoples Hall, which chronicles the lives of aboriginal people. Together, the two exhibitions take up Level One. The museum suggests that one spend up to ninety minutes visiting both.

On the middle level are the Canadian Postal Museum, which shows the importance of communication through the mail, and the Canadian Children's Museum, which introduces young people to the cultures of the world. There are also temporary exhibitions, for example, on the life of hockey immortal Rocket Richard, the joys of skating in Canada, the Dead Sea Scrolls and the treasures of Petra, the pink city of Jordan. The CMC has an IMAX theatre and, outside, a Japanese Zen Garden and "the Canada Garden" of native plants and flowers.

On Level Three is the Canada Hall. It covers "a thousand years of history" through life-size exhibits and costumed characters, from the Vikings to the present. Here, for example, is life aboard a seventeenth-century fishing vessel, creaking and groaning; here are the tents and cabins of settlers and pioneers; here are the storefronts in the Old West; here is an Alberta oil rig, a Saskatchewan grain elevator, and a reassembled (and consecrated) Ukrainian Church; here is a railway waiting room showing a black-and-white film of a nostalgic cross-country journey aboard the Canadian Pacific Railway. The museum suggests sixty minutes for the Canada Hall.

The permanent exhibition space in the Canada Hall is now three times what it was when it opened. But the trouble is less what the museum displays than what it does not. For all the boldness of its form, the diversity of its objects, and the relevance of its temporary exhibitions (which have become more topical under Rabinovitch's imaginative leadership), the museum is appallingly incomplete. While it says a great deal about aboriginal Canada, social Canada, and commercial Canada, it has little to say about political Canada. Astonishingly, in the 140th year of Confederation, the country's founders, creators, and lawmakers are largely invisible from the country's repository of memory and so is the history they made. The museum avoids controversy, studiously so, offering strained commentary on some of the seminal moments of our past. Some of them it simply ignores.

Wander through the exhibitions of the Canada Hall. When the curators decided to present "a thousand years" of Canadian history in a single gallery, they had to make choices. Having decided to commit "75 to 90 minutes" of a visitor's time to the Grand Hall and the First Peoples Hall, they decided to allocate "45 to 60 minutes" to the Canada Hall. It immediately says something. Museums are like newspapers and state dinners; *placement* matters. So does space. Where a story appears in a newspaper (front page, back page) and how many columns it receives (quarter page, half page) is a measure of its importance. So is where a guest is seated at the table in relation to the host. The Great Hall and the First Peoples Hall are on Level One, inviting the visitor to enter. The Canada Hall is on Level Three, challenging the visitor to find it.

What is striking about the Canada Hall is what is not there. The siege of Quebec – you know, that short, sharp morning skirmish in which a Briton named Wolfe defeated a Frenchman named Montcalm on the Plains of Abraham in 1759 – is noted on an explanatory panel. There is nothing substantial here about the meetings at Charlottetown that led to Confederation in 1867 or to the patriation of the Constitution in 1982 or the conscription crisis of 1917. Nothing substantial about the bombings by the FLQ in the 1960s or the rise of the Parti Québécois in the 1970s. Or the October Crisis. All this is too hot; in fact, one of the museum guides allows that she and her colleagues deliberately play down the Conquest and other uncomfortable questions when visitors raise them, which they do.

Walking into the Canada Hall is like stumbling onto a movie set. See the meticulous recreation of a British officer's room in nineteenth-century Montreal, based on a painting by artist Cornelius Krieghoff, including a pair of skates, a wine goblet, and a dip net. Or the bookstore in Winnipeg established by Frank Dojacek, a public-spirited Ukrainian who was a pillar of his community of immigrants. Or the Chinese hand laundry illustrating the plight of Chinese immigrants (who "washed laundry with their tears"). The expulsion of the Acadians is mentioned on a wall panel and the Winnipeg General Strike of 1919 is played up in the "social progress gallery." But a shoemaker at work in his house is more prominent in the museum than a clutch of Canadians at work in Parliament, from Sir John A. Macdonald to Pierre Trudeau. They too knew something about the national soul.

In 1999, stung by criticism of political correctness, the museum asked historians for an independent assessment. They found that too many people, places, and events were minimized or left out. K.J. Munro of Edmonton pointed out that the hall did not address the Hudson's Bay Company, the founding of Quebec City and Halifax, the creation of New Brunswick, the establishment of the Supreme Court of Canada, the hanging of Louis Riel, the introduction of Medicare, the adoption of the Canadian flag, or the referendums in Quebec in 1980 and 1995. Penny Bryden of Mount Allison University said there was no unifying theme. "Not only are the individual objects on display in the Canada Hall shown in an antiseptic environment that separates them from the broader historical context that gives them meaning," she said, "but in the gallery as a whole there are so many stages of development left unexplained that each exhibit becomes progressively more meaningless." Jacques Monet of Sudbury said parts of the exhibition were "sanitized," inchoate and confusing. He found it strange that, amid the replicas of images of so-called ordinary life, the visitor doesn't know "why these people came here, or why they decided to stay." Among his forgotten Canadians: Thomas D'Arcy McGee, Crowfoot, Nellie McClung, Henri Bourassa, Lester Pearson, Georges-P. Vanier.

(These sins of omission were not limited to the Canadian Museum of Civilization. When, in 1998, J.L. Granatstein became director of the Canadian War Museum on Sussex Drive in Ottawa, he was appalled at the commentary in the exhibition. There was almost no mention, for example, of the North Atlantic Treaty Organization, which Canada helped found after the Second World War. Historians rewrote the texts. In the new Canadian War Museum that opened on May 8, 2005, the narrative is clear, honest, and telling. In many ways, it is an antidote to the malady of the CMC, or, more charitably, a companion.)

Why is the Canadian Museum of Civilization the way it is? Rabinovitch, the owlish, cerebral public servant who has led it since 2000, says the museum was never conceived as a forum of political history. Its areas of expertise, as well as its collections and research, were centred on ethnology, archaeology, and anthropology. One of the reasons for the Grand Hall and the First Peoples Hall is that the artifacts displayed there comprised most of the museum's collection for its first 120 years or so. History did not become a part of its mission until 1964, and the emphasis was on social history. Rabinovitch says the innovation that the CMC has shown makes it "the most positive exception among Canadian museums, and perhaps museums worldwide." He notes the steps the museum has taken to enhance its political dimension: hiring its first curator with a mandate to develop political history; appointing a western historian; adding more detailed commentary on the fishery, black history, and Confederation; mounting a pointed contemporary exhibition on life in French North America.

Since the historians' review, the Canadian Museum of Civilization has re-examined and reconfigured things. It has added 40 per cent more content to the Canada Hall, such as that Chinese hand laundry and copies of head tax certificates. There has been an attempt to address more than the ordinary lives of people who seem to have been dropped into this enterprise, as if the heavens had simply opened. It now plans a permanent exhibition dedicated to great Canadians, turning over its entire top floor (one quarter of its permanent exhibition space) to those who made decisions and those who influenced them. It will be called *Face to Face: The Canadian Personalities Hall*. The tin-ear appellation notwithstanding, the exhibit promises to shed light on the people and events that the Canada Hall misses, which are far too many for a self-respecting national museum of 151 years. Promises.

As Rabinovitch argues, there are reasons that the country's biggest, most popular museum isn't addressing this country's political history. It might be the nature of its collection or the training of its curators or the weight of its past. It is also the difficulty in agreeing on the narrative; history is a minefield, a clash of interpretations among interested parties, which is why museums court controversy over the exhibitions they mount. Still, the reality remains: until the Canadian Museum of Civilization reorganizes and reorients itself, a visitor can come away without a clear sense of the great events and the great people of this country's past. It is staggering, really. And unlike in Washington or Paris, he could actually leave the national capital almost as ignorant as he arrived. In Ottawa, with some notable exceptions, there is no Lincoln Memorial or Pantheon or other soaring monument or museum to illustrate what went on here. If the country's history museum doesn't tell the whole story, no other will. As of now, it doesn't.

Ironically, though, the federal government had hoped to address lacunae in our knowledge of ourselves when it announced the creation of the Canada History Centre in Ottawa in 2003. Having been elected three times, Jean Chrétien was in his last six months in office. The centre would be part of his legacy. It would promote, exhibit, and interpret the great events and the great people of our past, both on display and online. More telling, it would be created in the Government Conference Centre, once the storied railway station in the heart of the capital, the venue of so many historical constitutional conclaves – including the one in 1981 that patriated the Constitution – and many first ministers' meetings. It would fill a need. "The Canada History Centre is being created to address a gap in the telling of our political and democratic history, which is often presented in a fragmented manner," said a background note. "The centre will integrate knowledge of Canada's political and civic past and will better equip Canadians to know who we are as individuals and as citizens of a great country and to participate knowledgeably in the Canadian democratic process." Predictably, there was much talk of inclusiveness in the purposes of the centre: that it would "reach out" to people, that it would promote debate "from diverse perspectives," that it would highlight important roles played by "aboriginal people, settlers and later immigrants," which included just about everybody.

Given what was missing in the Canadian Museum of Civilization, given the ignorance of national history among young Canadians and new Canadians, given the promise of renewal of a magnificent historic building, this seemed to be the right idea at the right time in the right place. After all, what was there not to like about a new museum in the national capital? Apparently, plenty.

For Paul Martin, the problem seemed to be that the museum would be a monument to Jean Chrétien. When Martin succeeded Chrétien in late 2003, he cancelled the project. Too expensive. No money. This was sadly predictable, a decision that suggested bad blood more than bad policy. What was less predictable was the hostility in some unexpected quarters toward the project.

One critic was John Jennings, a board member of the Canadian Canoe Museum in Peterborough, one of the country's many regional museums. "I was one of those who had to celebrate the cancellation of the Canada History Centre," he harrumphed. "Museums are having a horrible time." His view was echoed by John McAvity, the executive director of the Canadian Museums Association. When the federal budget came down in February 2004, McAvity said he could find only "one cause of satisfaction" in it: the cancellation of the History Centre. He was joined by Michael Robinson of the Glenbow Museum in Calgary, who was "proud to have campaigned to 'snuff the political history museum in its cradle.'"

Maybe they had a point. If Ottawa could not support other museums across the country adequately (public funding fell from 77 per cent of museums' revenues in 1999 to 63 per cent in 2004), why open a new one in Ottawa costing between $90 million and $125 million? That was reason enough for McAvity and company to cheer its demise. On the other hand, it might also have had to do with good, old-fashioned jealousy. Whatever, it was sadly Canadian to see this level of hostility. Legacy or not, Chrétien saw a need for a museum of this kind in the national capital. Yes, it had an awkward name, and yes, its mandate was unclear and its independence uncertain, and yes, it may have been executed badly. But the point remains: Chrétien wanted to raise the stature of Canadian history and he wanted to give an historic building new life. His idea stirred political rivalry and professional disdain. Ultimately, the money that would have been spent on the Canada History Centre did not go to the other museums; McAvity and his co-religionists were left with no new money and the country with no new museum. Some two years later, the Conservatives cut $4.6 million from the Museum Assistance Program, which aids small museums around the country. Parliament restored the money and the chastened new government promised a new museum policy, but it would not include a history museum.

Jean Chrétien, who collected Inuit art and played classical music in his office, also wanted to create a national portrait gallery. He believed that Canada should have a place to display historical art in its capital just as Britain, France, the United States, and Australia do in theirs. It was not a new idea; Vincent Massey proposed this in 1948. "Canada possesses no national portrait gallery where the likenesses of all the eminent figures in Canadian life could be found," he wrote in *On Being Canadian* almost sixty years ago. "Such portraits should be acquired not because of any artistic merit they might possess but as documentary records in whatever form they are available. Suitably housed and catalogued, the collection would be of the greatest value to students of Canadian history and of genuine interest to the general public."

The Portrait Gallery of Canada was to be created in the former embassy of the United States, a nineteenth-century jewel that sits at 100 Wellington Street, directly across from Parliament. It is one of the best examples of neo-beaux-arts style in Canada. The location is unique in the capital. Money was allocated, preparatory work began. The plan was to renovate the embassy and build an addition. All that stopped when the Conservatives came to office in January 2006. Some $9 million of the project's $45 million had been spent. No matter. By summer, the government had served notice that the project was under review; by autumn, it seemed as if it were cancelled, though there were reports that it would be situated in Calgary, within the corporate headquarters of EnCana Corporation, the wealthy oil conglomerate. Some suggested that the delay was bureaucratic, or a question of who would run the place, Library and Archives Canada, as is now the case, or the National Gallery. More worrisome, it may have been philosophical, that the government saw no need for such a building in the national capital.

Without doubt, there is. The purpose is less the art than the history, inviting Canadians to make the connection between their past and its faces, many of whom they do not know. It is an indispensable part of a nation's legacy. Sandy Nairne, the director of the National Portrait Gallery in London, wonders why there is even a debate on the question; he says it would be "a tragedy" if the project didn't proceed. "How can you do without it?" he asks. "No great country can think of itself without thinking of those who made it a great country." The reason, he explains, is that it creates a sense of nationhood. "Debates about nationality never finish. They carry on and everyone's part of it."

If there is any doubt about the need for a national portrait gallery or a national history museum, it was confirmed by *The Greatest Canadian*, a popular television series broadcast on the CBC in the autumn of 2004. Based on similar series in Great Britain and Germany, the show invited viewers to choose those Canadians who had made the greatest contribution to Canada. It was clear from many of the one hundred original nominees that the audience knew almost nothing about their compatriots, living or dead, who had built this country. As we know, historians have long said that Canadians are appallingly ignorant of Canada. *The Greatest Canadian* proved it. Many of the nominees were less about history than celebrity. They included singers, comedians, and even a mischievous broadcaster from Winnipeg who asked his listeners to mount a write-in campaign on his behalf.

The pantheon of the top twenty Canadians is revealing. The gallery of greats included David Suzuki, the scientist and broadcaster known for his strong views on global warming and other environmental threats (5); Don Cherry, the sports broadcaster whose opinions are as loud and tasteless as his sports jackets (7);

Alexander Graham Bell, a Scotsman who lived in the United States and Canada (9); and Wayne Gretzky, the magnificent hockey player (10). They are in league with more conventional choices: Tommy Douglas, the Prairie politician and father of medicare (1); Terry Fox, the one-legged athlete who died of cancer while running across Canada (2); Pierre Trudeau (3); Sir Frederick Banting, the co-discoverer of insulin (4); Lester Pearson (6); and Sir John A. Macdonald (8).

The next ten included Louis Riel, the Métis rebel; Jean Vanier, the humanitarian; Roméo Dallaire, the general who led the beleaguered UN forces in Rwanda; and Stephen Lewis, the former UN ambassador and AIDS crusader. The list also included country singers Shania Twain and "Stompin' Tom" Connors, Mike Myers, the actor, and Bobby Orr, the hockey legend.

"What a picture of Canada is on display!" moaned columnist Andrew Coyne. He had reason to despair. Only two writers (Leonard Cohen, Pierre Berton) were among the top fifty Canadians. Our prime ministers, even the great ones, got no respect; Laurier was forty-third, and King forty-ninth, just behind the less accomplished Diefenbaker (47) and Chrétien (45). Yes, deserving people did make the list. The Unknown Soldier (21) was a fitting choice, as were Nellie McClung, Canada's first social activist; Norman Bethune, the impassioned doctor on the front lines of the Chinese Revolution; and Sir Isaac Brock and Sir Arthur Currie, military leaders both. But for all of those so deserving, there were those who made this a farce. Pamela Anderson, the buxom actress? Senator Anne Cools, the former student radical? Ed Belfour, the Maple Leafs goalie? Geddy Lee, the rock musician? Avril Lavigne, the pop singer? Bret Hart, the wrestler? Rick Mercer, the comedian? With a list like this, the joke's on us.

Those on the list were only slightly more egregious than those left off it, such as C.D. Howe, the great minister in King's wartime cabinet, and Cornelius Van Horne, the builder of the railway. There was no Baldwin or Lafontaine, no Georges-P. Vanier or Roland Michener, no Robertson Davies or Margaret Laurence or Northrop Frye. There was no George Brown or Louis de Buade, Comte de Frontenac or Henri Bourassa. There was no one from the Group of Seven (though Emily Carr was there). No explorers, from Alexander Mackenzie and Pierre-Esprit Radisson to Samuel de Champlain. No public servants, such as O.D. Skelton, the esteemed public servant, who was the first undersecretary of state for external affairs, or Louis Rasminsky, the governor of the Bank of Canada. No entrepreneurs, other than John Molson. Lord Beaverbrook, Roy Thomson, and Timothy Eaton didn't make the cut.

You soon realize that this is a popularity contest, not a history test. This isn't measuring knowledge of the past but the present, which is why many on the list are living. For better or for worse, and largely for worse, they are in the Canadian consciousness. Tecumseh, the Shawnee war chief, Laura Secord, the heroine of 1812, Harold Rogers, the community activist, and Sir Sandford Fleming, the engineer and inventor, seemed to have slipped in by accident (or were planted by the organizers to prevent this exercise from becoming a total farce).

Then the winner was announced. That Tommy Douglas was chosen "the Greatest Canadian" is predictably Canadian. A man of courage, tenacity, and acuity, Douglas was the former Baptist minister and bantamweight boxer who was the reformist premier of Saskatchewan from 1944 to 1961. When he entered national politics as leader of the newly formed New Democratic Party, Douglas joined Lester Pearson in creating universal health care for all Canadians, against much opposition. Today medicare, like peacekeeping, has become a part of the Canadian iconography, a secular religion. We talk about it endlessly. It has all kinds of benefits to us, including making us different from the Americans and allowing us to feel superior. So it was no surprise that Canadians chose Douglas; in a sense, he is us. Said George Stroumboulopoulos, the hip broadcaster who nominated him: "Tommy's values became Canadian values, and when we choose to brag about our country, it's because of the things that Tommy gave us."

Another reason. It is a good bet that Canadians did not even consider John A. Macdonald in the top five because they knew little of him or his contemporaries. They remembered Pierre Trudeau and Lester Pearson, nation-builders both, and they knew of Banting. All would be legitimate candidates for the greatest Canadian, as were many others down the list, like Laurier and King. But that suggests a serious view of this competition and that would be a mistake. Elsewhere, they did take it more seriously, though. Three years before the CBC, the BBC asked its viewers to nominate their "great Britons." They responded enthusiastically. Their top ten: Winston Churchill, Isambard Kingdom Brunel, Diana, Princess of Wales, Charles Darwin, William Shakespeare, Isaac Newton, John Lennon, Elizabeth I, Horatio Nelson, Oliver Cromwell. Keen to know if this list truly represented what Britons think, the BBC commissioned a poll of two thousand respondents and found the results almost exactly the same for eight of ten nominees. The striking thing about the British list is that, beyond the top ten, it reflects men and women of stature. There are some dubious picks – pop musician Boy George (46), actress Julie Andrews (59), and footballer Bobby Moore (69) – but they are few. These are a thoughtful people, conversant with their past, making thoughtful choices. As essayist Mark Harrison put it in *Great Britons: The Great Debate*: "The clearest image to emerge through this snapshot of public opinion is that the British are sustained and stirred more by greatness forged in the white heat of history than by greatness conferred by the bright light of celebrity." Or, put more simply, Britons know their past and cherish it. *The Greatest Briton* was a wonderful, educational exercise. *The Greatest Canadian* was entertainment, frothy and frivolous. It was as forgettable as yesterday's entrée, a send-up of ourselves. Shame, that.

It isn't just the schools, the museums, and the government that fail us. It is also the professional historians, their books and periodicals. As J.L. Granatstein and Michael Bliss have argued, academic historians in Canada have stopped writing political and national history. They prefer to write labour history, women's history, ethnic history, and regional history, among others, often freighted with a sense of grievance or victimhood. This kind of history has its place, of course, but our history has become so specialized, so segmented, and so narrow that we are missing the national story in a country that has one and needs to hear it. Says Jeffrey Simpson of *The Globe and Mail*: "History departments now largely teach particularist histories of people defined by region, locality, gender or ethnicity. Political history is considered passé in many quarters, as is history on a grand scale. Micro-history has taken over, galvanizing some, boring most."

Leaf through the 2006 winter catalogue of University of British Columbia Press, one of the nation's largest academic publishers. Perhaps *The Culture of Flushing: A Social and Legal History of Sewage* has its place in the national œuvre; so might *The Culture of Hunting in Canada*. As the publisher says, it may be that the "uncontroversial reputation" of flushing is "deceptive" and that hunting is "a fundamental but understudied aspect of Canadian history." When you see these books in a catalogue, though, it's hard to know whether to rush to the bookstore in ignorance, or to the toilet in revulsion, or to the shotgun in despair. Think those are esoteric titles? Some of the other new books from UBC Press in 2006 included *Capital and Labour in the British Columbia Forest Industry, 1934–74*; *Nutrition Policy in Canada, 1870–1939*; and *Contact Zones: Aboriginal and Settler Women in Canada's Colonial Past*, which "locates Canadian women's history within colonial and imperial systems." All may have important lessons for us. More likely, they are dense, distant, and obtuse, written by experts for experts. In other words, they will sell few copies and reach few people.

Does this mean that all historians have to write about the big picture? Hardly. There is always room for novelty, personality, and discovery in exploring our past. But it is also true that there is less room than in other countries. A country as under-studied as Canada, which has so few books on so many important topics, can ill-afford this excursion into esoterica that seems to preoccupy so many professional historians. When critics lament the decline of political history or biography, as they do, they need only point to the paucity of fresh biographies on our greatest prime ministers, particularly those before 1950.

On Sir John A. Macdonald, for example, there has not been a biography of stature since Douglas Creighton's *John A. Macdonald: The Young Politician, The Old Chieftain* in 1955. The *Literary Review of Canada* ranked Creighton's two-volume biography thirty-first on its 2006 list of "the 100 Great Canadian Books" and said: "Hard though it is to believe, it is the first definitive account of Sir John A." It wasn't hard to believe. There are less comprehensive books, such as P.B Waite's *Macdonald: His Life and World* in 1975 and Donald Swainson's *Sir John A. Macdonald: The Man and the Politician* in 1989 and Patricia Phenix's *Private Demons: The Tragic Personal Life of John A. Macdonald* in 2006. On Sir Wilfrid Laurier, there has not been a big biography since Joseph Schull's *Laurier: The First Canadian* in 1965. More recently, Richard Clippingdale wrote *Laurier: His Life and World* in 1979 and Laurier LaPierre wrote *Sir Wilfrid Laurier and the Romance of Canada* in 1996. On Sir Robert Borden, a large figure of Edwardian and post-Edwardian Canada, we have *Borden: His Life and World* by John English in 1977 and *Robert Laird Borden: A Biography* by Robert Craig Brown in 1975 and 1980. On Richard Bennett, not an eminent prime minister, we have P.B. Waite in 1992 (*The Loner: Three Sketches of the Personal Life and Ideas of R.B. Bennett, 1870–1947*).

Mackenzie King is probably the most under-studied. The biggest work is the three-volume *William Lyon Mackenzie King,* which was written by R.M. Dawson and H. Blair Neatby. Among others, there is also J.L. Granatstein's *Mackenzie King: His Life and World* in 1977, C.P. Stacey's *A Very Double Life: The Private World of Mackenzie King* in 1976, and Joy Esberey's *Knight of the Holy Spirit: A Study of William Lyon Mackenzie King* in 1981. Yet there is very little of substance in recent years on a prime minister who was more than twenty-one years in office. It is astonishing in a country with so many seats of higher learning and so many historians filling them. Then again, King is simply forgotten. When the Bank of Canada reissued the fifty-dollar bill in 2004, it put out a press release explaining in detail the depiction of Thérèse Casgrain and the leaders of the women's rights movement known as "the Famous Five" in 1929. Of King and the front side of the bill, it said nothing. He'd been there for years, it was true, but did anyone know why?

Historians and journalists became more interested in the prime ministers in post-war Canada, though not until Lester Pearson. Louis St. Laurent, whom some historians call one of Canada's finest prime ministers, is portrayed in only one book: *Louis St. Laurent, Canadian* by Dale Thomson, published in 1968. John Diefenbaker was the subject of Peter C. Newman's *Renegade in Power: The Diefenbaker Years*, which revolutionized political reporting when it was published in 1963. There was also a later biography of Diefenbaker, *Rogue Tory: The Life and Legend of John G. Diefenbaker*, by Denis Smith, published in 1995. Other than these, there is no full biography, though friends and foes have written reminiscences and recriminations.

Thanks to historian John English, the life of Lester Pearson is recounted fully and eloquently in two volumes (*Shadow of Heaven* in 1988 and *The Worldly Years* in 1992). Historian Robert Bothwell offered his less ambitious portrayal in 1978 (*Pearson: His Life and World*), as part of a general series on the prime ministers of Canada. There have been oral histories and other books, but once again, no big biography beyond English's.

Pearson's successor, Pierre Trudeau, is the great exception to the historical rule in Canada. No political figure in our past has been written about as much as he. In 2006 alone, he was the subject of the first of a two-volume biography by John English (*Citizen of the World: The Life of Pierre Elliott Trudeau*) and the first of two volumes (*Young Trudeau: Son of Quebec, Father of Canada, 1919–1944*) by Max and Monique Nemni. Earlier, Trudeau was the subject of biographies by Richard Gwyn (*The Northern Magus: Pierre Trudeau and Canadians*, in 1980), George Radwanski (*Trudeau*, in 1978), and Michel Vastel (*The Outsider: The Life of Pierre Elliott Trudeau*, in 1990). Christina McCall and Stephen Clarkson wrote a two-volume study (*Trudeau and Our Times: The Magnificent Obsession* in 1990 and *The Heroic Delusion* in 1994). There are a host of more recent books on this northern colossus.

But Trudeau is in a class by himself. As subjects of biographers, his successors do better than his predecessors. Brian Mulroney was the subject of a major treatment by John Sawatsky in 1992, now dated. Jean Chrétien was the subject of a two-volume study (*Chrétien: The Will to Win*, in 1995, and *Iron Man: The Defiant Reign of Jean Chrétien*, in 2003) by the able Lawrence Martin. The popularity of political journalism has produced some books on recent politicians. The rise of Paul Martin was chronicled in two books by journalists Susan Delacourt and John Gray and his fall was chronicled by journalist Paul Wells. All were engaging and informative, though none was a classical biography. Interestingly, the life of Stephen Harper is explored in detail by author William Johnson, who wrote *Stephen Harper and the Future of Canada* before Harper became prime minister.

One of the reasons we have little biography may be that we have little autobiography. There isn't the same tradition of writing magisterial memoirs in Canada as in Britain or the United States, and our prime ministers have left few of them. Macdonald, Laurier, King, and St. Laurent did not write their memoirs, though King did leave his titillating diary. Pearson and Diefenbaker each left memoirs. Trudeau did not, at least not in a diligent way, preferring to edit the transcripts of television interviews. Kim Campbell did write an account of her short stewardship she might have called *From Here to Obscurity*. Mulroney is writing a memoir and so is Chrétien. As for ministers, there is less tradition of looking back, at least not any more, and we suffer for it. Donald Fleming, Diefenbaker's finance minister, produced more than anyone wanted to read. Paul Martin Sr. wrote three volumes on his long career in public life, and that seems to have exhausted almost everyone since.

On the whole, Canada knows more about its public figures today than those of two or three decades ago, but it is still not nearly enough, and much different from America and Britain. Every autumn and spring, bookstores in the United States are full of new interpretations of George Washington, John Adams, Thomas Jefferson, Benjamin Franklin, Alexander Hamilton, Franklin Roosevelt, and Harry Truman. Just when one thinks there is nothing new to say about the Founding Fathers, David McCullough or Joseph Ellis comes out with a crackling new book. When Theodore Roosevelt seems old hat, Edmund Morris publishes a masterful two-volume biography. In America, even dead white males get a second act, and Americans love it. Doris Kearns Goodwin published a dazzling interpretation in 2005 of the leadership of Abraham Lincoln that no one had imagined. Ten years earlier, she brought the same kind of originality to the White House of FDR and won the Pulitzer Prize. The indefatigable Robert Caro is still turning out volumes on the life of Lyndon Johnson, which he has been writing since 1976. The Kennedys remain a cottage industry; so is the Civil War, the Second World War, and the civil rights movement.

The British are not dissimilar. In his retirement, Roy Jenkins, the erudite politician, turned out a splendid volume on Winston Churchill. Martin Gilbert, the great man's biographer, has made a career of chronicling Churchill's life, as well as the epochal events of the twentieth century. The British appetite for the past is not limited to the last century or two; Amanda Foreman, a young historian, published *Georgiana, Duchess of Devonshire*, a portrait of the eighteenth-century English chatelaine, to much acclaim in 1999. That's what good historians do: they rescue the forgotten and give them new life.

It isn't enough to argue, as the apologists do, that Canada is smaller than the United States or Britain, and that consequently our past is not as interesting. Yes, we are smaller, but there is a long, vivid history out there, if only we were inclined to discover it. Much of it has been told not by historians but by journalists, such as Peter C. Newman, who wrote the history of the Hudson's Bay Company, and Pierre Berton, who wrote the history of the Canadian Pacific Railway, as well as the War of 1812, Vimy Ridge, and the Klondike. These are the two great popularizers of the important events and figures of our history. We owe them a debt. If only the professional historians could bring the same passion to our past that Newman and Berton have.

"History loves company" reads an advertisement for the Historical Hotels of Canada. It is catchy but insincere. Hotels may love company but history doesn't. Not in Canada. We don't think it is that important. The problems of history, as we have seen, go beyond the scholars who won't write what people will read; the curators of museums who won't take risks; the civil servants in education ministries who won't mandate history in the schools; the politicians who won't make something more of our historic sites. It is about taking ourselves seriously. We abuse our past in Canada. Or we deny it.

In 1982, we did away with Dominion Day. Just like that. A member of Parliament decided it was a colonial remnant, an insult to Quebec and multicultural Canada. So, one Friday afternoon in

July, when the House of Commons was almost empty, it passed a seemingly innocuous private member's bill ("An Act to Amend the Holidays Act") changing the name of the national holiday celebrated on July 1 from Dominion Day to Canada Day. The bill had been around since 1980, attracting no attention or public comment, before it was suddenly recalled for debate that day.

There were thirteen members in the chamber at the time, not the twenty required for a quorum. But no one asked for a count, a quorum was deemed to exist by the speaker, and the bill soon received unanimous consent. It all took five minutes. The Senate approved it three months later. In the debate, our lawmakers saw "dominion" as too British, an imperial imposition. They seemed to regard "dominion" as an emblem of colonialism in the way some dim-witted Americans tried to ban the use of "niggardly" because they thought it had racist overtones. In truth, "dominion" was suggested not by the British, but by Sir Leonard Tilley of New Brunswick, who took it from the eighth verse of the seventy-second psalm of the Bible, which says, "He shall have dominion also from sea to sea, and from the river unto the ends of the earth." Its roots or reason didn't matter to the high priests who sat in the House of Commons that lazy summer afternoon. They happily went about their historical cleansing. Dominion Day became Canada Day, a term of crushing banality. As Robert Sibley put it brilliantly in an essay in the *Ottawa Citizen*, this was "a case of identity theft, an act of historical vandalism." Actually, it was an even greater affront than that: a renunciation of the past, a misreading of history, laden with political correctness and historical ignorance.

If we do not deny history, we apologize for it. The latest apology for the sins of our ancestors involved the head tax on the Chinese. In June 2006, Stephen Harper offered the nation's regrets for "the racist actions of our past." Wrapping himself in sackcloth and ashes, Harper said he was sorry for a government that imposed the head tax between 1885 and 1923. He said that Canada's failure to acknowledge "these historical injustices has prevented many in the community from seeing themselves as fully Canadian." So he offered symbolic payments of twenty thousand dollars to the few remaining victims. The tax was racist, and it was wrong; issuing apologies for the acts of others, as Brian Mulroney did for the seven hundred or so Japanese Canadians interned in the Second World War, is a way of coming to terms with our past. The problem is there have been other injustices in our past, and the victims – such as Jews, Italians, Sikhs, and natives in residential schools – no doubt have their grievances too, and will soon be seeking compensation for their injustice.

In some ways, we try to address memory, but not hard enough. Television has its uses. The Heritage Minutes made by the Historica Foundation, a non-profit organization that promotes Canada's history, are a superb way to popularize our past. On a good day, The History Channel helps, too, but running imported dramas like *JAG* and *Over There* doesn't tell Canadians much about Canada. The CBC produces some excellent documentary and drama, but it has to be careful; history is incendiary. The broadcast of the biopic *Prairie Giant: The Tommy Douglas Story* was scheduled for mid-January 2006, during the last week of the federal election campaign. It was postponed until after the election because the CBC was "concerned about the appearance of partisanship." Imagine, the broadcast of a documentary on the life of "the greatest Canadian" was delayed because revisiting his battle to balance the budget and introduce health care might enlighten the uninformed and tip the scales in a political campaign. What could be more dangerous? Months later, the rebroadcast of *Prairie Giant* was cancelled because the family of Jimmy Gardiner, the former premier of Saskatchewan who was depicted in the drama, complained that the interpretation of him was false and demeaning. After reviewing the material, the CBC agreed. *Prairie Giant* was felled, again, by rubber bands and peashooters.

One of the misapprehensions in Canada is that Canadians do not know much about their history because they are uninterested. Actually, that isn't so; when Canadians are given an opportunity to learn more about themselves, they embrace it. With enthusiasm. Mark Starowicz, one of Canada's most innovative broadcasters, recalled that when he and others began work in the 1990s on *Canada: A People's History*, they had modest expectations. It was the first television series on the history of Canada, he said, and the conventional wisdom was that Canadians thought their history boring. So he was astonished when the thirty-two-hour series aired in 2000–1 and became the most highly viewed documentary in the history of the CBC, with ratings rivalling the Olympics and the Stanley Cup playoffs. The two books based on the series became bestsellers, as did the video sets. "It seemed as if we had been prospecting in the fields of Canadian identity and memory when we unconsciously drilled into a pressure dome that blew us away with its intensity," he says.

There is a lesson here: if you offer, Canadians will accept. In other words, if the country were to teach its history, preserve its historic places, mark its anniversaries, remember its leaders, and create museums and memorials, it would find a public. The challenge isn't demand, it is supply. This isn't simply nostalgia or sentimentality; it is a deep desire, in a world that is changing, to understand some of the fundamentals about ourselves. In opening new museums or creating new monuments, we continue to write our biography every day. The alternative is a book of blank pages. We can choose that, too, and we might. If the happiest nations are those with no history, as someone once said, the cheerful amnesia that now engulfs us could bring us a lifetime of contentment. But at what cost?

Chapter 4

The American Canadian

In the spring of 2003, two months after Canada refused to join the invasion of Iraq, Michael Adams published *Fire and Ice: The United States, Canada and the Myth of Converging Values*. Adams is the co-founder and president of Environics Research and Communications, which has been conducting public opinion surveys in thirty countries since 1970. Adams seems to survey everything from philately to falconry; it is a matter of professional pride to him and his fellow pollsters to think that *anything* is measurable. Beyond *Fire and Ice*, Adams has written three other books, including *Sex in the Snow: Canadian Social Values at the End of the Millennium*, which was a bestseller in 1997. When his book on Canada and the United States appeared, Adams was a respected authority on matters political, social, and cultural, at the top of his game.

His reputation brought credibility to *Fire and Ice*. It needed it. Adams was challenging the belief that Canadians and Americans are becoming more and more alike. The argument of cultural and economic integration had been made persuasively by Michael Bliss and Jeffrey Simpson, among others. "Canadians, whether they like or acknowledge it, have never been more like Americans, and Canadian society has never been more similar to that of the United

States," said Simpson in *Star-Spangled Canadians: Canadians Living the American Dream*, published in 2000. "If the two countries are becoming more alike, and they are, this drawing together does not arise because Americans are changing. Canadians are the ones whose habits of mind, cultural preferences, economy, and political choices are becoming more American – without being American." At the beginning of the new century, Simpson argued that culture and communications had shrunk the attitudinal and institutional differences between the countries, "which means in every sense that Canadians have become more American in their outlook, values and structures" (with the exception of religious and moral issues).

Yet *Fire and Ice* was saying the opposite: Canadians were not becoming Americans. The two peoples were actually drifting apart, becoming less and less like each other. Not for Adams the hoary notion that we are all North Americans, alike in everything but dialect. Not for him the soothing orthodoxy that the border is an artificial separation of two peoples of similar instinct, imagination, and ideals. Rather, he finds, we are turning into something quite different. "Canada is becoming the home of a unique postmodern, postmaterial multiculturalism, generating hardy strains of new hybrids that will enrich this country and many others in the world," he wrote. The differences are pronounced. "You've got this shy, deferential people becoming more liberal, more autonomous, more inner-directed, more tolerant of diversity than Americans," Adams said in an interview in 2004. "It seems counterintuitive."

It is. Every one of the 208 pages of *Fire and Ice* – particularly the sixty-three numbing pages of charts, figures, and appendices – struggles to pull Adams's stone sled up the hill of conventional wisdom. "The hypothesis is there, that we're probably converging," Adams said. "Historians were saying it, public opinion polls said that Canadians thought they were becoming more like Americans. You know, we drive cars to and from work. We aspire to suburban houses with pools in the backyard, we don't spend enough time with our families. We both say that our family is the most important thing in our life. So many signals that would be saying, we're converging. And it was that hypothesis that I was testing."

Adams conducted three public opinion surveys, in 1992, 1996, and 2000, based on fourteen thousand interviews in both countries. He found a growing gap in cultural and social values. In a range of questions on authority, patriarchy, faith, and other values, he reported significant differences. For example, in the United States, 49 per cent of those over age fifteen agreed with the statement: "The father of the family must be master in his own home." In Canada, the figure was 18 per cent. In the United States, 31 per cent agreed with the idea that when one is feeling tense, a little bit of violence is "no big deal." In Canada, it was 14 per cent. Among Americans, 38 per cent thought men are "naturally superior to women," in contrast to 24 per cent of Canadians. One-quarter of Americans agreed that "non-whites should not be allowed to immigrate to this country," while only 13 per cent of Canadians agreed. And so on.

From these acorns grow great oaks. Adams paints a picture of the American as materialistic, vulgar, violent, and superficial. Canadians are less so. In Canada, he reports that minivans outsell SUVs by a ratio of two to one. In the United States, it's the reverse. "This is a stark difference whose roots can be traced directly to the differing values of our two countries," explains Adams, suggesting that Canadians care more about the environment. It wasn't that Adams was the first to explore the nature of these two peoples living on either side of the forty-ninth parallel; pondering the differences between Canadians and Americans is an old obsession. What Adams did was give it new life, inviting his compatriots to re-examine their self-image at the very moment the direction and leadership of the United States were losing favour in Canada. And he did something else. He cast a light on a corner of our national character: our ambivalent and tortured relationship with the

Americans, our struggle to understand them, our moral superiority in dealing with them.

The thesis of *Fire and Ice* and the response to it in Canada are revealing. The book received good reviews and signal honours. It was a national bestseller. Even the wonkish Paul Martin was impressed; he called the book a "very accurate portrayal" of social conditions. This was a serious, seminal work.

But there is another story to tell. It is less flattering to the book, to its author, and to us. When you revisit this debate a few years later, in a different political and cultural climate, when you ask about the conclusions of *Fire and Ice*, you wonder about its credibility. Then, when you reread the many tributes, you wonder about our critical judgment. In hailing the book as Canadians and their cultural interpreters did, you come to see the insecurity here. You see anew the narcissism of small differences and our smugness over big ones. And, in the end, you realize something important. This isn't really about Michael Adams at all. It's about us.

First, there were the reviews. One of the realities of publishing in Canada is there are few marquee places to review books and few marquee names to review them. Beyond *The Globe and Mail* (whose weekly tabloid is the best book review in English Canada), the *Toronto Star*, the *National Post*, the *Ottawa Citizen*, and the Montreal *Gazette*, few newspapers have literary supplements. The best in French Canada is *Le Devoir*; its weekend book review runs eight or more pages. But most newspapers devote little more than a page or two to books, if that. Books get a fair hearing in the *Literary Review of Canada*, an ambitious monthly of high quality run on a shoestring, as well as the venerable *Quill & Quire* and *Books in Canada*. All have small circulations, however. There is also *Policy Options*, a provocative periodical, and the academic journals that publish reviews, such as *The Canadian Historical Review*, the *Journal of Canadian Studies*, and *International Journal*. The trouble is that only experts read these periodicals, where reviews often appear long after publication. *Canadian Foreign Policy*, published three times a year by Carleton University in Ottawa, can take two years to publish a review of a bestselling book in its field. By that time the book may be remaindered.

Fire and Ice made a splash in the northern pond. Under the headline "We're nice and getting nicer," Oakland Ross enthused in the *Toronto Star*: "*Fire and Ice* provides a persuasive and arresting antidote to the popular wisdom du jour – the notion Canadians as a people are hanging up their snowshoes, wiping away their coy, deferential smiles, and forsaking both publicly funded medicine and weird, six-character postal codes, to pledge allegiance instead to the dark trinity of gods that increasingly seems to rule America – the triple-headed Hydra of money, materialism and the military." Ross, a fine novelist and former foreign correspondent, says the findings of the book "tell a rather gratifying tale." He is so taken with this "engaging . . . paean to the virtues of being Canadian" that he gushes appreciation like the hapless, stammering Gomer Pyle of the United States Marine Corps: "Why, thank you, sir," Ross enthuses. "Merci. Grazie. Obrigado." Playfulness aside, Ross's article raises no flags about Adams. Other than noting that Adams polled before the terrorist attacks on the United States of September 11, 2001, this interpreter accepts every conclusion at face value. He repeats the shopworn clichés and threadbare stereotypes about the polite Canadian and the rude American and sees "a clear and quantifiable trend" in the nature of the two peoples. After all, as Ross assures the readers of the country's largest newspaper, Adams has the numbers.

The *Winnipeg Free Press* was also warm. Scott MacKay, the president of a local polling firm, found the book "a good read." He had only one caveat: that Adams makes no secret of his personal bias and his "shocking and almost entirely negative characteriza-tion of American society may cause the reader to fear that his case has been built on selectively assembled data." A similarly favourable review in *Spiral Nature*, an American journal, called the book an entertaining and insightful look into the Canadian and American psyches, though it, too, cast doubt on the "impartiality" of the author. "Without slandering America, there is a discernible favouring of Canadian ideals and values – completely understandable as Adams himself is Canadian," it said.

To Thomas Axworthy, the erudite former principal secretary to Pierre Trudeau, Adams "acutely" described the chasm in values between Canadians and Americans. *Fire and Ice* had a personal resonance for him. "I have been teaching part-time in the United States for nearly 20 years, and my personal experience is in complete accord with Adams's statistical insights," he wrote in *The Globe and Mail*. At Harvard University in the mid-1980s, Axworthy recalls, the ethos of the New Deal was still in place and liberals such as Senator Edward Kennedy could still be elected president. No longer. Their view has been replaced by tax-cutting, neo-conservative, religious activists, and the only way moderates like Bill Clinton can win elections is to appeal to that conservative majority. Meanwhile, Axworthy argued, the liberal-social democratic centre had expanded in Canada. So, when Canada disagreed with the United States over the International Criminal Court, the anti-landmines treaty, the war in Iraq, or the Kyoto Accord, as the governments of Jean Chrétien and Paul Martin did, they were reflecting national values, just as George Bush's policies were reflecting American values. "Demography may not be destiny," declared Axworthy, "but values certainly are."

There were more bouquets to come. In May 2004, a year after it was published, *Fire and Ice* won the Donner Prize, which is awarded each year to the best book on Canadian public policy. The prize was established by the Donner Canadian Foundation, one of the country's largest charitable organizations, in 1998. The purpose of the prize is "to encourage an open exchange of ideas and to provide a springboard for authors who may not necessarily be

well-known, but who can make an original and meaningful contribution to policy discourse." The winning book must address an
important subject, must offer a sound, original, and authoritative
analysis, and must be "a well-written, well-presented book that can
be read and understood not only by experts, but also by interested
and informed laymen." The prize is said to be the richest and
most prestigious of its kind in Canada. In a country that doesn't
see non-fiction in the same glamorous light as fiction, the Donner
is extraordinary. The winner receives $35,000, the finalists get
$5,000, and the award is presented at a splashy banquet. This is a
serious prize.

The Donner citation called *Fire and Ice* "an outstanding work
that deserves pride of first place." Said Grant Reuber, the chairman
of the jury of eminent Canadians: "Thought-provoking and well
written, *Fire and Ice* addresses a critical issue that underlies many
current policy arguments. . . . Adams's research challenges conventional views and will be widely used by those who make policy
decisions – his research is key to understanding how our fellow citizens perceive the world around them." In 2003, the Donner final-
ists included a book on how journalists influence the news, one
on the challenges of public policy in agriculture, and a study of the
Senate of Canada. In the eyes of the prize jury, none was as good as
Fire and Ice. The jury members were not the only ones persuaded
that *Fire and Ice* would shape public policy; economist Mark
Lovewell of Ryerson University said: "Will the book change
Canadian public policy? Definitely yes."

With the endorsement of a major prize, the applause of the
critics, and a solid record of sales, the stature of *Fire and Ice* was
assured. When the *Literary Review of Canada* announced in 2005
that the book had been chosen one of the top one hundred
Canadian books of all time, Adams had particular reason to be
proud. Although the LRC thought Adams inferred "too much from
too little," it said that the book identified "differences that have

become too large to ignore . . . revived professional research on, and public interest in, comparative values as a way to foretell the political future of North America." That *Fire and Ice* was number ninety-nine out of one hundred books (listed in chronological order) didn't matter. *Fire and Ice* was there, now deemed a Canadian classic to sit on the bookshelf beside *Lament for a Nation*, *Renegade in Power*, and *Survival*. And that was that.

What's wrong with this picture, then? A trained sociologist and seasoned pollster, the creator of a large and successful firm with more than three decades of experience, has a hunch about Canadians and Americans. He takes three major surveys over a decade or so on national attitudes on both sides of the border. He adds up the results, he reaches a conclusion, he writes it up. His book challenges the orthodoxy. It sells thousands of copies, receives warm reviews, wins plaudits from the cognoscenti.

So, what is there to criticize here? Well, for starters, the book's curious methodology, its thinly veiled bias, and its tiresome self-righteousness. And that's just Adams. The public reaction to the book – the sales, the reviews, the Donner Prize, the endorsement of the *Literary Review of Canada* – that's us. Surely it is fair to ask how Adams went about his work, why he struck the tone he did, and what his findings really say. It is also fair to question how closely the critics examined *Fire and Ice*, and why their encomiums to its theory of divergence – that supposedly yawning gulf between Canadians and Americans – fell on receptive ears in Canada in 2003.

First, it is important to know that not everyone was as enamoured of *Fire and Ice* as *The Globe and Mail* and the *Toronto Star*. Some critics found its conclusions unproven and unpersuasive. One of the early dissenters was David Frum, the Canadian conservative journalist, author, and former speechwriter to George W. Bush. Frum, who lives in Washington, D.C., is unafraid to smash icons. Having learned that Adams had declared a new orthodoxy, he bought the book, read it, and reread it. His conclusion? It is "an intellectual card-trick." In a biting commentary in the *National Review Online* on November 9, 2003, Frum looked at the methods in the surveys and found that Adams asked the same questions on both sides of the border only about half of the time. Adams did not reveal the questions he asked; from the "sample" gleaned from the author's website, however, Frum declared the questions "tendentious" and "slanted." Moreover, Frum was disturbed that Adams creates "value profiles" by methods he does not reveal.

Frum questioned invoking values or culture to explain differences. He worried when Adams noted that SUVs outsell minivans two to one in the United States while minivans outsell SUVs on the same scale in Canada. Adams suggested this proves that Canadians are more conscious of the environment than Americans. Really? Frum argued that SUVs usually cost more than minivans, and Americans are richer than Canadians, who naturally opt for the cheaper option. How could Adams ignore money, Frum asks, when trying to explain why people buy what they buy? (Curiously, sales of minivans in Canada have dropped 29 per cent since 1999 and are now surpassed by small cars and pickup trucks. Crossover utility vehicles (not SUVs) were expected to surpass minivans in 2006. They are now the biggest growth segment in Canada.)

The most devastating critique of *Fire and Ice* came from Joel Smith, a professor of sociology at Duke University in North Carolina. Smith is professor emeritus at the university; he has taught for more than fifty years and has an impressive record of publications and professional achievement. In a review published in the *American Review of Canadian Studies*, he parsed Adams's numbers and analyzed his methods with the authority of a trained sociologist and found both woefully deficient. Some of Adams's methods Smith called confusing, if not misleading. He pointed out, in the language of his discipline, the absence of "sample frames," methods of "data collection," and "refusal rates." While Smith was sympathetic to the argument that the two peoples are different, he dismissed this book as a credible antidote to the thesis of convergence: "At best, this is an op-ed piece spun into a book; at worst, a polemic. Despite its pseudo-scientific trappings, the basic message is only Adams' personal views on where the two countries are heading. The book fails to meet the standards of acceptable social science." Smith said that while Adams cited the work of several scholars who have written on this question, he never explained where they went wrong, as a scholar should. Smith found the pollster's interpretations "inconsistent and arbitrary." He pointed out the absence of questionnaires and tests of significance, and noted that appendices that purport to explain the value analyses did not. "The presentation of data," Smith wrote, "can be likened to a well-decorated store window in front of an empty store." More generally, Smith found the whole project "conceptually muddy." He asked what "values" are, and wondered why Adams had listed 101 of them. He accused Adams of a kind of intellectual dishonesty – using "scholarly credentials and the guise of reputable social science to promote personal views." His withering judgment? "*Fire and Ice* is a polemic masquerading as a report based on a scientific study and analysis."

Smith's trenchant review did not appear until March 2005, almost two years after *Fire and Ice* appeared. (Eighteen months later, Adams had not seen it.) Yet, here was the view of a respected scholar at one of his country's finest universities. Reading his scathing deconstruction of *Fire and Ice* makes you wonder how many of the early reviewers asked how Adams conducted his research, let alone questioned the credibility of his conclusions. Unable or unwilling to make an assessment, they accepted it at face value.

As for the Donner Prize, who knows? Prize juries are inscrutable. They make strange choices. Although there were fewer books entered that year, a shortlist of four was chosen from among sixty books. The jury was surely qualified to assess a work of this complexity. Its members that year were Donald S. Macdonald, the former minister of finance and royal commissioner; Claude E. Forget, the former minister of health in Quebec; Paul Boothe, a professor of economics at the University of Alberta; and Elizabeth Parr-Johnston, the former president of the University of New Brunswick. It wasn't the first time that an obscure or dubious book won the prize. In 2001, the winner was Marie Mc Andrew, a professor at Université de Montréal who had written a study of ethnic and cultural diversity in Quebec schools. One generous commentator said that her study "was virtually unheard of in English Canada until its selection by the Donner jury." As it has never been translated into English, a fair guess suggests that it still is.

In other years, the prize has gone to reputable scholars such as John F. Helliwell, Tom Flanagan, and Thomas Courchene. There is nothing wrong with recognizing unknown academics or rewarding eminent ones; this we should welcome in a country with few intellectual rewards for this kind of unsung labour. The jury that chose Adams was obviously smitten with the thesis of *Fire and Ice* and convinced of its impact on public policy in Canada. So were the editors of the *Literary Review of Canada*. It is always hard to divine who wins these prizes and who makes these lists. *The Hockey Sweater*, the beloved children's tale by novelist Roch Carrier, was not among the *LRC*'s top 100. Nor was *Generation X* by Douglas Coupland. Nor was any book by Yann Martel, Michael Ondaatje, Mavis Gallant, or Alistair MacLeod.

The real question raised by the success of *Fire and Ice* is why it did so well in Canada. What was it about this meditation on the Canadian psyche that seemed to resound so deeply? Why did smart people seem to abandon their critical faculties and fall in love with the theory of divergence in the face of evidence to the contrary? The answer may be as simple as this: *Fire and Ice* told us what we wanted to hear.

Recall the time. *Fire and Ice* was published on May 13, 2003. On March 17, 2003, Prime Minister Jean Chrétien had announced that Canada would not join the United States and "its coalition of the willing" in the liberation of Iraq. The decision was greeted enthusiastically in many quarters in Canada, especially Quebec, which has a history of opposing intervention in foreign wars. While there were strong pockets of support for the war in other parts of Canada, particularly Alberta, a narrow majority of Canadians (nowhere near the numbers who were against the war in subsequent years) seemed to agree. Sentiment in Canada was running even more strongly against President George W. Bush, whom Canadians had never liked; polls showed that had Canadians voted in the presidential election of 2000, they would have elected former vice-president Al Gore, the Democrat. In 2004, after four years of the Bush administration, they would have again chosen the Democrat, John Kerry.

The United States was unpopular in Canada in the spring of 2003. It may have been another outbreak of the virus of anti-Americanism that has deep historical roots in Canada. Or it may have been a personal antipathy toward the president himself. The distinction did not seem to matter. Relations between Canada and the United States had been sour for two years. It began with the reality that Bush, whose political experience was limited to six years as governor of Texas, had come to office with no knowledge of – and no instinct or inclination for – Canada. It did not go unnoticed in Ottawa that his first foreign visit was to Mexico, not Canada. Traditionally, visiting Canada first has been seen as a gesture of respect for America's closest ally and biggest trading partner. Things got worse after September 11, when Canada had taken in some twenty-three thousand stranded passengers whose airplanes were diverted to Newfoundland and other places. Beyond that, Canadians offered blood and money to help at Ground Zero, while one hundred thousand gathered on Parliament Hill in Ottawa in a heartfelt expression of solidarity with the United States. Yet Bush did not mention Canada among the thirteen nations he thanked in his address to a Joint Session of Congress on September 20. The next year, when an American fighter pilot accidentally killed four Canadian soldiers in Afghanistan, Bush waited a day before expressing his condolences. In the president, Canadians saw an ideological, religious, untutored conservative from the Southwest, as far from them geographically and culturally as a president could be. They disliked his intention to open the Wildlife Refuge in Alaska to oil drilling and resented his headstrong positions on mad cow disease and softwood lumber.

It wasn't always this way. A few years earlier, Jean Chrétien and Bill Clinton had been good friends. Both were centrists who had come to power in 1993, and they were proof of the pattern in bilateral relations that Democrats usually get along well with Liberals while Republicans usually get along well with Conservatives. So it was here. As Opposition leader, Chrétien had attacked Brian Mulroney, his gregarious Irish predecessor, for being too cozy with George H. Bush; he knew that Canadians want their prime ministers to keep a respectful distance from the Americans. Yet he and Clinton were close enough that Chrétien once flew to Washington unannounced to play a clandestine round of golf with Clinton. However, with the election of George W. Bush, the Republican, there was no natural rapport with Jean Chrétien, the Liberal. Despite some similarities in style – both were folksy, inarticulate, instinctive populists with little interest in the fine points of public policy – the two didn't hit it off. When Bush tried to charm Chrétien, he innocently allowed that he liked Conrad Black, whom Chrétien loathed. It was said that Chrétien was called "Dino" in the White House. By 2003, Washington was disappointed that Ottawa had chosen to stay out of Iraq. The Americans were also annoyed at how Chrétien had announced it: he had stood up in the House of Commons in Question Period and delivered his terse renunciation. Fellow Liberals jumped to their feet around him, applauding triumphantly. His words were carried live in the United States by CNN. Whatever Canada's reasons for staying out of Iraq, which would look wiser and wiser as things went bad, Chrétien appeared indifferent to the United States as it prepared to go to war.

Bush had been aggrieved with Canada since Françoise Ducros, Chrétien's infelicitous press secretary, was overheard in the press-room calling him "a moron" in November 2002. The prime minister was slow to repudiate Ducros (she eventually resigned), which seemed to indicate that he saw nothing wrong with her remark. In Washington, the president was not amused with this, or a string of other insults from Canada, including an outburst from Liberal MP Carolyn Parrish in February 2003, in which she spat: "Damn Americans . . . I hate those bastards." It was no real surprise, then, when Bush cancelled his first official visit to Ottawa, scheduled for May 6, 2003. Officially, Bush had pressing commitments arising from the war in Iraq, but he could still host John Howard, the prime minister of Australia, who was a steadfast ally. As it happened, Bush found time to appear with Howard at his ranch in Texas on the same day that he was to be visiting Chrétien in Ottawa. The point was noted in Canada.

All this was happening at around the time *Fire and Ice* appeared. As Scott MacKay wrote in the *Winnipeg Free Press*, the book's timing was "perfect" because "Canadians have perhaps never been so focused on their place in the world vis-à-vis the United States . . ." He might also have said that never had Canadians been so skeptical of the United States and its motives. And if their doubts needed ballast, here was a tome by a respected pollster, packing daunting charts and surveys that seemed to confirm just about every prejudice, suspicion, and instinct they had about their neighbours. Timing? This was a godsend for Adams.

But if Adams was telling Canadians what they wanted to hear about the Americans that spring, his audience was not recently converted. Just as anti-Americanism has waxed and waned over Canada's history, so has a sense of moral superiority. Dean Acheson, secretary of state under Harry Truman, had identified it among Canadians in the late 1940s and early 1950s. He had been particularly irritated by Canada, and its foreign minister, Lester Pearson, who had been pressing for a diplomatic rather than a military settlement to the Korean War. This angered Acheson, who called it meddling; he thought that Canada did not understand the burdens of the United States, as the leader of the free world in the Cold War. In 1951, Pearson had written Acheson that the U.S. should "take more notice of what we do and what we say." Acheson's impatience, unconstrained by diplomatic sensibility, comes through in a memo he wrote during the Korea debate: "If you think that after the agonies we have gone through here [in Washington] to get agreement on this matter, we're going to start all over with our NATO allies, especially you moralistic, interfering Canadians, then you're crazy."

Acheson, whose mother was a Canadian, visited Canada often, socialized with Pearson, and knew the country better than most Americans. He was one of the giants of twentieth-century American diplomacy – brilliant, tough, self-assured, patrician, intolerant of foolishness and fakery, unafraid to use his tart tongue. In 1964, out of power but not out of breath, Acheson contributed an astringent essay to an innocuous collection on Canadian-American relations. There, he inveighed against Canada's self-righteousness. He called his essay "Canada: Stern Daughter of the Voice of God," borrowing a line from Wordsworth. It has resonated ever since. Unconstrained by a political correctness that did not yet exist, it captured neatly the sense of a country that complained too much that it was taken "for granted" by the United States and was too ready to lecture it.

That sententiousness that Acheson saw fifty years ago has been around since the nineteenth century. "We are free from many of the social cancers that are empoisoning the national life of our neighbours," declared the *Canadian Methodist Magazine* in 1880. "We have no polygamous Mormondon; no Ku-Klux terrorism; no Oneida Communists; no Illinois divorce system; no cruel Indian massacres." Not all of this was true – the Europeans had made the Beothuk of Newfoundland extinct by the nineteenth century – but Canada had not the history of violence of the United States. This allowed Canadians to develop a certain hauteur. Says historian J.L. Granatstein: "Canada may have been poorer, but it was better, an attitude that remained all through the 20th century and into the 21st." This smugness comes and goes in public opinion and manifests itself in differing ways in our politics. It has been used by prime ministers from Sir John A. Macdonald to John Diefenbaker, who denounced the United States and loathed JFK (who loathed him, too), to Jean Chrétien. Slow to understand the moral question of September 11, Chrétien mused gratuitously about the size of the U.S. deficit and its inadequate foreign aid.

Allan Gotlieb, one of the most able diplomats of his generation, finds moral superiority a current in Canada's foreign policy. When the Liberal government published its highly anticipated foreign policy review in 2005, he said, "The drafters have been clever to expand it to say that it is in Canada's national interest to save the world. There's a good deal of high-flying rhetoric, statements about how great we are. It raises unrealistic expectations. It's not a very big lurch to start thinking about yourself as a moral superpower. Why aren't we changing things then? It's important to use restrained language and lower expectations."

In the last federal election campaign, Paul Martin could not resist chiding the Americans over their commitment to the Kyoto Accord, the international protocol adopted in 1997 to reduce global warming. On December 5, 2005, at an international conference on climate change in Montreal, Martin said the United States lacked "a global conscience" for reneging on its obligations under Kyoto. The inconvenient truth was that the United States had been more faithful to Kyoto than Canada; while its emissions had risen by 13 per cent since 1990, those north of the border had risen by 24 per cent. Martin's remark was cheap, playing the anti-American card to win votes. It was also false, a huge distortion of fact that author and columnist Paul Wells called "a whopper . . . as big as Britain." Rebuking the Americans on Kyoto – fully aware that Canada's record was even worse than America's – was trafficking in hyperbole and hypocrisy. Later in the campaign, the Liberals would air a series of advertisements making much of the alleged ills of the United States. None of this won them the election, but Martin's allegation drew an acidic response from David Wilkins, the courtly, mild-mannered South Carolinian who was the newly arrived American ambassador in Ottawa. Wilkins needed no direction from Washington; he listened carefully to Martin, got off his exercise bike, and hit back hard. "It may be smart election-year politics to thump your chest and constantly criticize your friend and your number-one trading partner," he told an audience at the Château Laurier Hotel in Ottawa a few days after Martin's comments. "But it's a slippery slope."

Later, Wilkins said that "Canada never has to tear down the United States of America to build itself up." That provided a second opportunity for the prime minister to whack the Americans. "I'm going to call them as I see them," Martin growled in a lumberyard in British Columbia. "I am not going to be dictated to." The burly, leather-jacketed Martin was looking like a stevedore and sounding like one, too; it was an election campaign and our boy was ready to rumble. "What happened over the next few days could only happen in Canada," wrote Wells in *Right Side Up: The Fall of Paul Martin and the Rise of Stephen Harper's New Conservatism*, his engaging account of the 2006 election campaign. "Liberal support, which had been sagging, took a bounce." Of course it did. It was why Stephen Harper and the Conservatives, who had promised to restore civility to the relationship, were not beyond a little American-bashing themselves. Just days after his election, Harper rebuked Wilkins for asserting his country's position on Arctic sovereignty. It seemed like a harmless restatement of long-standing policy. Wilkins was taken aback. Then again, he had been in Ottawa only seven months and he was still learning the political uses of anti-Americanism in Canada.

What did all this prove? Principally, that rounding on the Americans plays well in Canada, which is why politicians do it, pandering to the lesser instincts of an insecure people. As Paul Martin tried to accentuate differences between the countries on Kyoto, Canadians like to emphasize their differences in attitude and inclination, particularly when they tend to flatter themselves. This is what Adams does subtly in *Fire and Ice*. "Americans pursue heaven on earth by fleeing their cities in search of bucolic bliss," he says. "Canadians, on the other hand, prefer to congregate in their cities, albeit with frequent escapes to cottages, cabins, chalets . . ." What he is trying to prove here is uncertain if unpersuasive, given that Canadians are thought to have among the highest rates of second home ownership in the world. Or, this assertion: "We find Americans better at making a living than living itself." This presumes a desperately unhappy people on the verge of exhaustion or suicide. When his findings were challenged by critics, the amiable Adams said that he didn't intend to slag or smear Americans. Engaging and successful as he is, perhaps he didn't. With a touch of defensiveness, he allowed that he does business in the United States, owns half a vineyard there, and, of course, counts many Americans as friends. But it is hard to read *Fire and Ice* without feeling that Americans simply do not live as enlightened, progressive, and wholesome an existence as Canadians.

Actually, Wilkins was mistaken when he said that Canadians don't have "to tear Americans down" to build themselves up. In a sense, we do. You do this when you feel inferior. "Inferiority complex is a tiresome phrase, but a useful one," wrote the sonorous Vincent Massey in 1948. "It can still be applied not unfairly to some of our people as they look at our great neighbour, but in a healthy mind, physical disparity should not cause a sense of inferiority. We can never equal the United States in terms of size. It will always build higher buildings; it will always have larger crowds. American life has pace and magnitude and glamour. It has immense vitality and exuberance, too, but these things must not blind us to the quality of our own life . . ."

Canadians have long known this. Tearing Americans down, as Wilkins puts it, makes Canadians feel better about themselves. The key to feeding our skepticism is creating differences. That the differences may be narrow, that they may be overstated, that they may not even exist does not matter; inventing and nourishing those differences sustains an irrepressible and indispensable Canadian nationalism. This is the purest form of narcissism that manifests itself in other ways in the Canadian character. We see it conspicuously in our view of the Americans.

Fire and Ice would have us believe that we are utterly different from the Americans and becoming more so. The counter-argument is that we have created a comforting mythology about our differences. One of the hoariest beliefs, for example, is that the United States is a melting pot and that Canada is a mosaic. This is one of the great, self-evident truths about America in Canada, as reliable as a Newfoundland fog and a Prairie horizon. It is stamped early upon impressionable Canadian boys and girls, who declare it as adults. Like other Canadian conceits, though, this reflects a sense of moral superiority. The argument is that Canada welcomes immigrants and allows them – nay, encourages them – to retain their language and customs. *We* let them be who they are. *We* do not ask them to assimilate. The mosaic may well be true in Canada (even if it has consequences for a pluralistic society with little unity). But is the melting pot true of the United States? Not necessarily.

The melting pot never assumed that immigrants would entirely give up their identities. The term comes from a play of that name by Israel Zangwill in 1908, when the United States was absorbing the greatest wave of immigrants in its history. Much as immigrants would be shaped by their new country, he thought, their new country would be shaped by them. That is what has largely happened; many immigrants have largely resisted assimilation. In *Beyond the Melting Pot*, the classic study on American ethnicity published in 1963, Nathan Glazer and Daniel P. Moynihan found that Jewish, Italian, and Irish immigrants of New York City never entirely lost their identity, and African-Americans and Puerto Ricans even less so. Glazer reconfirmed those findings when he revisited the subject in 1997 in his book, *We Are All Multiculturalists Now*. Arthur Schlesinger, the author, historian, and champion of liberalism, reached a similar conclusion sixteen years ago. He was anxious enough about the failure of immigrants to adapt to the United States that he wrote a harsh critique of multiculturalism in 1991. In 2004, Samuel P. Huntington, the controversial political scientist, noted the shift in the pattern of immigration to the United States; instead of a fairly even distribution from Europe and Canada in the post-war era, most immigrants to the U.S. were now coming from Mexico and Latin America, and they were less likely to integrate.

If Mexican, Chinese, and Indian newcomers are jumping into the bubbling melting pot and emerging as red-blooded Yankees, it is not evident in the country's schools. On August 27, 2006, *The New York Times* reported that the 55 million students enrolling that autumn were the largest number in America's history "and in ethnic terms, the most dazzlingly diverse since waves of European immigrants washed through the public schools a century ago." It reported the pressure on schools in Loudoun County, Virginia, in particular, where the sons and daughters of Hispanics, Asians, and African-Americans are transforming a school system that was once wholly white into one that is cosmopolitan. Thuy Nguyen, a sixteen-year-old junior from Vietnam, told the *Times*: "I'm jumping around, talking to the Caucasian clique and the Middle Eastern clique. I have friends from El Salvador, Mexico, Peru – one girl is half Korean and half Puerto Rican, she's cool – and from India, Pakistan and Afghanistan." In Loudoun County, enrolment has tripled over the last fifteen years; the number of Asian students has multiplied twelve-fold and Hispanics seventeen-fold. The county is twenty-five miles from Washington. It is a magnet for international families and known as "a place that nurtures cultural differences as schools across America are rapidly becoming more diverse," said the *Times*. Look at the numbers: in 1973, 78 per cent of students in public schools were white and 22 per cent were minorities (including blacks, Asians, and Hispanics). In 2004, 57 per cent were white and 43 per cent were minorities. Predictions are that minority students will outnumber white students in America in a decade. This has already happened in six states. Is this a melting pot?

"This skewed level of immigration is without precedent in U.S. history," wrote Patrick Luciani in the *National Post* in 2005. He examined the melting pot, in particular the impact of Hispanics. "If anyone thinks that all these Hispanics are assimilating according to some cookie-cutter, melting-pot formula, they haven't been paying attention." The rise of Hispanic America is the greatest challenge to the melting pot. In 2007, Hispanics are a strong visible minority – if not a majority – in Florida, California, Texas, Arizona, New Mexico, and Nevada. Beyond the South, the West, and the Southwest, pockets of Hispanics can be found in New York, New

Jersey, and Washington, D.C. Unlike other large groups that have come to the United States, Hispanics are integrating slowly. Of the 41 million in the United States in 2004, 31 million are said to speak Spanish at home. That reality is behind the push in some places to introduce official bilingualism. Use an automatic teller machine in a major city. Chances are the instructions will be in Spanish as well as English. As Hispanics grow in numbers, they have become political, forcing governments to address a host of social and economic issues such as illegal immigration, migrant labour, language, welfare, and education. In a country in which political power has shifted to the Sunbelt, Hispanics will become increasingly pivotal. If you want to imagine the political future of America, watch the finale of *The West Wing*, the highly acclaimed drama that ended in 2006 after eight seasons. Who succeeded President Josiah Bartlet of New Hampshire on Inauguration Day? Why, Congressman Matt Santos of Texas, an Hispanic American. Of course.

The rise of Hispanic America alarms some in the United States. Patrick Buchanan, the conservative commentator who ran three times for president, fears for the loss of the Southwest, culturally and politically, to Mexico. In *State of Emergency*, he sees America becoming "a conglomerate of races and cultures" like the Roman Empire. "The country I grew up in was culturally united, even if it was racially divided," he told *Time* in 2006. "We spoke the same language, had the same faith, laughed at the same comedians. We were one nationality. We're ceasing to be that when you have hundreds of thousands of people who want to retain their culture, their own language, their own loyalty." Buchanan, a tribune of the American Right with a deft pen and a stentorian voice, is characteristically alarmist. But if that school in Virginia is any measure, it is unlikely that his fears are shared by most Americans. That the changing nature of immigration will alter the Canadian perception of America is equally unlikely, though. "The Canadian myth system likes to reinforce notions like our supposed 'multicultural-ism' which is different from the American melting pot," says Angus Reid, one of Canada's leading pollsters. He says many of his surveys over the years "suggest that if anything, Americans were more tolerant of ethnic diversity." Yet it is comforting to Canadians to believe, as Michael Adams tells them, that they are "more toler-ant of diversity than Americans." Or to cling to the self-satisfying belief that Canadians have got immigration right and Americans have got it wrong.

Myths die hard. Misconceptions about America take root in Canada and flower in our well-watered imagination. There are many. The Americans are spenders. We are savers. The Americans are fat. We are trim. The Americans have a disorderly, undemocratic politics. We have a measured, democratic politics. It is useful to consider some of these much-trumpeted differences at the heart of *Fire and Ice* and ask: are we really so different, after all?

Spenders and Savers. Americans like to consume. They are an industrious, energetic people with a genius for making money and a joy in spending it. They are hard-wired for buying and selling; commerce is written into their genetic code. "Fight terrorism," warned the late-night comics after September 11, "Go shopping!" Americans have never needed much encouragement. They work long hours, take few holidays, and like to spend almost everything they make. Their ability to produce and consume, fed by an instinct for innovation and salesmanship, is breathtaking. It has helped make Americans the richest people in the world. If they ever really believed Benjamin Franklin's stodgy aphorism "a penny saved is a penny earned," they abandoned it in the post-war era.

Canadians are more prudent. We have always been less wealthy, less comfortable with publicity and promotion, and less vulnerable to it, and simply less likely to acquire things. Perhaps it is the Anglo-Saxon in us – not that it makes us more virtuous. Yet the gap in personal savings rate – the difference between disposable incomes and expenditures – has been narrowing in recent years. In 2001, Canadians saved 5.7 per cent of their disposable income, a decline of two-thirds since 1984. The Americans saved 2 per cent of their income. (In thrifty Scandinavia, the Swedes were saving 4.9 per cent, the Finns 3.5 per cent, and the Norwegians 8 per cent.) In the last quarter of 2004, however, something dramatic happened in Canada: the personal savings rate fell from 1 per cent to -0.6 per cent, the first time that it had gone below zero since the federal government began collecting figures in 1961. Moreover, the personal savings rate in Canada had fallen below that of the United States.

The reasons for the decline aren't clear. It may be that Americans tend to borrow more because they can deduct their mortgage interest against their income. Canadians, for their part, may feel wealthier when housing prices rise and may have been more inclined to spend money in recent years as real estate soared. Another explanation may be that incomes may not be rising that much in Canada, and Canadians are now inclined to borrow or use savings to maintain a standard of living to which they have become accustomed. Some are inclined to dip into their registered retirement savings plans to finance a first house, and many are not contributing to retirement savings (unused RRSP contribution room increased four-fold between 1992 and 2004). Whatever the cause and the consequence, Canadians are saving less money. If frugality was a point of distinction between us and the Americans, it is no longer.

The Fat and the Fit. Once the world saw the Ugly American. Now it sees the Obese American. This is more than a cliché; in fact, many Americans are fat. Some authorities call obesity an epidemic in America, suggesting that half the population is overweight. One of the reasons is diet. Food is relatively cheap in the United States and Americans like to eat. They eat often (snacking is displacing formal meals), they eat badly (fast food rules), and they eat heartily (portions are large).

Here, too, Canadians consider themselves on the side of the angels. Like much of the world, they sneer at the corpulent American trying to squeeze into the airplane seat next to them. While the Canadian may not be the renowned sixty-year-old Swede, that human specimen, nor is he the thirty-year-old American, that sad-sack couch potato. Now that is becoming an illusion, too. Canadians have become more overweight since the 1980s. About a third of Canadians are considered fat. More alarming, the rate of growth in obesity is about the same on both sides of the border. If this is true, we are going the way of the Americans, and it will have repercussions for Canada's health system and public policy. The *Ottawa Citizen* editorialized in 2006: "It is getting harder and harder to be self-righteous and denigrate the Americans for their super-sized lifestyle – a lifestyle we evidently share."

Black Knights and White Knights. Americans are aggressive and direct, say Canadians. We see ourselves as kinder and gentler. By some measures, such as the rates of crime and violence in Canada, this is true. But is it true of politics? Our politicians are fond of accusing each other of launching "American-style" attack ads. Or warning of changes to our system that would "Americanize" Canada. As columnist Andrew Coyne of the *National Post* says: "Among the many things Canadians think they know about their neighbours to the south is that their politics are a disgrace. 'American-style' is almost invariably a curse-word in this country, and never more so than when it comes to the theory and practice of democracy."

The image of American politics in Canada is largely negative: the influence of money, the length of presidential campaigns, the apathy of voters, the distemper of debate, the disputed election of 2000, the disenfranchisement of the underclass, the broken voting machines. Frank McKenna, Canada's former ambassador to the United States, called American politics "dysfunctional," characterized by paralysis and parochialism. In many ways, this is true. Money matters (presidential candidates are now opting out of the public finance rules to spend without limit), campaigns are long, the Electoral College is archaic. In their session between 2005 and 2007, the House of Representatives did little but address corruption and gridlock. Unsavoury things do happen in American politics; there was such anxiety over allegations of irregularities in the presidential election of 2004 in Ohio (where a reversal of some sixty thousand votes would have given John Kerry the presidency) that the state delayed destroying the ballots until an investigation was complete. Yes, the stakes are high in the United States, and yes, politics isn't always pretty.

But undemocratic? Canadians shouldn't be so confident. Jeffrey Simpson called Canada "The Friendly Dictatorship" in his book by that name in 2001. He argued that the leader of a majority government – which is what Canada had for all but nine months between 1974 and 2004 – was in complete control of the executive and the legislature. The prime minister has a wide range of powers, he noted, from setting the date of elections and the duration of campaigns to making prominent appointments, including the governor general and the judges of the Supreme Court. Few of his decisions can be checked by Parliament when his party controls it.

In the United States, the courts and Congress act as a check on the power of the president. He is enormously powerful, of course, but he may be constrained by Congress in a way a prime minister in control of Parliament may not. Beyond the broader constitutional issues, there are other ways in which the American system is more democratic and responsive. Take presidential campaigns. To win the nomination of one of the two major parties, a candidate must run a gauntlet of primaries and caucuses in several states, in several regions, over several weeks or months. To be a serious contender, he or she must raise money, build an organization, draft policy, and win endorsements. Candidates must have the stamina to run in many states, often at the same time, wooing voters and debating rivals. It is a gruelling, enervating process that eventually allows voters in most states to register their preference. And all that is before the national campaign, in the autumn, which is a two-month marathon of its own, including a series of highly publicized televised debates.

In Canada, you could become leader of one of the two major parties without any such test. In fact, Paul Martin won the leadership of the Liberal Party of Canada with 93 per cent of the delegates at a national convention in 2003. They were chosen by riding associations, often in raucous meetings in which the credentials of voting members were challenged and the membership recruitment questioned. John Manley, the candid former deputy prime minister, called the process "corrupt" and withdrew from the race. Martin was so powerful that he frightened other candidates away, which had also happened when Kim Campbell entered the contest for the leadership of the Conservative Party in 1993. Untested in their leadership campaigns, Campbell was defeated in the general election and Martin lost his majority and then his minority, too.

The American electoral system cannot guarantee the best candidate will always win, but it has let the people into the "smoke-filled rooms" once filled with party bosses and powerbrokers. In many ways, American politics is lively and inventive. Despite its flaws, Americans have a robust, responsive democracy. They elect representatives to a number of offices, from sheriff to district attorney, in a country with a staggering number of elective positions. They vote for their member of the House of Representatives every two years and their president every four, and a third of their Senate every two years. They can recall and replace sitting politicians, which is what the voters of California did in 2003 when they tired of their governor. They express views on many issues in binding referenda. They expect their representatives to hold confirmation hearings to review the credentials of judicial nominees, as well as cabinet secretaries, ambassadors, and senior officials. They also expect those representatives, sitting on other committees, to use their powers to investigate, subpoena, and question all manner of people and issue a report. This happens all the time.

In Canada, we tend to disparage much of this; confirmation hearings are inevitably seen as a "circus," as if they were irredeemably disorderly. Sometimes they are. We have few referenda in Canada, as if consulting the people were a dangerous thing. We have no provision for petition, review, or recall. We have no history of public hearings on governmental appointments. We do have a broader range of parties in our national legislature – including one of left-of-centre federalists and one of left-of-centre secessionists – but the two major parties are historically centrist, probably with fewer differences between them than those between the Republicans and the Democrats. Our federal elections have no fixed dates and campaigns are measured in weeks, not years (though that's not always a bad thing). Our televised debates among the party leaders can degenerate into unseemly shouting matches, as they did in 2004, when the loftiest vision was offering the shortest waiting time to see a doctor. Canadians like to think of their politics as more civil, and fortunately we have had nothing to compare with the "swift boat" tactics that were used by Vietnam veterans to help sink John Kerry's candidacy in 2004 or the malicious advertising used in the senatorial races in Virginia and Tennessee in 2006. But our parties make sulphurous accusations against one another, and we use attack advertising – as the Conservatives did relentlessly against Stéphane Dion in early 2007 – in campaigns that deny any claim to sainthood. As for voter turnout, it is only marginally higher in Canada.

On the whole, we see ourselves as more democratic. It isn't necessarily so.

In some ways the Americans have become more like us, as in their pattern of immigration; in some ways we have become more like them, as in our levels of obesity and savings. However, in its politics, and the language and practice of politics, Canada is moving toward the United States.

We are now setting election dates in law. This is new to parliamentary democracies. Since 2000, British Columbia, Ontario, and Newfoundland have established fixed election dates, and the federal government wants to do the same in national elections. It proposes holding elections every four years – the first would be October 19, 2009 – with a mechanism to allow for the vagaries of parliamentary government, such as the resignation or the defeat of a government on a vote of non-confidence. The impact of fixed elections would be to create a political season beginning as much as a year before the vote. Campaigns would no longer be frenzied interludes of five to eight weeks. They would begin earlier and end later, as they do in the United States.

At the same time, in Canada, we are discussing appointing senators only from among those who have been elected, and limiting their terms of office to six or eight years. Senators now serve to the age of seventy-five. There are no term limits in the United States Senate, but there are for the presidency and some state offices. Canadians are sensitive to importing American practices. When Stephen Harper unveiled this proposal to a committee of the Senate in September 2006, Senator Jim Munson asked if this would lead to the "Americanization" of the system, and columnist Susan Riley of the *Ottawa Citizen* asked whether this was "the first step toward the Americanization of the Senate?" People have also wondered about placing an "American-style" honour guard by the Tomb of the Unknown Soldier. As governor general, Adrienne Clarkson refused a request imposing "a presidential-type installation on our unpresidential system" when Paul Martin wanted to move the swearing-in of his government from Rideau Hall to Parliament Hill. "I believe in modernization . . . but I do not believe in Americanization," Clarkson declared in her memoir, *Heart Matters*. When the Conservative government asked focus groups to preview its first budget speech in 2006, they thought its reference to living "in a sometimes dangerous world" sounded "too American." The wording was changed.

More and more in matters political, for better or for worse, we are doing as the Americans do. The Conservatives have begun asking Parliament to review the prime minister's major appointments. The first hearing of a high court nominee was held in February 2006, shortly after the new government appointed Judge Marshall Rothstein of Manitoba to the Supreme Court of Canada. This hearing was a charade; the government named Rothstein and invited Parliament to question him after the fact. Constitutionally, Parliament has no power to block the appointment. Members could only ask and listen; the televised hearing was like off-Broadway political theatre. But Rothstein's appearance before Parliament was a first in Canada. Although the tone was warm and the questions polite, it drew comparisons to the "circus-like" confirmation hearings around the appointment of high court judges in the United States – and, invariably, more gnashing of teeth and tugging of forelocks over inevitable Americanization.

Then there are the small things, some introduced by the Conservatives in their first year in office. It was novel in Canada to invite guests to sit in the Visitors' Gallery for the Speech from the Throne or to serve as a backdrop for a nationally televised speech by the prime minister (several sat behind Harper as he spoke to the nation from the Hall of Honour of Parliament on September 11, 2006). In the United States, presidents routinely invite guests to their State of the Union Address and identify them to dramatize a point in the address. The Conservatives are now using people as political props, too. When Harper greeted President Hamid Karzai of Afghanistan on September 23, 2006, he arranged a guard of honour and intended to join his guest in reviewing it. This has always been the role of the governor general, the commander-in-chief. When word leaked out and Harper decided not to join Karzai, it may have been because he was accused of borrowing an American practice. And had Karzai wanted to pay his respects to Canadian soldiers killed in Afghanistan, he could have visited the National Military Cemetery of the Canadian Forces, where some are buried. Before 2001, Canada had no such cemetery. As the *Ottawa Citizen* reported, it was the dream of General Maurice Baril, the former chief of defence staff, to create a military cemetery in Ottawa "like the one in Arlington, Virginia, where fallen soldiers could be buried with their comrades, on their home soil." And we did.

American influences are also appearing in the language of politics. We are increasingly describing our institutions in American terms. It is no longer uncommon to hear politicians and journalists speak of "the administration" rather than "the government" in Ottawa as if it were Washington. "Prime Minister" has yielded to "Mr. Prime Minister" like "Mr. President." We tend to use honorifics long after people have left office, as they do in the United States. Allan Gotlieb is sometimes called "Ambassador Gotlieb" and Peter Lougheed is sometimes called "Premier Lougheed" though in Canada we do not retain these titles. Other Americanisms are also heard, though less frequently. The media have called Laureen Harper, the unpretentious wife of the prime minister – with absolutely no encouragement from her – "Canada's First Lady." The prime minister's airplane has been called "Canada's Air Force One." Mr. Harper is given to saying "God Bless Canada" at the end of speeches. When he visited Afghanistan he told the troops that Canadians do not "cut and run." For that, he was accused of sounding "American."

Are we becoming more like the Americans in our political outlook and attitudes? In some ways, yes. At one time party leaders in Canada could lose elections and live to fight again and again. Lester Pearson ran three times as Liberal leader (1958, 1962, 1963) before he became prime minister. Robert Stanfield ran three times as Conservative leader (1968, 1972, 1974). Today the major parties allow their leaders no more than two tries (John Turner, Kim Campbell, Joe Clark, Paul Martin) before discarding them. We don't tolerate losers any more. In the United States, the Democrats and Republicans once renominated candidates who had already run and lost once before (Grover Cleveland in 1892, William Jennings Bryan in 1900 and 1908, Thomas Dewey in 1948, Adlai Stevenson in 1956, Richard Nixon in 1968). They no longer do. Although Canada is becoming impatient with losers, too, such intolerance is thought to be thoroughly American. Jill Ker Conway, the brilliant historian from Australia who became the first woman vice president of the University of Toronto, was always struck by how her colleagues in Canada dismissed American mores. When she once comforted a friend who had lost an academic battle, she found his answer revealing: "I've lived in the United States too much," he said. "I don't enjoy to lose [*sic*] any more."

Perhaps the greatest American influence on Canada of the last generation is the Charter of Rights and Freedoms, which celebrated its twenty-fifth anniversary in 2007. A bill of rights, entrenched in the Constitution and subject to judicial review, was radical when it was introduced in 1982; it was said to be "grafted" upon the parliamentary system. A quarter century later, Canada is a different place. Through the Charter, Canadians are aggressively asserting their rights and making Canada a more litigious country, in which the courts have become ascendant. Like the United States.

On May 9, 2005, two years after *Fire and Ice* appeared, *The Globe and Mail* reported an Ipsos-Reid poll in a banner headline on its front page. It found that, while fewer Canadians and fewer Americans saw each other as the close and warm friends they once did, they shared many of the same attitudes. In fact, in speaking of Canadians and Americans, the report concluded – wait for it – that "their core values were rapidly converging." The poll found that on attitudes toward possession of marijuana, civil liberties in the face of terrorism, protection of the poor, caring for the elderly, and spending on the environment, there was a remarkable similarity of views on both sides of the border. In some cases, there were surprises; when asked whether people from diverse backgrounds would be better off if they became more like the majority, 44 per cent of Canadians said yes in contrast to 38 per cent of Americans who answered the same way. For those who never accepted the thesis of divergence, the poll suggested another reality. "I think Adams has blown this way out of proportion," said pollster Angus Reid in 2006. "When we look globally at the country most like the USA, it is us." Reid points out that there are huge regional differences in Canada and the United States that make this difficult to measure. But he says there is not that much difference in the values of someone who listens to CBC Radio and someone who listens to National Public Radio.

A survey published by *Maclean's* in October 2005 carried the headline, "Closer than you think." It also found the conventional wisdom – that would be divergence – grossly overstated. "Despite everything you've heard in recent years about our crumbling relationship with the United States, most Canadians and Americans want the two countries to get a whole lot closer in the years ahead," *Maclean's* reported. Citing a poll by SES Research, the company that predicted the outcome of the 2006 federal election with pinpoint accuracy, it found a desire for "more co-operation, not less. And when it comes to our perceptions of each other, the two nations are still defined more by our similarities than our differences, and often don't live up to our shared stereotypes. Perhaps most remarkably, on many issues that supposedly divide us, Canadians think a lot like Americans do." The poll found high levels of support for co-operation in security and a belief that both nations represent their ideal in human rights, whatever the excesses of the war on terror.

These are only two of the soundings on cross-boundary attitudes in recent years contradicting *Fire and Ice*. There were other polls showing fewer differences, including several done by Frank Graves of Ekos, another prominent pollster. He says the question of whether values are becoming more alike or different is complex: "What is clear is that the fragile Canadian psyche deeply craves to believe the differences are large and widening and this is most likely rooted in the narcissism of differences which comes from being the smaller and less visible player." When asked to explain the difference between his findings and others', Adams defends his thesis and argues that diverging values do not mean vanishing mutual interests. When David Frum attacked his book, Adams responded politely and unapologetically that his arguments were "not meant to be remotely ideological."

In 2006, Adams followed *Fire and Ice*, which was not published in the United States, with *American Backlash: The Untold Story of Social Change in the United States*. Here he looks at American values alone, without reference to the peaceable, perfect kingdom to the north. His view of America is harsh here, too, as it is in *Fire and Ice*. As an interpreter of America, Adams wryly puts himself in the company of de Tocqueville. "Hubris would suggest that I am the great-great-great-great-grandson of Alexis de Tocqueville," he told the Montreal *Gazette*. "He was a count. I hope I can count. That's the one thing we might have in common. That we both count on counting."

So where does this lead us? If *Fire and Ice* identified a new trend in society that would influence public policy, as Mark Lovewell and others predicted, it is hard to see where. Having read Adams, perhaps Jean Chrétien was emboldened to embrace gay marriage in his last months in office. Perhaps Paul Martin felt free to flay the Americans over Kyoto. Actually, Canada may now be moving in another direction. What happened to "liberal values" when Canadians elected a Conservative government in 2006 that promised to reopen the debate over gay marriage? Or to withdraw from the Kyoto Accord? Or to tolerate the growth of private health care? Or to play down peacekeeping, as critics have charged, and fight in Afghanistan in an "American war"? A few years ago, when Adams was conducting his polls, gay rights, Kyoto, universal health care, and peacekeeping were our emblems of distinction. They were what made us different; they were supposed to reflect our progressiveness and accentuate our differences with the United States. Yet, electing the Conservatives does not necessarily mean that our values have fundamentally changed, either. It means that our *politics* have. It suggests that our differences with the United States are more political and institutional than personal and ideological.

One of the mistakes that Canadians make about the Americans is to think that they know them and understand them. We don't. The perception among Canadians is that America is a monolith that thinks only one way. It isn't and it doesn't. It is true that George W. Bush is a conservative whose views have had unhappy consequences for the environment, labour rights, stem cell research, the Supreme Court, and foreign policy. But the idea of a Republican Ascendancy, as imagined by presidential strategist Karl Rove, has not come to pass. In November 2006, Americans returned control of both houses of Congress to the Democrats. Some of the more conservative Republicans – Senator Rick Santorum of Pennsylvania, for example – were defeated. The United States remains a divided country that has twice come close to putting a Democrat in the White House over the past eight years, and that kept both houses of Congress almost evenly divided before reinstating the Democrats (and several committee chairmanships to northern representatives closer in outlook to Canada).

It may well be that Americans are more conservative than Canadians, but remove the South and Quebec, and America looks much like Canada. When it comes to enduring values, the ones that matter, the two peoples embrace democracy, the free market, human rights, and the rule of law.

While twenty-six states have banned gay marriage, California and others allow legal unions. While Texas has the death penalty, Massachusetts, Michigan, and Minnesota are among twelve states that effectively don't, reflecting a trend against capital punishment that has seen the number of executions drop by 46 per cent since 1999. While South Dakota was outlawing abortions (voters overturned the ban in November 2006), a woman in Prince Edward Island cannot get an abortion there, and in New Brunswick and Nova Scotia, she may have to travel long distances. Once Canada was alone in banning second-hand smoke in the workplace and other public areas; now 52 per cent of Americans in twenty states are covered by such legislation.

Much of this we deny. It is a peculiarly Canadian complex. That there is subtlety about Americans frustrates our natural instinct to create or seek difference, to draw those self-satisfying easy and sharp distinctions. If we are really less different vis-à-vis the Americans than we think, we are less certain about our identity, which is largely based on what we are not.

The American Canadian does not know how to come to terms with this. His world is defined by his neighbour, largely because of economic, commercial, and political decisions made a generation or two ago. He may work in a branch plant or a subsidiary run by Americans, who own or control much of the national economy. He may sell his goods, services, or resources to Americans, who buy some 76 per cent of his country's exports and accept without complaint, year after year, a colossal trade deficit with Canada. Either way, the capital, investment, and market of the United States is the fundamental reason he enjoys one of the highest standards of living in the world. Beyond the influence of economy, he lives with the dominance of culture. He watches American movies and television, wears American jeans, listens to American music, reads American books and magazines. He drinks coffee at Starbucks, eats hamburgers at McDonald's and ice cream at Ben and Jerry's. He aspires to the American Dream, whether it is represented by a minivan or an SUV, and the greatest obstacle to achieving it isn't desire but money. At the same time, he is content to live under the suzerainty of the American Empire, huddling under its nuclear umbrella and outsourcing national defence to the Pentagon. That he does not have to spend much on the military, in relative terms, means that he can spend more on the social programs he values. He accepts this subsidy happily from the Americans while reminding them of the generosity of his social programs and scolding them, as Jean Chrétien did, for their fiscal irresponsibility.

The American Canadian sees no contradiction in living this life, which he accepted when he welcomed American investment and embraced American culture. Lord knows, there were critics. Many doubted the country's wisdom. George Grant, Kari Levitt, Mel Watkins, Pierre Berton, Peter C. Newman, and a host of others mourned this embrace, warned of its consequences, and wondered what it would mean for an independent Canada. Their laments felled forests and filled bookshelves. Of course, that debate was decades ago, and its embers were extinguished by the free trade agreement in 1989. Having fallen into the arms of America – slowly, incrementally, unconsciously – the American Canadian still wants to deny it. How else to explain a people who live in an American world, enjoying its manifold advantages, while seeming to dislike it so?

J.L. Granatstein calls this anti-Americanism, plain and simple, woven so deeply into the Canadian soul that we barely notice any more. He calls this enduring, unwavering, soft-spoken suspicion, distrust, and hostility toward Americans "the founding myth of Canada and remains the state religion, accepted, tolerated and even encouraged." Granatstein argues it has always existed in Canada – he wrote a history of anti-Americanism in 1995 that made the same list of important books in the *Literary Review of Canada* as *Fire and Ice* – and argues that it always will. He quotes Frank Underhill, the eminent historian, who described this antipathy for Americans among Canadians a half century ago: "The Canadian is the first anti-American, the model anti-American, the archetypal anti-American, the ideal anti-American as he exists in the mind of God." Perhaps so. We know that putting distance between ourselves and the Americans, creating distinctions beyond those that already exist, is fundamental to asserting ourselves. Indeed, it is a matter of survival. As an historian, Granatstein can cite example after example of this, in decade after decade, by governments of either political stripe. Collectively, it says something about us. Anti-Americanism was a reality to Clifford Krauss of *The New York Times*, who says he encountered more of it in his four years in Canada between 2002 and 2006 than he did when he covered Central America in the 1990s. His predecessors, who lived in Toronto as he did, found a spirited anti-Americanism in Canada's largest city, too.

It is entirely predictable, then, that this psyche should produce a market for Michael Adams. In a sense, he is its creation. Armed with the numbers, speaking a certain language, it isn't surprising that he struck a chord among Canadians. That his methodology has been questioned, that the differences are often statistically insignificant, that subsequent surveys contradict him, that events since reflect more convergence than divergence – all matter not. We believe what we want to believe. Canada and the United States as distinct as fire and ice? The differences are closer to ashes and water.

Whether Canadians are really, deeply, and congenitally anti-American, though, is unlikely. Historian Norman Hillmer, who has co-written *For Better or for Worse: Canada and the United States into the Twenty-First Century*, believes that at root, we are not. If we were, he asks, how could we have come this far? Much as we may have at times sought to stress our differences, there have been times that we have seen only similarities. Indeed, Granatstein thought the free trade agreement would spell the end of anti-Americanism. Not so. Hillmer sees us as paradoxical, narrow-minded, even hypocritical, but not anti-American. He is closer to the truth.

If Canadians were really anti-American, we would have to denounce ourselves, or everything about our country and our place in it. We are contradictory, inconsistent, and, yes, occasionally hypocritical. When it comes to the Americans, we say one thing and do another – happy to enjoy the fruits of prosperity and security gained by the good fortune of living beside the most benevolent neighbour God could have given us. Canadians, bless us, are not bothered by our inconstancy or ambivalence. Canadians do not mind it when our politicians put distance between ourselves and the Americans – we even encourage it – as long as those spend-thrift, overweight, aggressive vulgarians continue to underwrite our prosperity.

If Canadians felt the way we say we do, and had the integrity of self-aware people, we would not have made the choices we have as a country. We would not have wooed American investment, we would not have welcomed American trade, we would not have consumed American culture, we would not have contracted out our national defence. An honest people as uncomfortable with the character of its neighbour as Canada has been with the Americans would never have created NORAD or joined NATO. Canada would have developed nuclear weapons after the Second World War, which it could have done, maintained a larger standing army, and opted for multilateral rather than bilateral trade. It would have placed much greater restrictions on foreign ownership and imposed airtight rules on imported films, magazines and books, radio and television. All these were choices Canadians could have made if we wanted to differentiate ourselves from the Americans. Of course, we were smart enough not to close our borders and detach ourselves from continental defence, which would have been expensive. By refusing to do any of those things, which would have been hard but honest, we retained our right to gratuitous criticism, our penchant for sanctimony, and our licence to pass judgment. At the end of the day, though, Canadians are less anti-American than un-American. It is less antagonism than skepticism. As the British are Euro-skeptics, Canadians are Ameri-skeptics.

All this claims a corner of the Canadian character. It is one of those ironies that after all those years of trying to create one country, of trying to embrace what John Diefenbaker called "the unhyphenated Canadian," we still have the French-Canadian, the English-Canadian, the African-Canadian, the Italian-Canadian, the Chinese-Canadian, the Indo-Canadian, and other representatives of language, race, or ethnicity. The greatest of the hyphenated Canadians today is the one that we are whether or not we admit it, for better or for worse, now and forever. It is the American-Canadian.

Chapter 5

The Casual Canadian

In 1946, a national organization called the Canadian Council of Education for Citizenship published *A Pocketful of Canada*. Less a book than a literary curio, it is a digest of history and geography, poetry, prose and prayer, art, music and mythology. It is what a Canadian of sixty years ago was expected to know about the great dominion presented in sketches, odes, vignettes, and rhapsodies from explorers, clergymen, poets, novelists, journalists, and other random chroniclers of the Canadian experience. These included Bruce Hutchison, Bliss Carman, Archibald Lampman, Hugh MacLennan, Stephen Leacock, and Susanna Moodie. It has looks and style, this little book; its title is stamped in gold on a sky-blue cover and its pages are adorned with wood engravings. There are essays on Indian art, crafts in French Canada, an introduction to Canadian architecture, an exegesis on Canadian painting, sculpture, and music, even the words and music to *God Save the King* and *O Canada*. There are letters, articles, and addresses by Jacques Cartier, Joseph Howe, Sir John A. Macdonald, Sir Wilfrid Laurier, Edward Blake, and J.W. Dafoe. There are photographs, maps, charts, tables, and excerpts from historical documents too: the Treaty of Paris, the British North America Act, the Statute of

Westminster. In a spirited introduction, the chairman of the council's executive committee, H.M. Tory, D.Sc., LL.D., F.R.S.C., declares the purpose of the book is "to reflect the spirit of Canada. The spirit of a nation is hard to define, but it is expressed in the life and thought of the nation's people."

The council was a product of the adult education movement of the 1930s, when it was fashionable for public-spirited Canadians to foregather regularly to discuss current events. It was created in 1940 by the Bureau of Public Information, an arm of the government, presumably as a mild form of propaganda. Its compendium is compact though by no means complete (there are no selections in French, for which its editor apologizes), but it does reflect, to a degree, how Canadians saw themselves in 1946. The material has been chosen, says the editor, because "it is thought to be characteristically Canadian, in mood or content, or both."

In its pages, however, there is no mention of ethnicity or pluralism. "Multiculturalism" would not enter the vernacular until the 1960s. There is no discussion of "whose" memory or "whose" suffering. It was 1946. If, as British television presenter Jeremy Paxman thinks, Britain was more certain of itself a half century ago, so was Canada. Things were clearer. Self-definition was easier in a more homogeneous society. And it made it easier to produce a book like this, a mirror to a people.

While it is nowhere mentioned in *A Pocketful of Canada*, something of historic importance to Canada took place the year it was published. On May 14, 1946, Parliament passed the Canadian Citizenship Act. For the first time, Canada defined being Canadian and wrote it into law. Before then, there had been no citizens of Canada, *per se*; Canadians were British subjects living in Canada. Having won greater autonomy from Britain under the Statute of Westminster fifteen years earlier, Canada had decided to set out the terms and conditions of its citizenship. On January 1, 1947, the day the new law came into force, journalist Blair Fraser mused about the novelty of it all on CBC Radio. Before then, he said, to be called "a Canadian" was no more than "a kind of a regional tag, like a bluenose or a sourdough." You were "a Ukrainian-Canadian or an Italian-Canadian." Now, he said with pride, you could call yourself a *Canadian*.

The architect of the law was a young Paul Martin Sr., who had been appointed secretary of state in 1945. He would be an urgent and progressive voice in Canada as cabinet minister, senator, and emissary for the next third of a century. After the war, Martin had made an emotional visit to the military cemetery at Dieppe, where some nine hundred Canadians were killed in the disastrous raid in 1942. Moved by their sacrifice, Martin returned home and launched "a crusade . . . to incorporate into law a definition of what constituted a Canadian." This wasn't just a matter of legal clarification, he recalls in his memoirs, *A Very Public Life: Far From Home*. It was in keeping with Sir Wilfrid Laurier's vision of the nation, a sentiment propelled by a surging post-war nationalism determined to banish the vestiges of Canada's imperial past. As the country began asserting itself in the world, Canadians bristled when they were registered as "British" at birth, marriage, and death. They resented having "British subject" stamped in their passports. As T.S. Ewart, a lawyer, fumed in a letter in August 1945 to the *Ottawa Citizen*: "These stupid regulations are caused by the inability to recognize the change in status of our country from that of a colony . . . [to an independent nation]."

As a student of the law, Martin had a jurist's interest in elucidating the status of aliens and British subjects as well as notions of nationality in laws that had been passed by Parliament in 1910, 1914, and 1921. But there was something bigger here. The Citizenship Act was a rite of passage for Canada. "In two world wars," Martin recalled in his memoirs, "we had borne our serious and full responsibility; our fighting men had brought honour to their country. For the unity of the country and for the fulfillment of its potential, it was of the utmost importance that Canada should give its people the right to designate themselves Canadian citizens in law as well as in fact." Fundamentally, the debate about citizenship wasn't about residence, naturalization, revocation, or other matters. "Citizenship means more than the right to vote; more than the right to hold and transfer property; more than the right to move freely under the protection of the state; citizenship is the right to full partnership in the fortunes and in the future of the nation," Martin told the Commons on April 2, 1946. Citizenship was about loyalty, community, maturity, unity. It was about nation-building. It still is.

Paul Martin Sr. fervently hoped the Canadian Citizenship Act would foster a broader sense of nationhood among Canadians. While the country was less diverse than it is today, it had divisions of region, religion, and language. Tensions over conscription in English and French Canada, for example, had smouldered during the Second World War. Martin was well aware of Canada's fragility. In the debate over the bill, parliamentarians talked of eliminating "the hyphenated Canadian"; this meant not only "English-Canadian" and "French-Canadian" but also "Chinese-Canadian" and "Scottish-Canadian." The hope was that citizenship would become the big tent in which newcomers to Canada would gather, abandoning old prejudices as they fled the nationalist storms raging across the post-war world.

Six decades later, that goal remains elusive. One of the reasons is that citizenship doesn't have the same gravity in Canada as it does in other countries. The Canadian Citizenship Act was part of a process of national self-definition that would lead, in the decades to come, to a native-born governor general, a new national flag, a reworded national anthem, and, most significantly, a renewed constitution. It defined a Canadian, established criteria for immigrants to become Canadian, told Canadians how they could lose their citizenship, assured men and women of equal status. It gave special treatment to British subjects and extended citizenship, with conditions, to naturalized immigrants living in Canada. They would have to wait five years and be of "good character," but they could become citizens. At the same time, the law eliminated dual citizenship, which allowed a Canadian to hold the citizenship of another country.

The second Citizenship Act, which came into effect in 1977, addressed flaws in the first and added some of its own. Dual citizenship was reinstated, a seminal decision that reverberates today. The residency requirement for citizenship was reduced from five to three years. Most important, citizenship was considered "a right" for qualified applicants rather than "a privilege." This law has stood for thirty years, despite promises by successive governments to change it. It has created a weak, amorphous idea of citizenship, easy to get and hard to lose. Today Canadian citizenship has become more about rights and benefits than duties and responsibilities. Hugh Segal, a sagacious observer who now sits in the Senate, says that one of the defining characteristics of Canadians is that we are "demanding" in what we expect of ourselves and our society. Perhaps that is generally true, but not when it comes to new Canadians in their new country. In truth, we don't demand very much of them.

Richard Gwyn, the columnist and author of *Nationalism Without Walls: The Unbearable Lightness of Being Canadian*, thinks our citizenship is hollow. "The lightness of being Canadian starts with the fact that it's the easiest citizenship in the world to obtain . . ." he writes. "What's striking is that we ask, and expect, so little in exchange for that blue passport." Three years isn't much time for residency, he argues, particularly if you don't have to spend more than 183 days of each year here. Other nations ask five years; Switzerland asks twelve years. Prospective Canadians need not even spend the required number of days here; if you could avoid having your passport stamped upon entering the United States en route to winter in Florida, for example, who would know you've left the country and who would ask? A prospective citizen is supposed to speak English or French, and take a test (unless you're under eighteen or over fifty-five) that measures the applicant's knowledge of Canada. Neither requirement seems to be very difficult. Up to 2005, an immigrant over sixty years old did not have to take the test or meet the language requirement. In announcing the government's decision to lower the age by five years in 2005, Immigration Minister Joe Volpe went to Toronto and gathered a crowd to give the change a sense of occasion. "We become Canadians by doing what Canadians do," he said, surrounded by seven fellow Liberal MPs and one hundred cheering Sikhs.

Having offered citizenship, we ask little in return. A witness before a parliamentary inquiry in 1994, quoted by Gwyn, put it this way: "My parents were immigrants, and my aunts and uncles as well. They were not told what it means to be a Canadian citizen. They were just told, essentially, 'pass the tests, pay the taxes, and that's it.'" The citizenship oath itself is spare: "I swear (or affirm) that I will be faithful and bear true allegiance to Her Majesty Queen Elizabeth the Second, Queen of Canada, Her Heirs and Successors, and that I will faithfully observe the laws of Canada and fulfil my duties as a Canadian citizen." Critics have argued that the oath asks too much allegiance to the Queen and not enough to Canada. Some want the Queen dropped altogether, though that prospect would surely send Canada's monarchists to the ramparts. The Liberals have tried three times in the last decade (1998, 1999, 2003) to amend the act and rewrite the oath. Each of their bills died. One of the proposed citizenship acts would have required new citizens "to more directly express their loyalty to Canada and Canadian values." The amended oath read: "From this day forward, I pledge my loyalty and allegiance to Canada and Her Majesty Elizabeth the Second, Queen of Canada. I promise to respect our country's rights and freedoms, to uphold our democratic values, to faithfully observe our laws and fulfil my duties and obligations as a Canadian citizen."

We ask less here than other countries. In the United States, new Americans take the "Naturalization Oath of Allegiance to the United States of America." It asks a new citizen: a) to renounce all allegiance to "a foreign prince, potentate, state or sovereignty"; b) to support and defend "the Constitution of the United States against all enemies" at home and abroad, "to bear arms on behalf of the nation and perform non-combatant service" when required; c) to do work "of national importance under civilian direction"; and d) "to do all this freely, without mental reservation . . . so help me God." In Australia, a fellow member of the Commonwealth more skeptical of the monarchy than Canada, the long-standing oath of allegiance was replaced in 1993 by a "Pledge of Commitment." It reads: "From this time forward, under God, I pledge my loyalty to Australia and its people, whose democratic beliefs I share, whose rights and liberties I respect, and whose laws I will uphold and obey." A second pledge, presumably to offer a choice, makes no reference to God. In Canada, we do not mention God, like the Americans. But we do mention the Queen, unlike the Australians.

Despite attempts, Canada has been unable to define more clearly and fully the expectations of citizenship. The Liberals had been preparing to table legislation in 2005 before they were defeated. The same year, a parliamentary committee reaffirmed the idea of citizenship as a right rather than a privilege. It also concluded that with rights come responsibilities. These, too, await definition in law. However, on its website, Citizenship and Immigration Canada elaborates. It says citizens have an obligation to "vote in elections; help others in the community; care for and protect our heritage and environment; obey Canada's laws; express opinions freely while respecting the rights and freedoms of others; and eliminate discrimination and injustice." That's a tall order for anyone, especially for a new Canadian. Sure, we expect everyone to vote, obey the law, and pay taxes, which would seem to be the bare minimum of citizenship. As for helping others in the community, protecting the environment, and eliminating discrimination, these are all desirable, too. Indeed, if all Canadians, new and old, subscribed to this notion of citizenship, Canada would be a more serious place.

But Canada is a fragmented country, and one of the reasons is its cavalier view of citizenship, which fosters a sense of entitlement among those who desire it. Should that be so? We make citizenship ever easier to acquire; the most recent proposed legislation would have required immigrants to live in Canada for three of the last six years to be eligible for citizenship, instead of three of the last four years, as is the case now. Should that be so? We allow Canadians to hold dual citizenship, imposing no obligations or expectations. Should that be so?

In the exquisite way that our political culture mirrors our national character, the question of dual citizenship has become a contentious issue in Canada three times in recent years. The first was in the summer of 2005, when Paul Martin designated Michaëlle Jean Governor General of Canada. As it happened, Jean had officially become a citizen of France only weeks before the prime minister offered her the job. Reflecting on those events in January 2007, sixteen months after her appointment, Jean recalled that acquiring French citizenship had been almost accidental. Her husband, Jean-Daniel Lafond, was born in France, and he and Jean had wanted their young adopted daughter, Marie-Éden, to have the same citizenship as his two girls from a first marriage. When the French Consul in Montreal suggested that Jean take out citizenship too, so that the whole family would have it, Jean thought "why not?" But dual citizenship wasn't something she either desired or pursued and contrary to published reports – which went unchallenged – she had not become a citizen when she married Lafond. Although there were whispers in Montreal that Jean wanted to work as a broadcaster in France, she says she had no plans to move to France, where she and her husband own a house. Whatever her intention, acquiring another passport was hardly unusual in 2005; Jean was one of an estimated five hundred thousand Canadians – we don't know exactly how many – with two, three, or more citizenships.

But when she accepted her vice regal appointment, expectations changed. As governor general, Jean would be the Queen's Representative in Canada, the country's de facto head of state and the head of its armed forces. No longer would she be Michaëlle Jean, private citizen; she would be Her Excellency the Right Honourable Michaëlle Jean, Chancellor and Principal Companion of the Order of Canada, Chancellor and Commander of the Order of Military Merit, Chancellor and Commander of the Order of Merit of the Police Forces, Governor General and Commander-in-Chief in and over Canada.

Not that that seemed to matter. Martin was unconcerned about her dual citizenship. Before her appointment, he asked her: "You're a French citizen, aren't you?" She said, "Yes, I got the papers a few weeks ago." He replied: "Well, in Canada, I don't think it would be a concern for Canadians. So many Canadians have dual citizenship." The issue did not come up at her news conference on August 4 when Martin announced her appointment. Later on, *The Globe and Mail* reported that news of her dual citizenship had been "mostly met with a shrug." Few Canadians seemed to care, apart from a lone demonstration of a noisy claque of protestors on Parliament Hill and the executive of the Royal Canadian Legion, which asked Jean "to clarify how she can proclaim her true allegiance to the Queen of Canada while pledging loyalty to France as a citizen of that country." It appears now that Jean showed no inclination to renounce her citizenship before the appointment, one of those personal choices designees make to avoid any suggestion of impropriety. (Adrienne Clarkson and John Ralston Saul, as well as Roméo LeBlanc and Diana Fowler, for example, had chosen to marry before the announcement of their appointments to Rideau Hall.) Nor did Jean appear immediately ready to renounce her citizenship *after* the announcement. Two weeks later, when she issued a written statement denying allegations that she and her husband had separatist sympathies, she did not mention her dual citizenship. On August 17, CTV News reported that "it doesn't appear to be a pressing matter." What didn't appear to be "a pressing matter" was the public position of the Government of France, where the nineteenth-century civil code forbids a French citizen from holding public or military office in another country. CTV had learned that the obscure provision that could theoretically cost Jean her French citizenship would not be invoked; rather, the network found that France had "never asked anyone to renounce their citizenship in the past and they [the French] don't really have any plans to renounce her citizenship in the future."

Well, that was a relief; the *French* would not strip Jean of her citizenship. She would be welcome to exercise all its rights and privileges even as she performed her duties as head of state of Canada. So, if she wanted to use the special lane for French nationals at Charles de Gaulle Airport in Paris to clear customs, *ça ne fait rien*. Publicly, Ottawa was as uninterested in the citizenship question as Paris. On August 19, Martin's spokesman said of Jean: "The Prime Minister is aware she holds dual citizenship . . . It's not a barrier to serving." Canadians felt much the same way. If they could hold dual citizenship, so could their commander-in-chief. Didn't ninety other countries around the world allow it, too? Their indifference was echoed by the Official Opposition (Bev Oda, the Conservative Party's heritage critic, had no objections) and the Monarchist League of Canada. Dual citizenship? Who cares?

Apparently, Jean did. On September 25, two days before her installation, she issued this written statement: "In light of the responsibilities related to the function of Governor General of

Canada and the Commander-in-Chief of the Canadian Forces, I have decided to renounce the French citizenship that I acquired for family reasons in 2004. France acceded to my request by decree on September 23, 2005." A spokeswoman for Jean told the *Ottawa Citizen* that Jean had "applied to the French government to give up her citizenship shortly after her nomination was announced in early August. The process was complete only last Friday." If that was so, then, it wasn't until France had agreed to allow her to renounce her citizenship that Jean felt free to do it. That raised questions. Why did she not announce her *intention* to renounce? What would she have done if France had not issued its decree? For seven weeks she was unable to say: "I am giving up my French citizenship. As governor general, with constitutional responsibilities, I don't want any misunderstanding." Her terse, narrow explanation – which, out of politeness or protocol, few in the opposition or the media questioned – suggests that Jean did not really want to renounce her citizenship and did not understand why she should do so. On the day of her statement, a spokeswoman explained that Jean worried that it might appear "kind of strange" if she were to remain a French national as vice-regal representative. "She just wanted to be sure," the spokeswoman said. "She thought it would be better [this way]."

Jean revisits the tempest over her citizenship with equanimity. She reveals that she had not made any comment on her dual citizenship before she became governor general because no one had asked her about it; in an earlier conversation, she allowed as well that she was reluctant to make it a subject of public discussion. But her silence didn't mean that she had not decided to act, she says. "So I thought, well, what comes with the responsibility of the Governor General? Commander-in-Chief of the Canadian forces. Commander-in-Chief of Canada. And that is a very specific responsibility. It is not the same for others [politicians]. Could I be under two flags? And I started to think about it and right away it appeared to me that if some people are uncomfortable about it in Canada, maybe I should do something. So I talked to the French ambassador here. If I decide to renounce, I asked, is it a precedent?" The ambassador told Jean that it was not possible to renounce citizenship; it had to be withdrawn. So a special commission was struck in France to investigate her case. As Jean recalls, the commission studied the constitution and found that she could indeed renounce her French citizenship. "As soon as I got the answer," she says, "I made it public."

When Jean had actually decided that she should not keep her dual citizenship – before she was designated in August, "shortly" after she was designated (as her spokeswoman said), a fortnight or so later when critics were calling her a sovereigntist, or much later, in September – is uncertain. But there is reason to believe that she had to be persuaded. Although Martin had told Jean that her dual citizenship didn't matter, he seemed to change his mind later and felt that Jean should not keep it. Unwilling or unable to raise this with her himself, he asked intermediaries to approach her. They told Jean that it would be unwise to remain a dual citizen as governor general, emphasizing, in particular, the difficulty of being commander-in-chief. What if there were a boundary dispute between Canada and France in the waters off St. Pierre and Miquelon, for example, and she had to order Canadian sailors into action against the French? Upon further reflection, Jean decided to renounce. Curiously, when she did so, she offered no reason other than her responsibilities as commander-in-chief. Whenever and however she made up her mind, her decision did not seem easy or instinctive. What we know of this train of events, publicly and privately, suggests that she came to this view reluctantly and that she was prepared to await the approval of the French. In her uncertainty about her citizenship and her deference to authority, Jean was the Casual Canadian.

The issue of dual citizenship also simmered during the month-long war in Lebanon in the summer of 2006. Between forty thousand and fifty thousand Canadians were in the country when the Israelis began bombing on July 12, and it raised legitimate questions about the obligation of their government to rescue them. "MPs squabble over cost of saving dual citizens," said a front-page headline in the *Ottawa Citizen* on July 19. How many of the Canadians in Lebanon were temporary visitors and how many were residents was unknown. The difference was important to those who argued that the government had no obligation to evacuate permanent residents of that country, even if they held Canadian passports, and even less obligation to pay for their travel. These Canadians had chosen to be in a place with a history of conflict, the critics said. They were not "accidental tourists."

Still, Canada decided to bring out its people. So did the United States, Britain, and France. With more nationals at risk and fewer resources in the region, Ottawa organized an extraordinary evacuation. It contracted a small fleet of ships that would sail many times from Beirut to Cyprus and Turkey, where refugees were met by consular officers and put on flights home. Any Canadian who showed up in Beirut with a Canadian passport (or even without) was offered passage home. Like the United States Marines, Canada would leave no one behind. It was genuine and generous. "The safety and security of Canadians is of the utmost concern of this and any government," said Peter MacKay, the minister of foreign affairs, a few months later. "Put simply, there is no higher priority."

Stephen Harper called it "the largest evacuation of Canadian citizens from another country in our history." In Paris, returning from the G-8 Summit, he saw an opportunity and seized it. Leaving the press corps behind, Harper, his wife, and his photographer climbed aboard his capacious military airplane and flew to Nicosia. Once there they sat on the tarmac for twenty-four hours awaiting the passengers from the first of the boats. But when the Canadians finally arrived and the big schoolbus took off with the Harpers aboard, only eighty-eight of the seats were full. Many of the evacuees knew nothing about Canada and had no interest in going there; they wanted to stay in Europe, the prime minister's offer notwithstanding. Among the passengers was Abbas Hachem, his wife and four young children. En route, he chatted with Harper and offered him advice on handling Israel. When Hachem arrived in Ottawa, he was arrested, charged with defrauding six Canadian banks of seventy thousand dollars in 2001, and jailed for a day until he was released on bail. Hachem had not been removed from the flight in the first place, we learned later, because he was not considered a security risk; it was decided that he could fly home with his family "for humanitarian reasons." Hachem was delighted to be in Canada, whatever his troubles with the law. "It is a very important thing to live in a safe place," he said. When Field Commander Harper's plane arrived in Ottawa in the hollow of the night, Minister MacKay and his officials were there to meet it. "I recall the expression of thanks from our fellow citizens as they disembarked from the plane and their joy at being home," MacKay recounted later, beaming like a boy scout.

Not all of his fellow citizens plucked from Lebanon were as exultant. Many were displeased that the rescue had taken so long and said so, loudly. The censorious *Globe and Mail* noted "the fumbles in plucking Canadians from Lebanon" and blamed the government for dawdling. "While other nations had chartered vessels and informed their citizens, Canadians were simply getting busy signals or being asked to stand by – until Ottawa contacted them." Reporters being reporters, not a discouraging word from the evacuation went unrecorded. "It's been disgusting, the way we have been treated," barked one evacuee. A man who had led his family out of the country without the government's help vowed: "They won't get our vote again." Others brought their own catalogue of complaints. The beleaguered diplomats at the Canadian

Embassy in Beirut did not answer calls. The boats were dirty, the toilets overflowing, the food scarce, the seas choppy. If the sheets were not four-hundred-thread Egyptian cotton and the pillow on the bed had no chocolate mint on it, blame the government. They did.

Canada's mid-summer mission had a touch of the surreal – Harper of the Levant flying to the rescue, his earnest minister at the ramp like a greeter at Wal-Mart, the legion of carping Canadians on the nightly news. The shame here was that this sideshow overshadowed a remarkable rescue, by sea, from an embattled country half a world away. In the end, Canada brought 14,982 people from Lebanon (of whom 200 or so were from France, Germany, Australia, Mexico, and other countries). On a lone voyage from Tyre, there had been more foreigners on board than Canadians; Canada took them anyway. The Department of Foreign Affairs answered some 45,000 phone calls and 12,000 emails. A force of 358 public servants, many of them interrupting their summer holidays, was assembled in Canada, Cyprus, Lebanon, and Turkey to meet the demand. The government issued 1,808 emergency passports and arranged transport on 66 chartered flights and 31 ferry passages. All told, the cost was about $96 million. Yet in a country careful with money, Canada waived fees and brought all its citizens home, not just to ports in the Mediterranean. "Canadians would not be expected to pick up and choose whether they could be taken out of harm's way based on their ability to pay," said MacKay. "Our job was to protect all Canadians and we did so." Harper said that given the emergency, "we would spare no expense." This was Canada, too. Decent. Diligent. Kind.

Naturally, this biblical exodus raised questions. Just what was Ottawa's obligation here, anyway? The new government promised to examine this. "Canadians want to know that citizenship means something, that we're not just a port in the storm," Citizenship and Immigration Minister Monte Solberg told a parliamentary committee in November. He said that if someone were absent from Canada and not paying taxes but would draw social benefits in the future, "I would think that Canadians would feel that this is unfair." Later in the month, to another audience, he said: "There are concerns in general – not just about dual citizenship but citizenship period – and what are the obligations that Canadians have toward their country."

Of course, Solberg knew that many of those evacuees had ties with Canada in name only. It is likely that they were Lebanese Canadians who had spent enough time in Canada during Lebanon's civil war in the 1970s to qualify for citizenship and had returned to Lebanon afterward. Or, they had acquired Canadian citizenship through marriage or as young children. According to the minister, who wasn't sure himself, about half of the evacuees (some seven thousand) went back to Lebanon after the war. "If at some point we feel that the children aren't in peace and safety, we will leave again for Canada," Zeina Mawassi, who had returned to her border town of Aytaroun, told *Maclean's* four months later. "When we had a problem, we went to Canada. When it was safe again, we went back to Lebanon." Mira Nahouli, an investment banker who was born in Beirut, raised in Montreal, worked in London and had returned to Beirut, said she has freedom because of her dual citizenship: "The best present my father ever gave me was a Canadian passport. Unfortunately, when you live in a country like [Lebanon], you need a way out."

Governments have obligations to their citizens, however circumscribed, to safeguard their interests around the world. That's why Canada maintains a consular service. Canadians on holiday, at work, or living abroad temporarily ought to expect their government to help them in a time of crisis. The assumption is that such protection is part of an implicit understanding with their government. Few questioned the assumption among expatriates, politicians, advocates, and editorialists that the government of

Canada had an obligation to rescue its citizens from a war zone and absorb the costs. And that *all* citizens, regardless of where they lived, could expect that of their government. Indeed, by the summer of 2006, this was conventional wisdom in Canada. In a poll by Ipsos-Reid conducted in July, at the height of the crisis, eight of ten respondents thought "Canadian citizens had a right to expect the government to evacuate them from a dangerous area . . . ." In other words, international rescue is a right of citizenship. "Canadian citizens are Canadian and we're going to do what we can to protect them," declared Solberg in August.

This idea of citizenship was not how Paul Martin Sr. had imagined it after his visit to Dieppe in 1945. It would be safe to say that Canadians do not recall Dieppe when thinking of their citizenship. Dieppe is about duty, honour, and sacrifice. It is doubtful that they imagine bearing arms or performing national service – as new Americans swear to do upon becoming citizens – though as citizens, they may well be expected to fight for their country. These days, Canadians are more likely to think of Dunkirk, where some three hundred thousand British soldiers were miraculously pulled from the beaches of France in 1940. At the time, a grateful Winston Churchill declared that, "Wars are not won by evacuations." They aren't, but elections are. Citizens have expectations and governments have obligations, and each is keenly aware of the other. One of the less benevolent reasons that the government brought everyone out of Lebanon, at no cost, was the price of leaving them there: pictures of trapped Canadian men, women, and children, killed or injured, risked alienating voters in urban, ethnic central Canada where the Conservatives dearly want to win seats.

In a sense, our idea of citizenship today is the reverse of John F. Kennedy's ringing appeal of a generation ago: the question is no longer what you can do for your country, but what your country can do for you. As students are no longer really students to universities and patients are no longer really patients to hospitals, citizens

are no longer citizens. Today everyone is a *client*. If that means res-
cuing you from Lebanon, Uganda, Kashmir, or any other place on
God's green earth, so be it. If that means maintaining a fleet of
ferries and airplanes or a bank of telephone operators awaiting
your call from the Andes, the Sahara, or the Amazon because you
have broken a toe, trekked into a tribal feud, or contracted malaria,
so be it. We don't stand on guard for Canada any more; Canada
stands on guard for us.

Well, not really. It hasn't come to this – not yet. But Canada
did go to extraordinary lengths to protect its own in Lebanon. No
questions asked. No money paid. All you had to do was flash a
passport, even if it was one of several you carry. No matter. As
columnist Terence Corcoran of the *National Post* sighed: "Let's see.
If there's a war in Lebanon, then today I'm Canadian."

This was the subtext of the flight from Lebanon and, once
again, it was a question of character. How to treat Canadians of
convenience? There are said to be 11.5 million Canadians, about a
third of the population, who hold valid passports. The government
does not know how many are living abroad, but some researchers
estimate 3 million and rising. They could be in Lebanon. They
could be in Hong Kong, from which tens of thousands came to
Canada before the colony reverted to China in 1997. Many have
since returned. Or they could be in Los Angeles. As Graham
Fraser of the *Toronto Star* asked, would Canada have to rescue the
200,000 to 320,000 Canadians who live in Hong Kong if China
imposed martial law on Hong Kong or attacked Taiwan? Would it
have to rescue hundreds of thousands of Canadians in California in
the event of a devastating earthquake? These places are home to
many Canadians who have no tangible ties to Canada; they do not
live, work, pay taxes, or own property here. What they have is a
passport they renew every five years. It sits in a drawer, as dormant
as their relationship with the country it represents. When things
go bad, they retrieve it. For expatriates, a Canadian passport is a

promissory note, an escape hatch, a bolt-hole. It turns the citizen into a petitioner. Martin Collacott, Canada's former ambassador to Cambodia, Syria, and Lebanon, who managed evacuations of Canadians during his career, says Canadians returning to their homelands are often demanding of Canada. "While they understandably feel at home in the surroundings where they grew up, in times of trouble they become very conscious of their status as Canadians and expect the federal government to come to their aid without delay." And why not if they see their passports as insurance policies. You may no longer pay premiums but you still expect gold-plated coverage. You're not only a client, you're "a stakeholder."

Dual citizenship has great advantages to a country like Canada, which generates 40 per cent or more of its wealth in trade; we benefit enormously from the expertise, experience, and entree to the world that citizens of other countries bring. In fairness, many dual citizens do pay taxes, own property, and maintain ties to Canada. As Canada grows through immigration, pressure to re-examine dual citizenship will rise. Governments tinker with this at their own risk. If they treat dual citizens in a different way, they may alienate new Canadians. To deny dual citizenship outright – as Iran, Japan, Norway, Pakistan, Thailand, and some forty other countries do – would be hazardous for a country built on immigration. However, there is a compelling national interest in reviewing it. The issue of dual citizenship flared once again in December 2006, after Stéphane Dion was chosen leader of the Liberal Party of Canada. Like Jean, he held French citizenship; in his case, it had come through his mother, who was born in France. Like Jean, he was in no hurry to give it up. "It's part of me," he said. "It's my mother who gave it to me. And like all sons, I love my mother and I love what she gave to me." No one was questioning Dion's loyalty to Canada, but once again, it was how it looked. Should a potential Prime Minister of Canada, the country's chief executive, have dual citizenship? On reflection, Dion thought perhaps not. He would give it up if necessary, though not necessarily for the most noble reasons. "If I see it's a liability for our winnability, I will do it," he said. He may not have to embrace this kind of expediency. For a day or so, his dual citizenship unleashed a frenzy of teeth-gnashing and forelock-tugging in Parliament. Then it went away.

What does all this say? We are a polite, phlegmatic people, willing to accept a head of state holding the citizenship of another country. We felt no urgency to press Jean on this question and we didn't think our government should, either. We were ready to let it pass with Dion, too. Perhaps it is our state of being. The question of Michaëlle Jean, Lebanon, and Stéphane Dion and dual citizenship shows us a side of ourselves. It says there is something sensible and decent about us – and something light, soft, and insouciant, too.

On June 26, 1963, at the height of the Cold War, President Kennedy made an historic visit to Berlin. It was a divided city in a divided Germany in a divided Europe. Kennedy understood the rhythms of history and knew the creases in the map of the world. As leader of the free world, he wanted to make a memorable statement about the Berlin Wall and its meaning. So, on that extraordinary day, having seen the Wall and peered into grey, lifeless East Berlin, he mounted a platform and spoke of citizenship as democracy and struggle. "Two thousand years ago, the proudest boast was *civis romanus sum* ['I am a citizen of Rome']," he declared. "Today, in the world of freedom, the proudest boast is 'Ich bin ein Berliner.'" Later, he said: "All free men, wherever they may live, are citizens of Berlin and, therefore, as a free man, I take pride in the words 'Ich bin ein Berliner.'"

Only minutes before, as Kennedy was entering the square filled with a million cheering Berliners, had he decided to phrase it that way. As Rome represented the ideal of citizenship in the ancient world, so Berlin did in the modern world. This was the frontier of freedom and before him were its stout defenders. Romans had known who they were in the world two millennia ago; in 1963, Berliners did, too. To Kennedy, they stood for something. Truth be told, you could probably find the same clarity and confidence, then and now, in a man or woman uttering: "I am an American." Or, "I am a Briton." Or, "I am a Russian."

But if a Canadian said "I am a Canadian," what would it stand for? What would it say? The question has no clear answer 140 years after Confederation, 90 years after the Battle of Vimy Ridge, 75 years after the Statute of Westminster, 60 years after the Canadian Citizenship Act, 25 years after the Charter of Rights and Freedoms. Each of these, in its own way, was an affirmation of Canada.

Whatever the uncertainty at this country's core, it hasn't stopped people from coming. In 2005, a total of 262,236 settled here; in 2006, the number was expected to be the same. In 2007, the government will admit the highest levels in twenty-five years. Four-fifths of them will eventually become citizens. No country welcomes more new citizens, per capita, than Canada; at 6.5 per 1,000, Canada has the highest rate of citizenship in the world. Canada absorbs about 215,000 new citizens a year, the second highest number after the United States. Some 84 per cent of eligible immigrants become citizens, in contrast to 40 per cent in the United States. People want to join us, to be sure, whatever it is that they are joining. In 2005, the top five countries from which new immigrants came were China (16 per cent), India (13 per cent), the Philippines (7 per cent), Pakistan (5 per cent), and the United States (3 per cent). These were followed by immigrants from Colombia, Britain, South Korea, and France.

Some of those who want Canadian citizenship have no doubt about what it means. Conrad Black, for example, renounced his citizenship in 2001 after a nasty spat with Jean Chrétien. As prime minister, Chrétien decided that Black could not retain his citizenship *and* accept a peerage in the House of Lords in Britain, where he already held citizenship. When the government told Black he had to choose, Black chose Britain. Five years later, he wants his Canadian citizenship back. His problem is that he is under criminal indictment in Chicago and his application cannot proceed until the case is settled. With the Liberals out and the Conservatives in, Black wants to be part of Canada again. He now speaks respectfully of Canada, even sentimentally. So does Robert Goulet, the singer with the baritone voice. He had moved to Edmonton from Massachusetts at thirteen, spent six years there and another seven in Toronto before returning to the United States. But he wasn't born here. "I feel Canadian," he maintains. "I tried to become a citizen for a long time, but it is driving me nuts. It's always red tape. My formative years were in Canada and I have so much love for Canada."

It says something about Canada that Black and Goulet – two luminaries with lives, fortunes, and reputations here – struggle for citizenship. Yet we offer it routinely to thousands of newcomers who barely meet its requirements. Or, we confer it upon profiles in courage such as the Dalai Lama, Nelson Mandela, and Raoul Wallenberg as an expression of our esteem. Or, we make the requirements of citizenship so elastic that Canadians can do anything they want with it, even running for office in their country of origin. This is what happened in the Italian national elections of April 2006. Vittorio Coco, a television personality in Toronto, ran for the Italian Senate and lost. Gino Bucchino, a Toronto surgeon, ran for the Chamber of Deputies and won. They were among eleven Canadians hoping to represent Italians living in North America. As elected representatives, they would exercise all the responsibilities of politicians in Italy while remaining citizens of Canada. This seems to present no problem to Bucchino. "Even though I am Canadian, I'm not really Canadian," he said with charming frankness.

Agreeing to let Italian Canadians serve in elected office in Rome was an unsurprising decision on our part, consistent with Canadians' studied indifference to citizenship. That this creates dual loyalties with far-reaching consequences, well, *que sera sera*. Not that all Italian Canadians embraced the idea. Tony Manera, the former president of the CBC, called it "a misguided" policy that risks bringing Italy's domestic political conflicts to a country that surely has enough of its own. "While Canada rightly encourages immigrants from all over the world," he says, "we must insist that, once they arrive in Canada, they leave their political baggage behind and assume their full rights and obligations as new Canadians to participate in the Canadian political process."

And what about those Canadians who return to Canada to live after half a lifetime away? Are they any less Canadian? For purposes of citizenship, no. For the purposes of politics, yes. Let us put it this way: after a prolonged absence, can an expatriate return home, run for Parliament, and lead one of the country's major parties? This was the question raised by Michael Ignatieff, the intellectual, author, and scholar who left Canada in 1978 for a career in academia and journalism in Britain and the United States. Ignatieff flourished abroad, winning prizes and praise. In late 2005, he came home and entered federal politics. Less than two months after winning a seat in Parliament, he announced his candidacy for the leadership of the Liberal Party.

Here is where it got interesting. In a country with a liberal view of immigration and citizenship, Ignatieff was dismissed in some quarters as a poseur and an outsider. He was a *foreigner*. At his nomination meeting in Toronto, jeering protestors chanted "American, American." To them and others, Ignatieff was not Canadian enough. He had been away. He did not know the country. "What rankles people is his 30-year exile from Canada and his unmitigated gall in presuming that his experience as a writer and U.S. university professor somehow qualifies him to lead Canada," sniffed Jon B. Johnson of Vancouver in a letter to the *National Post*. "With virtually no business, government or political experience in

Canada or elsewhere, it is astonishing that Mr. Ignatieff thinks he can saunter back to this country after three decades and presume that he has the skills and knowledge to lead our nation." That wasn't entirely wrong; even if Mr. Ignatieff was running rather than sauntering, he certainly felt that he could lead the country. In his campaign speeches, he evoked his breadth of experiences as a child, a student, and a professor in Canada, the visits he made, the books he wrote, the family and friends who remained here. "I don't feel I have been away at all," he said.

Ignatieff's candidacy revealed cross-currents in the Canadian character. The first is a resentment of success and a dismissal of his audacity to presume that what he achieved abroad could possibly compensate for his absence from Canada. He hadn't paid his dues. He had been spending more time hearing of the agonies of Catalans and Croatians than of Canadians. In this, we see the authentic streak of envy and resentment that has a proud pedigree in Canada (it is discussed in Chapter 7). The second current runs deeper. It is one of genuine respect, even reverence, for his credentials *because* they are earned abroad. After all, they are foreign rather than domestic, which could never be as good. Dazzled by his Oxbridge resume, intoxicated by his eloquence and erudition, Canadians were grateful that someone of his stature, even with no political or managerial experience, would agree to become the leader of the Liberal Party and the prime minister of one of the world's largest, oldest, and most complex countries. No wonder the Liberals made him the front-runner in their leadership campaign and the runner-up at their national convention. (This reverence for things foreign might be seen as a form of neo-colonialism. It surfaced when the Liberals asked Howard Dean, the chairman of the Democratic Party, to give the keynote speech at their convention, as they had asked Bono, the Irish rock star, three years earlier. Critics wondered why they could not find a Canadian.) Few Liberals seemed to know or care that Ignatieff had used "we," "us," and "our" when he had spoken of America while in America. Rather than a native who had never been away, he sounded then like a stranger who had never been here. Or far worse, a wannabe American. On these occasions he seemed reluctant, even embarrassed, to speak Canada's name. In *The Rights Revolution*, one of his many books, he said that writing the book had "deepened my attachment to the place on earth that, if I needed one, I would call home." Did he not need a home in his new universe? What was Canada, then? A default position?

Only in a country with so little self-confidence – or such wisdom – could so little political experience and so much national ambivalence go so far. Then again, this is the way of the Casual Canadian. An incredulous Jeffrey Simpson of *The Globe and Mail* was mystified by Ignatieff's meteoric political ascent: "Such ambition would be risible in any other serious country. Could anyone imagine a person who had lived 90 per cent of his time outside the United States returning to win a congressional seat, then several months later launching a campaign for a party nomination for president? Could one imagine anything like it in Britain, or France or Japan?"

Having lived in Canada, Conrad Black, Robert Goulet, and Michael Ignatieff understand the meaning of citizenship. Many immigrants do not. Theirs is a vague view of a country that is cold, safe, rich, dull, and nice. Canada is *terra incognita* to them. It is an empty vessel. And that is what makes it so attractive. Being Canadian doesn't demand much. Fundamentally, citizenship can mean anything and they can be anything – which may mean staying who they are in custom and practice, living the way they lived, in the language they lived, in Canada rather than in China, India, or Pakistan.

Once Canada was known for its winter or its wealth. Or the quality of its diplomacy, the bravery of its soldiers, or the prominence of its peacekeepers. Or its social democracy – universal health care, old-age pensions, and unemployment insurance. More recently, it has attracted attention for its openness to gay marriage and the decriminalization of marijuana. In 2003, *The Economist* cooed "cool Canada" as it pictured a moose in sunglasses on its cover. Today, Canada is about diversity. This is how others see us and how we see ourselves. It flatters us. We are the world's pluralistic society. We are the way of the future. Canada is multiculturalism; multiculturalism is Canada. As the boast of the ancient world was the sophistication of Rome and the pride of the modern world was the steadfastness of Berlin, the emblem of the post-modern world is the diversity of Canada.

If enough people tell you this, you come to believe it. Of course, Alexis de Tocqueville, Rupert Brooke, Rudyard Kipling, André Siegfried, and other observers of Canada weren't telling us this. But Alistair Horne and Andrew Malcolm were discovering it in the 1950s and the 1980s. And to other, more recent, observers, diversity is the essence of Canada. It is its mantra. When the British travel writer Jan Morris visited Toronto in 1984 and saw a city vastly different from the one she had visited thirty years earlier, it was as if her senses had taken flight: "Multiculturalism! I had never heard it before, but I was certainly to hear it again, for it turned out to be the key word, so to speak, to contemporary Toronto. As *ooh-la-la* is to Paris, and *ciao* to Rome, and *nyet* to Moscow, and hey you're looking *great* to Manhattan, so multiculturalism is to Toronto. Far more than any other of the great migratory cities, Toronto is all things to all ethnicities. The melting pot conception was never popular here, and sometimes I came to feel that Canadian nationality itself was no more than a minor social prerequisite, like a driving licence or a spare pair of glasses."

A decade and a half later, writer Pico Iyer visited Toronto, discovered multiculturalism, and fell as hard for it as Morris had. In polyglot Toronto, it seemed, every street, store, billboard, and restaurant reflected "the Multiculture," as he called it. Everyone was an ambassador of diversity. "Very nice city," says the turbaned taxi driver who drives Iyer in from the airport. "Very clean, very safe. Nobody here, he is from Canada. So nobody can say, 'You could not be here. You cannot come!'" Iyer, who was born in India, educated in Britain, and lives in America and Japan, travels the world chronicling the emerging international culture. He sees Toronto as the capital of the Republic of Diversity. "The hope of the Global Soul, always, is that he can make the collection of his selves something greater than the whole; that diversity can leave him not a dissonance but a higher symphony," he writes. "In Toronto, I wondered whether the same could be true of a Global City. And I felt, at another level, an instant kinship with this place where people seemed to speak another language I could understand." Blinded momentarily by the colours of the city's rainbow, Iyer speaks of Toronto embarking on a great multicultural project with "itself as guinea pig" and raising "the possibility, exhilarating to contemplate, that a city made up of a hundred diasporas could go beyond the cities that we knew."

Here is Toronto, then, a protectorate of pluralism. Morris and Iyer celebrate what Toronto is: the safest, most diverse city in the world. Almost half of Greater Toronto's population of 5.9 million was born abroad, and that percentage is growing as the region draws newcomers every year. Although Toronto is the seat of Canada's multiculturalism, it also flourishes in Montreal, Vancouver, Winnipeg, and other cities. In Canada, 5.4 million Canadians, or 18 per cent of the population, were born somewhere else. This has made Canada the second most heterogeneous country in the world, after Australia. The mix of language and culture that have flowered in the stony, forbidding north have brought energy, imagination, eclecticism, and wealth to Canada. Cast in law in 1971 and 1988, entrenched in the Charter of Rights in 1982, multiculturalism has an unassailable stature in our institutional architecture. Indeed, under Section 27, the Charter must be "interpreted in a manner consistent with the preservation and enhancement of the multicultural heritage of Canadians." Multiculturalism has transformed this country's self-image. It has made Canada a curiosity, an exemplar in the post-modern world. To some it is the *bel idéal* of the future itself. When Pico Iyer was in Toronto, he visited a mixed-race couple in a Portuguese neighbourhood – David, white and Jewish, Alicia, dark and Goan Christian – waxing rhapsodic about the diversity of their city. "Now the new form of nationalism is *multinationalism*," David says. "This nationalistic impulse is toward all nations. And I love it! It makes me weepy."

But even they say that multiculturalism isn't the emblem of inclusiveness that it appears to be. For all David's tears, multiculturalism is not embracing. David and Alicia don't know their neighbours. While they see, smell, and taste Portugal in the restaurants, markets, and shops of their neighbourhood, which they cherish, they don't know any Portuguese. Indeed, they and their neighbours live separate lives. "Multiculturalism actually increases the distance between us," allows Alicia. Other Torontonians whom Iyer meets say this isn't an accident; multiculturalism assumes a kind of self-policing and self-segregation. The doubt, indeed the argument, raised by multiculturalism is that it is turning Canada into an ethnic archipelago. We are living on islands of our own in the Sea of Canada – Chinatown, Greektown, Little Italy, Little India, Ste. Boniface, Westmount – associating with each other largely through trade and commerce. But we have nothing much in common. Canada is becoming "a community of communities" – the vision of Canada expressed by former prime minister Joe Clark – though surely not as he imagined it.

These forces have shaped us into our shapeless self. Yann Martel, the award-winning novelist, calls Canada "the greatest hotel on earth. It welcomes people from everywhere." A perceptive and apt description, it imagines a Canada in which everyone is a visitor, occupying a room, a floor, or even a wing, depending on his means. No one stays for very long because no one wants to make an extended commitment. A hotel is impermanence, by its very nature the most tenuous of loyalties. People come and go. In point of fact, this is actually true of Canada; some 30 per cent of immigrants are thought to return home after getting citizenship. George Jonas, the author and journalist who came to Canada from Hungary, picks up the metaphor. He warns of "turning a nation-state into a railway station in which passengers mingle, occasionally sharing a destination but no destiny." Indeed, when you consider the evacuation of Canadians from Lebanon, Canada is not only a hotel and train station, but a taxi service, too.

This compartmentalization of Canada emerges in unsavoury ways: in the grim, urban corridors where Jamaican, Haitian, and other street gangs fight each other; in the high-rise housing projects filled with Somalis and other struggling minorities; in the epidemic of violence against women in the Indo-Canadian community; in the desire of some Muslims in Ontario to use Sharia law; in the arrests of eighteen suspected terrorists, all of them Muslim, whom no authority would identify as such. Stephen Harper proudly tells the World Urban Forum in Vancouver in 2006: "We have avoided ghettoization – the bane of urban existence in so many places – the impoverished, crime-ridden, ethnically polarized no-go zones." By and large, he is right. But he overlooks the segregation of aboriginal Canadians in western cities and the alienation of visible minorities, their difficulty finding work and securing a place in society. There are reasons for worry. Michael Valpy, the journalist and author, sees trouble among second-generation minorities who are not entering mainstream society and risk becoming part of the underclass. Tarek Fatah, a broadcaster, warns of fundamentalist Islamists who use multiculturalism to present themselves as moderates to "hide their misogynist, homophobic and segregationist agenda." He warns that if Canadians don't redouble their efforts to integrate and promote a secular society, "we risk creating a fragmented nation, divided into twenty-first-century religious and racial tribes, suspicious of each other and longing for the home we left behind."

We do not discuss these sensitivities. But there are clear dangers. In *The Land Newly Found*, historians Norman Hillmer and J.L Granatstein marvel at how multiculturalism "keeps the world ostentatiously in Canada. That is its explicit aim: each of the country's varied cultures and races is to be promoted, not homogenized and forgotten." So heavily is it embedded in the consciousness, so sacrosanct in our house of civic worship, that multiculturalism is motherhood. When the Parliament of Canada published a list of some 40 (of 308) members of the House of Commons who were born outside Canada, this was astounding to European diplomats, but not to us. It is another form of validation. Here, look at us! See Alghabra and Ablonczy, Chan and Chow, Mark and Minna, Telegdi and Temelkovski. See how open we are!

And so we worship the deity of diversity. To some in Canada, multiculturalism is a fetish. It is not seen as a means to a unified society of universal values but an end in itself. The danger is that ethnic nationalism will trump civic nationalism, instead of the other way around. In the absence of competing visions of ourselves, multinationalism is defining Canada. This causes no anxiety to the incurious, bemused Canadian. The appeal of multiculturalism is that it is something that we can confidently say that we are rather than what we are not, in the same way we call ourselves peacekeepers, mediators, or moderates. "There is a whiff of smugness in our celebrating our success as a multicultural society," says Janice Gross Stein, one of Canada's leading thinkers. Indeed, smugness is becoming superiority.

And now the multicultural Canadian is evolving into "citizen of the world." Actually, the bicultural Pierre Trudeau described himself as that on a sign posted on his door at Harvard in 1948 and historian John English thought it so representative of the man that he chose it as the title of his two-volume biography. Jennifer

Welsh, a Canadian professor at Oxford, calls Canada a "model citizen" in her book *At Home in the World*. Guy Laforest, a well-travelled political scientist, calls Canadians "citizens of the world" and representatives of "peace, dialogue, negotiations and multilateralism." Call it what you will. Whether the new Canadian is a "citizen of the world" or Pico Iyer's "Global Soul," Canada has found its new vocation: the world's charter global citizen.

The risk in rushing to claim global citizenship – a noble aspiration, surely – is diminishing an unformed national citizenship. Some believe that official multiculturalism means encouraging new Canadians to live in their own worlds, importing prejudices and nursing antipathies, ignorant of what 140 years of nationhood has achieved on the upper half of North America. As Jan Morris noted more than two decades ago, citizenship in multicultural Canada seems to be little more than a driving licence. We may prefer wings to roots, but it has a cost. As we embrace a new order of internationalism – eating sushi, Jamaican beef patties, or vermicelli while watching Hindi or Australian movies – we risk losing our centre of gravity and our fragile sense of place. In inviting new Canadians to remain much as they are after they settle here – either through official sanction or benign indifference – we are in danger of reducing our Canadianism to a quaint, antiquated, nineteenth-century attachment, like English fox hunting. Indeed, you might even say that Canada is on its way to skipping a stage of its development. It is as if it never fully went from colony to nation or even from colony to colony. Instead, in the twenty-first century, it is leaping from colony to cosmopolis. For all of those efforts to define our Canadianism through our citizenship, our flag, and our constitution, for all the talk of universal values, we have still not become that united, self-assured nation. As a monarchy can skip a generation in crowning a younger sovereign, leaving a dutiful heir waiting all his life for a coronation that never comes, so can a country. In Canada, we are moving from one undefined, undeveloped level of citizenship to another. With no apologies offered to the conscientious Paul Martin Sr., we are hurtling from imperial subject to post-national cosmopolitan.

If multiculturalism is narcissism, it finds favour in the country's political culture. Consider the extraordinary ascent of Michaëlle Jean. When Paul Martin announced that he had chosen her as Canada's twenty-seventh governor general, she was a mystery to most Canadians. Michaëlle who? Outside of Quebec, where she had always enjoyed what she calls "a love affair" with the people, she was unknown to Canadians and Canadians were unknown to her. Unlike other governors general, she had not emerged from a national institution such as the armed forces, the foreign service, or Parliament. Her professional life had been spent at Radio-Canada, the French-language broadcaster, almost entirely in Quebec. While it is true that not every governor general has been a figure of eminence, it is also true that her predecessor was. Indeed, Adrienne Clarkson's appointment established a new standard of achievement, one by which Jean would be judged.

Jean's story is compelling. She fled an authoritarian Haiti with her parents at age eleven. Her father abused her mother. As a child, she was called "*une noire.*" She studied in Quebec and abroad, learned several languages, and found a place of prominence in television in Quebec, a lily-white medium. She also became a social activist in Quebec, particularly on behalf of homeless women. It must also be said that Jean is beautiful – luminous skin, high cheekbones, slender and fashionable. People liken her to Halle Berry, the American actress, but her sensuality evokes a hint of Josephine Baker, the American actress, singer, and dancer who seduced Paris after the Great War. Jean has playfully described herself as "hot." She rocks. In Canada, heads of state don't look like this.

Martin was enamoured of appointing a black woman to the office of governor general. "She really represents the story of Canada – the story of Canada in who she is, how she came here, and what she has done," he said. "She is a reflection of that great quality of Canada, a country which focuses on equality of opportunity." Liberal Senator David Smith, the silkiest of communicators, repeated the government's talking points: "It symbolizes what we are all about and the openness of our society." Well, both were right. Jean did represent the story of Canada: her flight from a poor, violent, desperate island in the Caribbean to the security and promise of the great frozen land. She also represented another story, which is our psychic need to declare where we came from, how we suffered, and how we succeeded. Victimhood validates us. (It is curious that in a country that celebrated the first appointment of a native-born governor general in 1952 as an affirmation of independence, today we celebrate those *not* born here, as if that were now more virtuous. Both Jean and Clarkson came to Canada as refugees.) In appointing Jean our vice-regal representative, we put her story in the shop window to display and admire. This is how we recognize "equality of opportunity" and "the openness of our society."

The chorus of self-congratulation would have had more resonance had Jean's appointment not looked like affirmative action. Listening to her explain why she accepted the appointment – an agonizing decision that she pondered privately for a month, an intense soul-searching a friend called "existential" – it becomes clear that her race and colour are at the heart of her self-image and her legitimacy as governor general. "So I wondered, you know, what difference would it make for someone like me to become governor general of Canada," she says. "The first positive answer was *this* would bring a lot of hope to a lot of people. That was very important. Because I arrived in Canada as a refugee. I am a black woman of slave descent. My ancestors were slaves. What would this mean not only to Canadians, but to the world? Those were fundamental positive aspects . . . I thought of so many children who could actually project themselves in a person like me and see that this is a country of so many opportunities. But I was also certain of the impact and the signal that it would send to the world. That I knew."

Could it be that the prime minister was so smitten with Jean's past and presence that he put aside his critical faculties? Martin presumably thought that being a successful black woman immigrant from Quebec was enough. If appointing Jean was the story of Canada, as he said, it was also the story of a political class so in thrall to multiculturalism that diversity could trump all else in selecting a head of state. A country of grey was becoming black and was proud of its sophistication. This isn't to deny Jean's estimable qualities. Her personal success was earned rather than conferred, and her tenacity, empathy, poise, and charm are beyond question. Her early tenure at Rideau Hall has been without accident or incident. Still, what we know about her appointment suggests it was impetuous.

When Jean Chrétien named Adrienne Clarkson, an unorthodox choice for an office traditionally filled by former politicians and diplomats, he gave her reason to believe that she emerged from a shortlist of candidates after vigorous examination. (Clarkson discusses this in her memoir, *Heart Matters*, recounting how she was vetted by Chrétien and his staff. Their "due diligence" raises doubts about the process that produced her successor.) Although Martin had become prime minister in December 2003, knowing that Clarkson would complete the anticipated five years in office (there is no defined term) in October 2004, he did not appear to have given serious consideration to the appointment of her successor, among the most important a prime minister can make. This is astonishing given the role a governor general may play in a hung parliament, which is what Canadians had elected on June 28, 2004. In this delicate situation, a governor general must understand the country, its institutions, and the Constitution (to this end, Clarkson studied the process and assembled a panel of scholars to advise her). Even when Martin asked Clarkson to stay on another year to ensure continuity during his minority government, we cannot assume he had a shortlist, let alone a leading candidate, for her replacement. We know this because Hélène Scherrer, Martin's principal secretary, told the *National Post* shortly after the announcement of Michaëlle Jean's appointment that she had proposed Jean's name to Martin in June 2005: "I said, 'Sir, I know who the next G-G is going to be.' And I just pronounced the name and he jumped on it right away. He said, 'You go and see her.'" That was on a Friday. On the Monday, he asked if Scherrer had seen Jean. Scherrer hadn't. "And he said, 'Yes, I want you to see her.'" Scherrer did. "Once he [Martin] was in love with the name and in love with the woman, he wanted her appointed as soon as possible," she recalled.

Between June and August, the Prime Minister's Office and the RCMP presumably scrutinized Jean. Perhaps they did not know or care that she had appeared to join others in toasting Quebec's sovereignty in an obscure film made by her husband, Jean-Daniel Lafond. Or they were indifferent to Lafond's association with former members of the FLQ, such as Jacques Rose and Francis Simard. Or they did not ask Jean her views on the sovereignty referendum of 1995. So great became the doubts about Jean and her husband by mid-August that Jean was forced to issue an extraordinary statement in response to media reports, declaring that she and her husband were "proud to be Canadian and that we have the greatest respect for the institutions of our country. We are fully committed to Canada." When the doubts refused to fade like a soft summer mist, the Prime Minister's Office dismissed them out of hand, as if such skepticism were "McCarthyism" or *lèse majesté*. *How dare you question the loyalty of the governor general designate!*

This is "a smear campaign"! If she's good enough for the prime minister, she's good enough for us!

Then again, Martin had "fallen in love" with Jean. Having met his criteria – a woman, a francophone, an immigrant, a visible minority – only cynics would suggest that the Liberals might have hoped that Jean's appointment would curry favour in heavily contested ridings in Haitian Montreal. Or how, as governor general, she might be an antidote to the long campaign waged by the Parti Québécois to win over immigrants to sovereignty. When a reporter asked Jean whether she was an example of "tokenism," she retorted: "I've never been a token, sir, and will never be." Here was some brio amid the bromides of her news conference. If the besotted Martin was unfazed by her friends and flirtations – not to mention that troublesome question of dual citizenship – it must be said that neither were Canadians. While there were some rumblings, somnolent vacationers looked up from their lawn chairs in the dog days of summer and looked away. Columnist John Ibbitson of *The Globe and Mail*, who seemed to have a schoolboy crush on Jean, noted perceptively that all Quebeckers of a certain age are nationalists and that half of Quebec voted "yes" in 1995, and "the rest of the country needs to accept this fact and move on." In a sense, the country did. Sympathetic commentators praised "the unsafe choice" and congratulated themselves on living in "a country where someone like Jean can be governor general." Even Ottawa's image-makers were agog. "She passed by in the hallway, and I felt her presence," gushed one.

But why had it come to this? If Martin had wanted a Quebecker as governor general, he could have picked one of greater personal and intellectual merit, with an unimpeachable commitment to federalism and an impeccable record of national service. At forty-eight years old, Jean was largely a stranger in the country and a stranger to it. Able as she was, she did not have the breadth of achievement or depth of knowledge of her predecessor, which we expect of a head of state. Unlike Clarkson, she was not a Member of the Order of Canada before she became governor general. Unlike Georges-P. Vanier, Jeanne Sauvé, and Jules Léger, her predecessors from Quebec, she did not have stature and recognition in English Canada. Curiously, though, her relative inexperience wasn't the reason for her own reservations about taking the job. Fundamentally, she wanted to be sure that she could make a difference; she also worried about abandoning a flourishing career. "I am very young," she says. "I am not at the end of my professional life. I had no good reason to leave my professional life." One observer said Jean was "unevolved." The job demanded not only someone who would make a difference but who *had* made a difference. The problem with Jean wasn't that she was black, but that she was green. That Jean may have been ill-prepared for the job didn't bother Martin, who seemed to see the job as ceremonial, which it largely is, rather than constitutional, which it sometimes is.

The debate dissolved on September 27, the day of Jean's installation in Parliament. Jean looked radiant and delivered an inspiring address. But journalists were soon asking her about the referendum of 1995, which was marking its tenth anniversary in October 2005. That surprised her. She refused to disclose how she voted then and she refuses to say so now. "Why should I answer?" she argues. "If we start that, if we start with that attitude – and I didn't want to fall into that trap of suspicion, you know, 'are you loyal or not?' – it was going too far. What is this? This was going too far. If you open that door, and you break the importance of the secrecy of the vote, my goodness, where are we going? Where are we going?"

Jean may decline to answer, but she should not be surprised if doubts follow her around Rideau Hall like a cranky footnote, right into the history books. She says the suspicions began with the rapturous applause her appointment received in Quebec, which set her up for criticism. ". . . It was unique in history for Quebeckers to be interested in that institution, and then to acclaim positively the appointment of 'une Québécoise.' It was too positive. The first survey said 89 per cent of Quebeckers were just thrilled. . . . 'Ah, wonderful! Positive! Good choice! Excellent choice!' Whoa, I had to pay for that, right?" She did, she says, when the sovereigntists began making hurtful accusations. Jean was an easy target. Without a public record to fall back on, it was hard to refute the allegations of that infamous toast. (She explains while others at the table may have toasted sovereignty, she was hailing the homecoming of a poet friend.) It didn't help that she was married to a husband who said in his book, *La manière nègre*: "So, a sovereign Quebec? An independent Quebec? Yes, and I applaud with both hands and I promise to be at all the St. Jean Baptiste parades." Or that he had hired Jacques Rose, a convicted criminal, to do work on their home. Or that he told Radio-Canada a month after he arrived at Rideau Hall: "We are both Quebeckers. We are Quebeckers, before being Canadians."

Here is Jean's credibility problem, and it explains why her popularity in English Canada (38 per cent) was much lower than in Quebec (71 per cent) on the day she was sworn in. It wasn't that she was a card-carrying member of the Parti Québécois, it is this mix of associations, proclivities, and nuances. She can argue, as she pointedly does, that ambiguity is the reality of contemporary Quebec and she personifies it. That may be so, and Canadians may have accepted it. It took some getting used to. After all, if vice-regal representatives have never looked like Madame Jean before, they have never sounded like her, either.

So perhaps it is just as well that she won't talk about 1995. Perhaps there are uncomfortable truths about this governor general that should remain unspoken. But you have to wonder about Michaëlle Jean: what if she had to deny a prime minister's request to dissolve Parliament and call an election? Or ask the leader of the Opposition to form a government? Would she have the experience, the wisdom, and the strength to manage a constitutional crisis triggered by a contested referendum and a unilateral declaration of independence by Quebec?

If Canadians thought that the Conservatives would be any more skeptical of multiculturalism than the Liberals whom they replaced, they were mistaken. On October 25, 2006, the prime minister announced that the federal government would support the establishment of the Global Centre for Pluralism in Ottawa. The purpose of the centre is to foster pluralism and diversity around the world. The government would contribute $30 million and the Aga Khan $10 million. So enamoured was Stephen Harper of the idea that he made the announcement in a joint appearance with the Aga Khan, the spiritual leader of the world's 15 million Shia Imami Ismaili Muslims. Harper said he was "honoured" the Aga Khan had chosen Canada as the home of the centre, which his organization would create. "Pluralism is not merely an ambition or ideal for this country," Harper said. "We actually walk the talk. Pluralism is the principle that binds our diverse people together. It is essential to our civil society and economic strength." He explained that the centre would promote pluralism internationally as a means to advance good governance, peace, and human development. This is what Canada does. The Aga Khan, for his part, called multiculturalism "Canada's gift to the world." He said that he chose Canada because "it epitomizes what can be achieved through a commitment to pluralism." He has long admired Canada's experience as a diverse society and thinks it has something to teach. "We now face a new and challenging moment in human history where secular, pluralist values and practices are not simply desirable any more – they have become essential, and not just for the future of the world, but also for survival itself."

And who could argue? One of the world's great philanthropists says that you are the world; actually, you are the future of the world. He chooses you to host his centre because your model is export quality, like German crystal or Irish linen. That's a compliment. What is there to criticize here?

Well, much. Never mind that Harper was so excited by this that he appropriated a commitment the Liberals had made eighteen months earlier and let it sound as though it were his own. Never mind that the government was "honoured" that the Aga Khan had "chosen" to receive $30 million for his centre from the government of Canada. And never mind that the centre would be housed in the former home of the Canadian War Museum on Sussex Drive, a heritage building the National Gallery of Canada wanted for expansion and one within spitting distance of the new headquarters the Aga Khan is already building on the capital's ceremonial mile. Did the country really need *two* institutions of this nature within a few blocks of each other? Why was the government supporting this at all? It had recently cancelled long-standing scholarship programs for Canadians studying abroad. It had also cancelled plans to build the national portrait gallery in Ottawa. This is an example of a mentality that denies money to a landmark cultural institution in the capital which is necessary while finding money for one which is not.

Once again, it was more important to reinforce a lofty self-image abroad than to foster a sense of self at home. It isn't that a centre for pluralism is a bad idea; in fact, it is a fine one – even if it is a mystery what it means and what it will do. But not here, not now, and not financed by the people of Canada. Had the Aga Khan wanted to build such a centre on his own, let him proceed with our blessing, as he is building a magnificent $200-million art gallery and spiritual centre in Toronto. But now a capital in need of institutions like a portrait gallery and a history museum – both cancelled by successive governments – has neither. What we have instead is a monument to multiculturalism. Rather than teaching our past at home, we prefer celebrating ourselves abroad. For Harper and the Conservatives, this is irresistible. They see votes here.

If the members of the Canadian Council of Education for Citizenship were to compile a book on the spirit of Canada today, it would not look like *A Pocketful of Canada*. Nor should it. More than sixty years on, the country has changed and so have its touchstones. The literary selections would no longer be limited to observers with Anglo-Celtic names like MacLennan, Mackenzie, Lampman, Campbell, Black, Graham. Instead, there would be excerpts from the work of Vincent Lam, the son of Chinese immigrants from Vietnam, whose novel won the Giller Prize in 2006. Or Rawi Hage, an émigré from Lebanon, whose novel was a finalist. There would be white, Anglo-Saxon names like Marshall McLuhan, Northrop Frye, and Margaret Atwood, sure. But there would be all manner of selections from Canada's literary rainbow – Mordecai Richler, Michael Ondaatje, Nino Ricci, Neil Bissoondath, Rohinton Mistry, Dionne Brand. Many have lived for years in Canada but write of where they came from, through their Canadian consciousness. In Canada, they have found the place and space to write, and sometimes government grants, too. This we salute.

But the danger is that in politically correct, self-conscious Canada, none of those old names would get in at all. They would be considered irrelevant dead white males. Instead of MacLennan's *Two Solitudes*, we have created four solitudes or six or eight or ten. Our literary digest might be called *A Handbook to Canada* or *A Survival Guide to Canada*, offering a post-modern sense of what the new citizen needs to know. In truth, we might say, not very much. Then again, in a country that seems to treat its citizenship as if every day were Casual Friday, we might not ask them to read anything at all. Worse, we might not even care.

Chapter 6

The Capital Canadian

In 1986, Jan Morris visited Ottawa. A wry and perceptive observer – some say the greatest travel writer of her time – she was preparing another in a series of essays on Canada commissioned by *Saturday Night*. She had always liked "the great white land" – which she had first seen by train on a cross-country lecture tour in 1953 – even if it was "one of the least magnetic places on earth." She particularly liked its cities and towns, enthusing about St. John's, St. Andrews, Montreal, Toronto, Saskatoon, Edmonton, Banff, Yellowknife, and Vancouver. An historian, novelist, and memoirist, the author of travelogues on Oxford, Hong Kong, New York, and Trieste, she had contemplated a book on Canada but could not find the literary shape for it. So she gathered up her dispatches from Canada, organized them geographically, and scribbled an admiring introduction. *City to City* was published in 1990.

Morris was enamoured of Ottawa. Like much of the untutored world, she had seen the capital of Canada as "less a city than an abstraction. We have no exact idea where it is, we are sometimes less than certain whether it is in fact a city, or some kind of province, and we speak of it . . . as a kind of generic or allegory." Ottawa was "a half-imaginary metropolis" in which she found "many another kind of allegory" that forms the spine of her adoring hymn. Hers was a strangely mystical interpretation of the cold, conservative capital. This flight of fancy could have only come from the redoubtable Ms. Morris, whose reputation gave her licence to be quirky. Only she could imagine Ottawa as a republic of mystery; to those who know it better, there is little emblematic about Ottawa, less that is enigmatic, and much that is as straight as the Peace Tower.

Morris saw Ottawa as an allegory of Canada, writ large; she looks at Ottawa and sees the land beyond. Everything becomes clear as she stands on the tip of Victoria Island, which lies just west of the city centre in the Ottawa River. Looking at the vista of the Gothic, coppered, chimneyed buildings of Parliament, she is dumbstruck, as many foreigners are. "The force that I feel down there is not exactly political, nor even economic, but something more elemental – an emanation of sheer size and space, of huge rivers and distant mountain ranges, of oceans far away, of illimitable grain fields and awful forests and frozen bays and wild cold islands. Half a continent looks towards Ottawa for its leadership – millions of square miles are centred upon those very buildings on the hill above me – from Niagara to the Northwest Passage the mandate of this city runs. Now that *is* Awesome!"

Her rhapsody is fine as far as it goes, which fortunately is no farther than the far shore of the great river. It is tempting to see Ottawa as Canada, as it is to see any capital as the captain of its country. This is especially so for the dazzled visitor looking for a quick and tidy conclusion. Journalists miss layered truths when they parachute into unfamiliar places; it is easy to fall in love with a metaphor made of a morsel. Morris is too smart to do that, though she comes close. That kind of rush to judgment may work in Ulan Bator, where we can divine the inner thoughts of an Outer Mongolian. But this we can say with confidence: Ottawa is *not* a metaphor for Canada. It is a mistake to judge Canada by Ottawa alone. The Capital Canadian is *sui generis*. He is peculiarly and uniquely a product of Ottawa. He is as indigenous to Ottawa as the Rideau Canal, the Bank of Canada, and Stornoway. He is of the place itself, period.

An Ottawan is not a Calgarian, a Haligonian, or a Torontonian. He or she reflects Ottawa and only Ottawa, the political, legal, and institutional manifestation of the country. So, to know the Capital Canadian is to know a part of the Canadian. It is one piece – albeit an important, indispensable piece – of our personality.

When Morris began comparing other cities of the world to Ottawa, the nineteenth-century lumber town wrested from the wilderness, she thought of Stockholm and Aberdeen. They seemed right in terms of their size, situation, climate, and temperament. But the more she thought about it, the more she could not imagine Ottawa as a Swedish or Scottish clone. She also dismissed the more obvious comparisons with Brasilia, Canberra, or Pretoria, which were also conceived as national capitals. Instead, she kept comparing Ottawa to another capital, a more unlikely capital. She kept thinking of Cetinje.

Ah, Cetinje. Once upon a time, it was the seat of the Kingdom of Montenegro. From 1878 to 1918, Montenegro was an independent country and Cetinje (pronounced set-in-ya) was its hub. Remote, majestic, and tiny, it sits in perfect splendour on the dry Karst Plain two thousand feet above the Gulf of Kotor, the most southerly fjord of Europe. In the country's golden interlude, Cetinje welcomed the world. For thirty years, diplomats, artists, and travellers flocked to the smallest capital in Europe. The major powers – Russia, France, Italy, Britain, the United States – built elegant chanceries and embassies along its tree-shaded boulevards. Many still stand. There was also the Grand Hotel, the Blue Palace, and the Royal Residence. Montenegro conjures up images of a mountainous kingdom of legions of strutting sycophants and courtiers and mustachioed generals in gold-buttoned uniforms with outsized epaulettes, all plumes and feathers, monocled, bemedalled and beribboned.

Today Cetinje is a town of fifteen thousand souls, delightfully compact and achingly beautiful. The French Legation is now a library, its books lying under sheets of plastic and coats of dust. The British Embassy is a school of music. Everywhere, from the crypts to the museums, you hear the footsteps of history and the whispers of intrigue. It is quiet on an afternoon in high summer, almost deserted. But Cetinje also gives the impression of biding its time, awaiting a return to glory, which may be imminent. In June 2006, Montenegrins declared independence from Serbia and subsequently entered the United Nations as the world's youngest country.

This is the Cetinje Morris remembered. And when her eyes fell upon the craggy, steepled, spiked capital of Ottawa, framed by the Gatineau Hills, our traveller could not help herself. She saw Cetinje. It wasn't that she saw Ottawa as a stage for *opéra bouffe*. Nor did she see Ottawans as the burghers of Ruritania, the fictional kingdom of central Europe (despite those ranks of uniformed bureaucrats in January swathed in beige, fur-trimmed parkas). It was something else, something more real, that turned Bytown into her Balkan outpost: ". . . Often enough the city seems to me, in its own self-deprecatory way, almost as exotic as Cetinje – almost as deeply in the middle of nowhere, almost as fiction-like in its nuances, just as resolutely equipped with the metropolitan trappings, as well supplied with home-grown heroes, and embellished at least as adequately with halls of government and diplomacy."

It is touching, this sentimentality. But the comparison between Ottawa and Cetinje is unfair to Cetinje, a kind of defamation for a city of its past. After all, here was a seat of royalty and an *entrepôt* of adventure. Small as it was, Cetinje was lively. It had colour. It was kicking. Things happened. In the early years of the last century, before the world redrew the map following the Great War and made Montenegro one of the six republics of the Federation of

Yugoslavia, before the regional capital of Montenegro moved to Podgorica, Cetinje was quite something. It had *character*, celebrated by F. Scott Fitzgerald and others. Ottawa, God bless it, has always had politicians and poseurs, but never peacocks or princes. No one could accuse it of having much life, either.

We know Cetinje. We know Ottawa. We know the difference. Ottawa is no Cetinje.

Oh, Ottawa has its virtues. Its greatest natural assets are the Ottawa River, a storied waterway of 1,130 kilometres that inspired Morris's Montenegrin Rhapsody. Or the Rideau Canal, which the British dug in the nineteenth century as a defensive measure. Today the canal follows the spine of the city for about eight kilometres, linking the Rideau and Ottawa rivers. To the north are the Gatineau Hills. To the east and south are woods and farmland, much of which actually lies within the capital's 4,662 square kilometres. You could say that Ottawa is in the middle of nowhere. It is an easy city to leave, which is one of its attractions. Within fifteen minutes you can be in the country, up to your neck in lake water or in drifts of snow. This is impossible in other capitals such as Washington, which sprawls along the Interstate leading to Philadelphia and beyond, or London, which seems to spill into the Fens. Not so Ottawa, where until a decade or so ago, there wasn't even a four-lane road to Highway 401, the east-west thoroughfare linking Montreal and Toronto. But not even this isolation could turn Ottawa into Cetinje.

Ottawa's appeal lies largely in Parliament, perched on the headland above the river. At its feet are the temples of Wellington Street. From Library and Archives Canada to the west, this ceremonial avenue winds past the Supreme Court, the Bank of Canada, the Confederation Building, the West, Centre, and East blocks of Parliament, the former American Embassy, the National Press Building, and the Langevin Block. It ends at the Château Laurier, the railway hotel of oxidized roof facing the old railway station, now the National Conference Centre. Here is the soul of the capital, representing knowledge, law, justice, and government. It gives Ottawa its mandate and its memory. It confers elegance, age, and history. The intersection of Elgin and Wellington streets is the finest view in town. Looking north, here is the façade of the old post office to the left, the Château Laurier to the right, the Peace Tower in the distance, its bells tolling. Here is the Cenotaph and nearby is the Rideau Canal. The scene is the modest country itself.

Within your vision, Ottawa offers its best. There are other noteworthy buildings farther afield, but most are here, on this eclectic avenue mixing gothic, art deco, and second empire. The climax is Parliament Hill, marked by the Eternal Flame, a soft, undulating greensward and a garden of statues. Beyond is the high promenade above the river and the world: the bridges to Quebec, the Canadian Museum of Civilization, the mechanical locks marching to the Ottawa River. In 1913, the visiting poet Rupert Brooke gazed upon Parliament (which would burn three years later) and exclaimed that the buildings "have dignity, especially of line; and when the evening hides their colour, and the western sky and the river take on the lovely hues of a Canadian sunset, and the lights begin to come out in the city, they seem to have the majesty and calm of a natural crown of the river-headland."

This is the postcard image of Ottawa. In the last half of the nineteenth century and the first half of the twentieth century, when these buildings were conceived, Canada's founders and builders had ambition and taste. They rarely seemed to think that anything was too big or too grand for this land of few people. It was that kind of confidence that inspired the Legislature of Saskatchewan, a Prairie palace erected in 1905 that rises from the flatlands like a mirage. In Ottawa, Regina, and beyond, they built with a belief in something larger, as if Canada would grow into it. Canada did. Years ago, that spirit made the nation's capital enduring and inspiring. It made Ottawa grand.

That Ottawa, anyway. Official Ottawa. Today, beyond the parliamentary precinct, the capital is an eyesore. It has been for some time. When Allan Gotlieb arrived in Ottawa from Oxford in the winter of 1957, he found the neo-gothic Parliament Buildings "spectacular" but was crestfallen at the rest of the city. "The town looked like an unkempt, decaying village," he wrote. "Hideous telephone poles leaning over the main street. A dismal place; to call it provincial would have been a compliment." On his first anniversary in the capital, he scribbled a note to himself in which he said that if he ever began to like Ottawa, it would be time for him to leave; he was sure that it wouldn't be "because Ottawa had improved but because his standards had fallen." Fifty years later, things are worse. Ottawa has suffered the desecration of a generation. It has endured a kind of blitz, an assault on its aesthetic from jackhammers, wrecking balls, and cement mixers. What charms it once had have been lost in a canvas of concrete. What has emerged beyond Parliament Hill is a shapeless, featureless skyline. Where there once was a variety of wood, brick, and stone, there are now cavities, carbuncles, or crematoria. It is as if the successors of Langevin and Cormier and other architects who imagined Ottawa had a finely honed instinct for the ugly. This is true of what has been built by both the public and private sectors, though the federal government is largely responsible; to accommodate a growing bureaucracy (some 113,000 civil servants work on both sides of the river), it has thrown up monstrosities designed by the *cum laude* graduates of the School of Brutalism. David Gordon, an urban planner and author of a forthcoming book on the city's development, calls them "the best collection of third-rate office towers in the country."

Even Jan Morris, enraptured as she was twenty years ago with the parliamentary precinct, saw the ugliness advancing like a red tide. ". . . The federal centre of Ottawa in all its jagged majesty seems to me still one of the most satisfying of all architectural ensembles," she writes. "It is however no longer sacrosanct in its uniqueness on its hill, but is invested on all sides, even from across the river, by siege-works of the ordinary." Ordinary? She was too polite. The catalogue of the soulless includes the tall hotel with its 1970s restaurant revolving like a lazy susan, the boxy, dysfunctional public library, the clutch of anonymous office blocks with bland food courts in their basements. It isn't that these siege-works are ordinary; it is that they are awful.

It gets worse. At Sussex Drive, where Wellington Street becomes Rideau Street in its descent to the eastern neighbour-hood of Vanier, things deteriorate fast. Once the city's shopping promenade, the home of Eaton's, Freiman's, and Morgan's, Rideau Street has become a pastiche of tattoo parlours, shawarma shops, gas stations, convenience stores, and money marts patronized by drifters. In the 1980s, a shopping centre went up at Sussex Drive and turned Rideau Street into a bus mall with glass shelters; in gleeful collaboration, the shopping centre chased away the inde-pendent stores and the bus mall chased away the shoppers. The disastrous bus mall was reversed, but the street never recovered.

The contagion spread to King Edward Avenue, which inter-sects Rideau Street on its way into Sandy Hill. This nineteenth-century thoroughfare was once appealing, even majestic, with trees, dignity, and synagogues built by the Jews of Lowertown in the early twentieth century. A plan to turn King Edward into an expressway in the 1970s was defeated. It was a hollow victory; today it is a six-lane roadway, an interprovincial transit corridor between Quebec and Ontario. A study in 1999 found that fifteen thousand trucks a day enter the city's downtown, many of them on King Edward. Smelly, dusty, and noisy, the avenue is an expressway in all but name. Residents have long complained that the corner of Rideau and King Edward is dangerous; a pedestrian was run over by an eighteen-wheeler there in September 2006. In an editorial a few days after the accident, the *Citizen* thundered that the street was "the most obvious example of bad urban planning in Ottawa" and said it should be an issue in the municipal election that fall. It wasn't. Ottawa remains a trucker's paradise.

Bank Street is no less a blight than Rideau. It is to downtown Ottawa what Yonge Street is to downtown Toronto – seedy and scruffy, with a massage parlour or two, fast food joints, and dollar stores. Try as they do to pretty it up with plants, curbs, sidewalks and streetlights, Bank remains a varicose vein. The same malaise overwhelms much of central Ottawa. You see it in the marches of Centretown, with its dull row-housing and rundown corner stores favoured by late-night thieves. You see it on the Queensway, the elevated expressway that cuts through the city like a rusting hacksaw. You see it on Bronson Avenue, Bank's ugly twin, with its empty storefronts, dirty laundromats, and discount computer shops. Bronson is now becoming an expressway to the airport, inspired by the success of King Edward Avenue. On the way, it passes Carleton University, which managed to dim its natural beauty – the Rideau Canal on one side, the Rideau River on the other – with a campus of remarkably insipid buildings all turned away from the water, staring at each other, forlornly.

An outsider sees this for what it is. One is Tyler Brûlé, the international style guru and founder of *Wallpaper*, the hugely successful journal of design. In the spring of 2005, Brûlé visited Ottawa for the first time in almost ten years. He knew it well; his parents grew up in the city, he summered at his grandmother's cottage on the Ottawa River, and he briefly attended high school in Ottawa. All of that made returning unsettling. "What I saw was nothing short of shocking," he wrote in the *Financial Times of London*. "As the capital of one of the world's most prosperous, liveable countries, Ottawa has become a national disgrace." His explanation? The lack of a master plan. "Defenders will argue that the city has a handsome parliament building and some nice-looking museums and ministries but this should be a given for a country with Canada's wealth and creativity," he sighed. "What Ottawa lacks is a cohesive, forward-looking brand vision that makes the visitor (and resident) feel like they're in a capital that fits with the country. An expressway cutting through the city centre is muffled by ugly sound barriers, box stores have been allowed to go up everywhere, modern residential architecture looks cheap and unchallenging and neighbourhood high streets that could be quaint lack any sort of restrictions on signage." Rhys Phillips, the architectural critic of the *Ottawa Citizen*, agreed with Brûlé: "I think he's too kind. At last someone has stood up and says the city sucks. Stand at the corner of Bank and Laurier and it looks like some tired little Prairie town on its last legs." For years Phillips has been an eloquent voice bemoaning the aesthetic calamity that an apathetic city has brought upon itself.

The problem is not just Bank Street or Rideau Street, the Queensway, or Centretown and its ordinariness. It is the failure of vision, over and over. Sparks Street, the east-west street one block south of Wellington, is another disappointment. Making it "Canada's first pedestrian mall" may have been a good idea in 1966, but it has failed miserably. Forty years on, Sparks Street sustains souvenir shops and tourist restaurants. It is deserted at night. In the early 1980s, the city introduced a Speaker's Corner, à la Hyde Park, to generate some buzz. It failed. No one wanted a soapbox in January.

Another lost opportunity is Nicholas Street. It is the gateway to Ottawa from the east-west highway and the city extends a limp hand in welcome. What might be a boulevard of wrought-iron railings, cheerful signs, and ornamental lighting is an expressway with concrete retaining walls. They hide a view of the Rideau Canal, the graceful waterway filled with skaters in winter and boaters in summer that runs alongside. Instead of creating anticipation, which a road into town should, Nicholas Street offers foreboding.

The city cannot help itself. When there are opportunities to act boldly, governments ignore them. That's the story of the Daly

Building, which sat next to the Château Laurier at the elegant corner of Sussex Drive and Wellington Street. An example of the Chicago school of architecture, it was built as a department store in 1905. Later acquired by the federal government, it fell into disuse. Despite spirited protests from preservationists, including a proposal from a renowned restoration architect, it was torn down in 1991. So, what to do with one of the last pieces of prime property on Canada's main street? What great public institution could we build there? The government leased the land to a developer to build an apartment house. An apartment house. There had been talk of including an aquarium or an interpretive centre – some public content in this most public of venues – but that never happened. What's worse, when the federal government learned that the developer was going to use "cheap" artificial stone on the exterior of the building – rather than the real thing used on the neighbouring Château Laurier – it ordered the change to stone and absorbed the cost of $1.2 million. Not that it really mattered. The new building, called 700 Sussex Drive, has the most pedestrian of appearances. It is now known as "Ottawa's power address," an enclave of rich people in million-dollar condominiums.

This decision, and so many others, are the genius of the National Capital Commission (NCC), the federal agency responsible for the development of lands and properties in Ottawa. The NCC has made so many mistakes that it has inspired a website called *NCC Watch*, which dutifully catalogues its "blunders," "waste," and "horror stories." There are many. Kitty-corner to 700 Sussex Drive, for example, is the National Conference Centre. It was a glorious beaux-arts railway station until it closed in 1966. The ornate old station has been the venue of constitutional discussions between the prime minister and the premiers, most memorably over the Meech Lake Accord. There was talk of turning the building into a sports hall of fame. More recently, it was designated as the site for the new history museum, a fitting use for a handsome heritage building. When a spiteful Paul Martin reversed Jean Chrétien's plan to create the museum, its fate became unclear once again. Given the government's record of indifference, it could end up as condominiums, too.

A stone's throw away is the National Arts Centre (NAC). It opened in 1969 as the country's centre for the performing arts. Despite its ups and downs, the NAC promotes and enhances the arts in Ottawa and beyond. Under the thrusting stewardship of Peter Herrndorf, its president and CEO, the centre has had a renaissance. But not even Herrndorf has been able to turn the cement box on the Rideau Canal into a jewel box. Its entrance is in the wrong place and it is simply ugly, reminiscent of a Stalinist detention centre.

If you follow Sussex Drive, which hugs the Ottawa River, you will discover a collage of the country: science, art, money, war, peace, diplomacy, power, and royalty. On the west is the Embassy of the United States, all bombproof glass and steel, the Peace-keeping Monument, and the National Gallery of Canada astride Nepean Point. On the east side are a few top-drawer shops and boutiques for the carriage trade. Farther along are the turreted Royal Canadian Mint and the former Canadian War Museum. Then there is Earnscliffe, the former home of Sir John A. Macdonald, now the residence of the British High Commissioner. Then the Embassy of France, the finest example of art deco design in the city. Both overlook the river, and both have pride of place, as the diplomatic representatives of Britain and France should in the capital. Between these are the stately premises of the National Research Council of Canada. At the end of the avenue, on the other side of a newly restored bridge, is 24 Sussex Drive, the residence of the prime minister, and Rideau Hall, the residence of the governor general. They face each other across a pretty roundabout designed by John Ralston Saul when he was at Rideau Hall.

This is the best of Ottawa, the kingdom of imagination. It works well architecturally, but there are lapses of judgment. How, for example, did we allow the construction of the castellated fortress known as the Lester B. Pearson Building? It houses the Department of Foreign Affairs. Its tone is forbidding. It has cement and steel barricades and heavy doors. Worse is the Royal Embassy of Saudi Arabia, just up from the department, and the Embassy of the State of Kuwait, across the street from what was the war museum. How these two illiberal nations came to occupy two of the most prestigious spots on the country's ceremonial mile remains a mystery. (Relations between Canada and Saudi Arabia were so strained a few years ago – the Saudis were accused of imprisoning and torturing a Canadian – that its envoys initially refused to occupy their new home.) Saudi Arabia is an autocracy. Kuwait is only marginally better. And so there they are, the desert kingdoms in spanking new legations, enjoying pride of place in the capital of Canada. It begs the question: How does a self-respecting country allow this to happen?

You might wonder how any of this happened in Ottawa. The indifference to the aesthetic. The mediocrity in architecture. The failure of planning. Ottawa is a city of 830,000, the fourth largest in the country and one of its wealthiest. It has many blessings – rivers and waterfalls, a recreational canal, a farmer's market, restful parks, two large universities, a nearby airport, national museums, lovely neighbourhoods. The Gatineau Hills are minutes away, offering walking, biking, boating, and swimming in summer and skiing and snowshoeing in winter. The Community Foundation of Ottawa called it "the quintessential Canadian bilingual community" – almost a third of the workforce speaks French. Its streets are safe. Its bicycle paths and ski trails are magnificent. Its air is clean. Its traffic is manageable. Amid the peace of a summer afternoon, a woman from Somalia sat on a park bench, and sighed: "So much bounty."

But it may be this bounty – the affluence enjoyed by the unionized public servant, the fatted diplomat, and the prosperous technocrats of Kanata – known as "Silicon Valley North" – that explains the inertia here. It shows. "The net result is a capital that looks like it has given up, or worse, feels as if it doesn't need to bother," laments Tyler Brûlé. Marion Dewar, the city's former activist mayor, felt the same resignation in describing the people and the politicians. "City council doesn't seem to be a council that invites people to get involved," she said in 2006, "and the people have given up." That is Ottawa – a city that has given up. It bumps along, living off its past, avoiding its future. They say that New York City is a place in a hurry, a town without foreplay. Ottawa is in no hurry at all. It is a town without climax.

Ottawa seems stubbornly impervious to outside influence, which is why it remains stunted. None of the panache of Montreal, 190 kilometres away, nor the variety of Toronto, 399 kilometres away, seems to seep into Ottawa. Allan Fotheringham, the acerbic columnist who held forth on the back page of *Maclean's* for almost thirty years, always marvelled at that. He would complain that it took national magazines three days longer to reach Ottawa than other major cities and that Ottawa had never heard of the *Toronto Star*, the country's largest newspaper. Hyperbole, of course, but he caught the city's determined detachment. "Ennui on the Rideau," Fotheringham called it. "Ottawa does not represent Canada, since nothing in Canada is so dull," he snorted. He wrote that in 1976. Things haven't changed.

But Fotheringham disliked Ottawa for the wrong reasons. He thought its restaurants were lousy, its shopping poor, its taxi drivers surly. Most of all, he hated the climate. "At the base of Ottawa's dullness is the beastly weather," he complained. "Ottawa's is masochism raised to public ritual. It is flagellation by public ritual. No wonder Mackenzie King fit in." Dr. Foth wasn't alone in feeling the chill. In 1976, Sharon Churcher visited Ottawa and wrote in the *Wall Street Journal*: "Though Ottawa is only 350 miles north of New York and lies near sea level, it is colder than Lhasa,

Tibet (12,000 feet up in the Himalayas), colder than Helsinki, Finland (which is much farther north), colder than Moscow, 'and Moscow is livelier,' says a staffer at the Soviet Embassy here." The weather doesn't seem to bother everyone, though. Ambassador Carlos Miranda of Costa Rica, the dean of the foreign diplomatic service, endured Ottawa for sixteen years before leaving in 2006. Philemon Yang, the High Commissioner of Cameroon, lasted twenty years. Both thought their governments had forgotten about them in Ottawa. This is quite possible.

The problem with Ottawa isn't the climate, however. If Ottawa was once a subarctic forest, Washington was a subtropical swamp. It got over it. In fact, the city's burghers endure the weather with good cheer, wrapping themselves in fur and fleece in the harsh winter and in seersucker in the humid summer. The real issue is complacency. This isn't peculiar to Ottawans; Canadians, in general, suffer from the same condition. "Our greatest failing is our unwillingness to face the reality of our second-rate performance in so many areas, and to do something about it," moans Thomas Homer-Dixon, the award-winning author of *The Ingenuity Gap*. "We are too comfortable about average, even mediocre." On the whole, Canadians are too ready to accept ugliness in their cities. What God has given them in Vancouver, Edmonton, Toronto, and Montreal and other cities, they have spoiled with the works of man. But that complacency reaches a higher order of refinement in Ottawa, like twenty-four-karat gold or twelve-year-old Scotch. You see it in the lethargy of a municipal government that has allowed the city core to rot. And in the somnolence of a federal government that permits authoritarian nations or self-interested developers to build on choice property and cannot itself find the ambition to build institutions worthy of a country of this size and stature.

In the rest of the country, Ottawa generates resentment, ridicule, or indifference. It is remarkable. At a public forum in Ottawa in 2005, a senior official of the Department of Public Works allowed that one of the reasons federal buildings are so uninspired in the capital is that taxpayers in New Brunswick don't want their tax dollars to be used to build monuments in Ottawa. That may well be the reason that governments won't imagine a grander capital. True, two decades ago they built institutions such as the Canadian Museum of Civilization and the National Gallery of Canada. But there is no imperative today to enhance the capital. When J.L. Granatstein was the director of the Canadian War Museum, he approached potential donors to support the construction of a new building to replace the old museum. Some balked when they learned that it would remain in Ottawa. The new war museum opened in 2005 to great acclaim, but it wasn't part of a grand design of public cultural institutions. In recent years, governments have cancelled the history museum, delayed the national portrait gallery, and ignored appeals for a new national library (its collection is threatened with water damage) as well as a new Museum of Science (it sits in a former bakery on a fast-food thoroughfare, miles from downtown).

The reason we don't think boldly about Ottawa is that we are not proud of Ottawa. We have none of the reverence for our capital that the French have for Paris or the British for London or the Italians for Rome. Vincent Massey, who opened Canada's first foreign legation in Washington in 1927, found that Americans wanted to look up to their capital. Canadians did not. ". . . Washington over the years has become a great and attractive city and the American, wherever he lives, takes pride in its embellishment," he wrote in 1948. "Our national capital as yet inspires no such pride in Canadian bosoms. We have indeed not outgrown a grudging attitude towards it."

There is a price for this. Canadians don't demand a vision of their capital from Parliament, and Ottawans don't demand a sense of their city from City Hall. Ottawa is happy with the ordinary. It is genteel and orderly, terrified of spontaneity. It has not had a big idea in years. No wonder it has no municipal concert hall and no rapid transit system. Its football stadium is crumbling and its team is in limbo. Its minor league baseball team is leaving. Its annual Tulip Festival is broke. Its farmer's market is uncovered and its riverfront is untouchable. Like misery, mediocrity loves company. Ottawa is happy to oblige, in one way after another.

A central library? Ottawa tore down its classical Carnegie Library in the 1970s and put up a blockhouse. It is now crowded and crumbling, held together by chicken wire and duct tape. The city has long acknowledged the need for a new central library but cannot find a way to build one. While Toronto, Vancouver, and Montreal have invested in bold central libraries, recognizing them as cathedrals of curiosity, Ottawa just threatens. It spends $44.26 per capita on its libraries, eleventh of any major city in Canada. A sports arena? The Ottawa Senators play in Kanata, a thriving community far from downtown, unconnected by light rail. Building an arena an hour in rush hour from the city centre where general parking costs ten dollars, may one day be seen as a stroke of staggering genius. The trouble is that day may not arrive for fifty years. A pedestrian footbridge? Someone decided that to link Centretown on the west side and Sandy Hill on the east side, a footbridge across the Rideau Canal was the answer. That the city was cutting services, that the bridge would cost $5 million, and that it was five hundred metres south of the existing Laurier Bridge didn't seem to give pause. Things became even more odd when the city began to look for sponsors for its Bridge of Sighs after it was approved by council and construction had started. *Cough up, dear donor, for a bridge that is going up whether you do or not.* No one did.

Ottawans do their part for the United Way and other charities, but they have few big donors. While the NAC's annual gala can raise a million dollars from heavy-hitters, the yearly fundraising dinner for the less glamorous Ottawa Public Library does well to break forty thousand dollars. No one could accuse Ottawa of being a town of big spenders, big hearts, or deep pockets. It is sensible, restrained, and level-headed in most things, which is good for snowstorms and bad for charities. Money must be spent prudently. On the whole, Ottawans do not want to pay for much more than fire, police, parks, schools, buses, ice rinks, and snow removal. They were so angry over tax increases – after years of a tax freeze – that they threw out their moderate mayor in 2006, the first time an incumbent had lost in memory. They replaced him with an amiable self-made entrepreneur who had never been to City Hall and wants the city run like a business. His inspiration for the city is not to raise taxes: to keep him honest he hired the former head of the Canadian Taxpayers Federation as his chief of staff.

Ottawa is easily satisfied in so many ways. Beyond stylish eateries such as Bectka, Stella, and Domus, the restaurants of the capital are unflavoured and unfavoured. Like so much else in town, fine dining is for somewhere else. Nowhere is the city's penny-pinching conservatism more obvious than while eating out. Despite an affluent population, the armies of automatons who work in the towers chow down in food courts that offer fare as exciting as the architecture around them. Or they gather in dark pubs and trattorias for office lunches where a designated calculator-in-chief dutifully divides up the bill among the diners. New things are resisted. As sushi colonizes Canada, staking a claim to virtually every corner from Halifax to Victoria, Ottawa resists its advance. Perhaps innovation and Ottawa don't go together.

To experience the uniqueness of Ottawa's cuisine, visit The Mill on the Ottawa River, which claims to be "one of Ottawa's most important landmarks." When Anne DesBrisay, one of the premier food critics in Canada, dined there in 2005, she anticipated an ordinary roast beef house. It so impressed her that she returned twice. In fact, it took her three visits to have the confidence to tell readers of the *Ottawa Citizen* that "The Mill is the worst restaurant that I have ever reviewed." Now, from a professional critic, that's quite a claim. A restaurant has to work hard to be so bad as to get a reviewer to return twice so that she could say: "Really, truly, I can't warn you away enough." More generally, that is the sentiment of Lesley Chesterman, a reviewer for the Montreal *Gazette*, who made the mistake of looking for a restaurant in Ottawa on Canada Day. The poor woman walked out of one restaurant recommended by her hotel concierge, rejected another, and ate at a third, which was "third rate." Of Ottawa she said: "Every city has its strengths and with Ottawa it is obviously not its restaurants." Needless to say, aggrieved restaurateurs howled, denouncing this uppity, insolent outsider. What does she know? This is usually the response to critics of any kind of Ottawa. True, Chesterman will never eat lunch in their town again, but then, she wouldn't want to.

Yet Ottawans are content with so many things. Maybe this is a virtue; fundamentally, they are the most appreciative of people. This is especially true of the audiences of the National Arts Centre who never saw a play, concert, or ballet they did not reward with a standing ovation. It does not matter if the violinist broke a string, the soprano fainted, the prima ballerina tripped, or Hamlet forgot to be. Before the first bow is taken the tweedy gentleman in D3 leaps to his feet, followed by the blue-stockinged dowager in A14 and the florid-faced adolescent in the ten-dollar seats. Soon they are clapping, standing, cheering in a very un-Ottawa sort of way. They have a kind of rhapsodic, post-coital look, their bodies quivering under their rumpled corduroy suits with the worn leather elbow patches and the matted, moth-eaten sweaters. Sure, they may not rise immediately for the Hallelujah chorus of Handel's *Messiah*, but they know how to show their gratitude at the end of a performance, *any* performance. Of them, let it be said: Ottawa is the standing-ovation capital of the world.

Looking at Ottawa, veteran journalist Val Sears finds "a place of paralyzed possibilities." He bemoans the inability of governments to find exciting uses for Victoria Island (where Jan Morris was awestruck) or the old railway station. Seldom has a city been so blessed with opportunity and so reluctant to embrace it. The farmer's market in Lowertown could be a year-round enterprise if the city would cover it, as they have in London, Ontario, and in Toronto. The riverfront could be developed in a careful, imaginative way. The downtown could be a model of innovation and light. But that takes elements of character that Ottawans do not seem to have.

This may be a problem of all created capitals, which is how Ottawa came into being. Brasilia is dull. So is Canberra. So was Bonn, during the Cold War. The latest entry is Nay Pyi Daw, the new capital of Myanmar, which used to be called Burma. Apparently the generals who have destroyed Burma want to do the same to Rangoon, the old colonial town. They have created Nay Pyi Daw on the road to Mandalay, which has "No people, no life," reported one unfortunate diplomat, which is how you might describe Ottawa.

Predictably, discouraging words about Ottawa are often attributed to an outsider, a disgruntled Torontonian or displaced Montrealer who has landed in Ottawa by accident and been forcibly held there. One of the city's perfervid defenders is Randall Denley, the *Ottawa Citizen*'s City Hall columnist. In a much-noted *j'accuse* in 2006, he argued how superior Ottawa is to Toronto. He called Toronto "dreadfully boring" without "a central idea" of itself. With the city's theatre scene "at low ebb," he declaimed, there is nothing "even remotely exciting" about it. As it happened, Soulpepper Theatre in the Distillery District had just opened in Toronto, followed by the city's striking new opera house a few months later. Surely this was satire. But no, dear Denley was dead serious. He actually believed it. It left only one question: if Toronto is *boring*, just where on the scale of human stimulation does that leave Ottawa? Denley, it might be said, personifies a defensiveness among Ottawans, which is why outspoken visitors like Tyler Brûlé usually make news. To Denley, the city is just fine, thank you very much – as long, of course, as taxes do not go up. Civic pride of this nature would be useful if it meant a commitment to make the place better. But more likely, as Denley correctly argued, Ottawa isn't really about going to the opera, eating out, or shopping, which is what you do in Toronto. It's about how quickly you can "go camping, cottaging or kayaking." In other words, Denley's measure of the place is how fast you can leave it.

After twenty-four years, Allan Gotlieb left it. He remembered that he had promised himself that it would be time to decamp if he became too enamoured of the place. "I stayed," he confided to his diary in 1981. "I began to like Ottawa. I remembered the envelope. I know it's time to leave."

After her sojourn of a few days, Jan Morris left Ottawa, too. She had fallen for the place, but then again, she was not living there. She describes, as only she can, descending the steps of Parliament Hill, warming to the morning chill, inhaling all around her. "Nothing seemed ordinary now! Cetinje would have stood and cheered! As I paraded that bright icy morning through the streets of Ottawa . . . it dawned upon me that if this went on too long, and if I were not extremely careful, I might start getting sentimental about the place.

"But fortunately I had to catch a midday flight, so it never came to that."

Chapter 7

The Chameleon Canadian

O ver the past few years, Irvin Studin, a young political thinker schooled at York University, the London School of Economics, and the University of Oxford, approached dozens of prominent Canadians and asked them to write essays on the meaning of Canada. He collected their contributions in *What Is a Canadian? Forty-Three Thought-Provoking Responses*, which was published in 2006. Studin was inspired by a similar thematic collection edited in 1958 by David Ben-Gurion, the first prime minister of Israel. Ben-Gurion asked: "What is a Jew?" and went to the great sages of Judaism for answers. To divine Canada, Studin went to its "sages" in government, letters, business, and academia. Naturally, as a Canadian, he tried to strike a geographical, ethnic, and linguistic balance, and naturally, as a Canadian, he apologized for falling short. Studin asked his respondents to open their essays with the declaration "A Canadian is . . ." He asked them not to write prescriptively; they could not say what a Canadian *should* be, but they could say what a Canadian is *not*.

As Studin learned, how Canadians see themselves today is at once different and the same as the way Canadians (and foreigners) saw themselves a century ago, a generation ago, and a decade ago.

There are those, for example, who say flatly that a Canadian is someone who cannot stop asking who a Canadian is, what Jake MacDonald, a Winnipeg writer, calls "this eternal, narcissistic, self-pleasuring celebration of our national identity." MacDonald writes that he wishes this exercise in self-love would get to "the money shot" so that Canadians can get beyond it. William Watson, an economist at McGill University, thinks that a Canadian is "as a rule too fond by half of contemplating what a Canadian is." They are not wrong.

Studin puts his contributors into three classes. The first is idiosyncratic. They define the Canadian as liberal, enlightened, diplomatic, tolerant, polite, generous, complacent, deferential, among positive qualities, or, more harshly, parochial and preju-diced. A recurring "circumstantial" trait is "lucky." The second class is socio-political. The Canadian is a creation of the state or an instrument of public policy, such as the Constitution, health care, and multiculturalism. For example, the "Charter Canadians" see their citizenship in the Charter of Rights and Freedoms. The third class are those who are alienated from Canada. They do not see themselves as Canadians at all but Québécois, exiles within Canada, who make the distinction between *le Canadien* and the Canadian.

Studin suggests a people of infinite variety (which is flattering, though not unique to Canada). To expand his eclectic catalogue of the Canadian, let us consider some elements of character that the sages do not address. Classed loosely, they are the tall poppy syn-drome (envy, resentment, jealousy); moderation (the instinct for the political centre); ambiguity (the value of vagueness); and civil-ity (decency and generosity). For examples, let us look again to our civic culture, where we find so much of ourselves.

The Tall Poppy Syndrome
The tall poppy syndrome is not peculiar to Canada. Some say it came from Australia or New Zealand, where the tallest poppy in a

garden was cut down because it rose above the rest. Some attribute it to Scandinavia, which has its own finely honed suspicions of success and self-advancement, or Japan, where a proverb suggests that "the nail that sticks out gets hammered down." Wherever it originates, the tall poppy is as Canadian as the Maple Leaf. It has become our national flower.

"Always a nation of sumkeepers, Canadians betray the flinty instincts of the envious sibling, on guard for any sign of someone else getting ahead, or enjoying the fruits of their success," writes William Thorsell, the head of the Royal Ontario Museum and the former editor of *The Globe and Mail*. Getting ahead is dangerous in Canada. Politically, this manifests itself in the uneasy relationship between the provinces, and the provinces and the federal government. It is always about money and power, about who gets what from whom, recorded in a ledger of debits and credits. Like the bearded clerks of Dickensian England, wielding sharp-nibbed pens in their drafty, dim chambers, the mandarins in Edmonton, Quebec City, St. John's, and every other provincial capital carefully scrutinize the balance sheet. Whether it is tax credits, transfer payments, or rights and powers, they protest the slightest disparity or inequity. This has become a practised, deep-throated wail we have come to expect from the premiers. When the flamboyant Danny Williams of Newfoundland didn't get his share of offshore oil royalties he said he was promised from Ottawa in 2004, for example, he lowered the Canadian flags flying from provincial buildings. Other premiers make a similar fuss, usually less histrionically. Their latest grievance is "the fiscal imbalance," the lament that provinces send more money to Ottawa in tax dollars than they get back in transfer payments. In a country this wealthy, this endless squabbling over the fiscal imbalance suggests a mental imbalance.

We see the tall poppy syndrome in the doubt, distaste, and disdain among clucking Canadians for those who set themselves apart – to be different, original, exceptional, fashionable – or *quelle horreur* – to be flashy, flamboyant, and rich. To stand up. To stand out. We have a thing about success, we Canadians. We resent it. This is perplexing, given our achievements as a people. The explanation may lie in our belief in the primacy of the collective over the individual, allowing one to succeed only as a group in Canada. Dare to achieve success on your own, as a freelancer or a striver, and you'll be cut down. Elizabeth Nickson, the writer and journalist, thinks that Canada badly needs more "ego-ridden exhibitionists with drive" even as she doubts that Canada has the capacity to produce them. "That, of course, is pretty much impossible given the fact that if anyone, and I mean anyone, raises his or her pretty head above the parapet, the number of shotguns levelled at them is awesome," she says. Resentment, envy, and jealousy colonize our consciousness, challenging the better angels of our nature.

Examples abound in the political culture. On October 14, 1957, Lester B. Pearson learned that he had been awarded the Nobel Peace Prize for having found a way out of the Suez Crisis. The Nobel committee said that he'd "saved the world." When a reporter called him with the news of the award, he was incredulous: "You mean that I have been nominated," he insisted. When he learned he had indeed won, he said: "Gosh!" The reaction of others was less innocent. As one legend had it, the very idea that the bow-tied, lisping "Mike" Pearson could win the Nobel Prize led one outspoken woman at a cocktail party in Vancouver to exclaim, "Well, who does he think he is!" In Ottawa, newly elected Prime Minister John Diefenbaker seethed. He had always resented Pearson's acclaim as an international statesman. By coincidence, Diefenbaker and Pearson, the future Opposition leader, were to dine with Queen Elizabeth in Ottawa that evening. As Pearson notes in his memoirs, he received almost as much attention at the dinner as the prime minister, who didn't like being upstaged. Diefenbaker did not attend the bipartisan parliamentary dinner given for Pearson in December before he left for Oslo to accept the prize. According to Diefenbaker's biographer, Denis Smith, "Diefenbaker begrudged that award." On Pearson's death in 1972, Diefenbaker privately told a reporter: "That man should never have won the Nobel Prize."

This kind of resentment emerges in other ways from the allegedly "nice" Canadian. Many an artist, actor, or musician has protested their withering treatment at the hands of reviewers. "Canadians, we eat our own," moaned a musician after a critic demolished his performance. Douglas Gibson, who has been in Canadian publishing for a generation, notes that Canada's critics are hard on second novels. "There is a feeling of reviewers lying in the weeds waiting to pounce," he says. So it was with Nino Ricci, whose first novel, *Lives of the Saints*, won the Governor General's Literary Award for Fiction. Three years later, his second novel, *In a Glass House*, was panned. He isn't alone in encountering that kind of hostility. But the tall poppy syndrome isn't necessarily limited to second novels. Paul Gessell, a veteran critic with the *Ottawa Citizen*, thinks no writer is immune. "First-timers who produce great novels run the risk of being too uppity for ultra-modest, mild-mannered Canadians," he says. "Writers, after all, are supposed to achieve success only after years of poverty and a run of barely noticed novels." In 1999, Robert Fulford, the former editor of *Saturday Night*, wrote a scathing commentary on *Shift*, a zippy magazine co-founded by Evan Solomon. The aggrieved Solomon accosted Fulford at an awards dinner. "I thought it was completely negative, condescending, and one-sided," he fumed. "I've always wondered what the tall poppy syndrome was, and it's you. What do you know about launching something new? You've always worked for elite, established institutions."

Peter C. Newman recalls how Marshall McLuhan "maintained his poise amid the customary slaughter dished out to our most

thoughtful writers by the butchers who pass for book reviewers . . ."
McLuhan, whose fame was international, was blissfully unaffected. "I experience a great deal of liberty here in Canada," he told
Newman. "I wouldn't get that in the States, because I'm taken
quite seriously there." Newman nurses a grudge of his own. His
extraordinary œuvre includes *Renegade in Power*, which revolutionized political reporting in Canada in the 1960s; *The Canadian
Establishment*, his trilogy of the country's business elite; and *Here
Be Dragons*, his eloquent memoir. Yet he has never been *nominated*
for the Governor General's Literary Award for Nonfiction. The
unkindest cut of all came in 2005 when Newman was invited to
attend the announcement of the year's nominees for the Awards.
Although Newman wasn't told that *Here Be Dragons* was a finalist,
he assumed so from the invitation. It wasn't. "Do I feel bitter
about it?" he asks of his successive snubs by the Canada Council.
"Darn tootin'. The GGs should not cater to popularity, but neither
should they reward obscurity as their main criteria. There ought
to be a balance."

Newman could have gone to the United States early in his career
– he had been repeatedly offered a job at *Time* – but chose to stay in
Canada, to which he had fled from Czechoslovakia during the war.
He was not one of those talented Canadians who was stymied in
Canada and sought success elsewhere. In the 1950s, Paul Anka, the
rising young singer, couldn't sell "Diana" in Canada. He took it to
the United States, where it was a smash. Margaret MacMillan took
Paris 1919 to Britain under a different title after it had been turned
down by publishers in Canada. Having won acclaim in the mother
country, it was finally published in Canada, where it won the
Governor General's Award in 2003. A young ambassador returned to
Canada after a highly publicized, much-praised posting to a difficult
country. The Department of Foreign Affairs refused his application
for promotion and offered him an acting position; some suggest that
his masters resented his sense of self-regard. Disappointed, he took

a top job with a leading international organization. And so it goes. Success obviously bothers us. When a newspaper reported an assault on a couple driving a luxury car in downtown Toronto, a letter-to-the-editor asked why the victims had been driving such a nice car. When the Bank of Canada asked focus groups to help it choose Canadians to put on the back of its new banknotes, the respondents called Lester Pearson "a partisan politician" and complained that Terry Fox, the one-legged marathoner who ran halfway across Canada before dying of cancer, had had "an abrasive personality." When Craig Kielburger, the child prodigy acclaimed for his efforts to help children in the developing world, was attacked in an article in *Saturday Night* in 1996, the magazine's editor called it "a great piece of journalism." Kielburger, then thirteen years old, called it "snide and derogatory." The article said that he had been using the Free the Children charity he had founded for his own benefit. He sued for libel. In 2000, *Saturday Night* settled out of court for $319,000. Ten years later, Kielburger thinks the magazine tried to make him look arrogant and patronizing because it disliked what he was doing and thought he was too young to be influencing governments. In ninth grade, Kielburger was too short to be a tall poppy, but he was cut down, anyway.

When *The Globe and Mail* invited contributions to a weekly feature it had created on the world's most overrated books, literary critic Bert Archer rounded on Timothy Findley, one of the country's most esteemed novelists: "The fact that he's considered a quality fiction writer and not just a creator of skilled but fundamentally pandering entertainment is not only a great Canadian confusion," Archer wrote, "it's the source of his strange brand of success."

No wonder Canada has few recognizable heroes. Other countries salute their soldiers, statesmen, scientists, writers, artists, athletes. Not Canada. In the Hall of Flags and Heroes in the headquarters of the Organization of American States in Washington, D.C., member nations designate a national hero to put on a pedestal. George Washington is there. So is José Marti and José de San Martin. Canada has no one. The Hall of Honour, in the Centre Block of Parliament, was supposed to honour Canadians. Today it has a plaque collectively honouring nurses and soldiers, but no individual – as if no one can agree on whom should be honoured there. Ask the Library of Parliament why or how this changed, and it cannot say. We have an excellent honours system in the Order of Canada, but we don't overdo it. We are more parsimonious than others in handing out awards; while there are about 3,000 living members of the Order of Canada, there are 125,000 members of the Legion d'honneur in France, which has less than twice the population of Canada. Peter C. Newman thinks Canada has few heroes, living or dead, because that would be boastful. "This country is fuelled by envy and deference, qualities that rank heroism as an emotional extravagance reserved for Italian tenors and one-album country-and-western singers," he wrote in 2000. "If God had meant us to be heroic, he wouldn't have made us Canadians. This is the only country on Earth whose citizens dream of being Clark Kent, instead of Superman."

At the same time, there are dangers in overstating the tall poppy syndrome. It may be that those novels that get lousy reviews deserve them. And although those much-maligned juries of the Governor General's Literary Awards have repeatedly overlooked Newman, they can also surprise, as they did in nominating writer Trevor Cole twice in three years for his first two novels. Ultimately, the failure of judges to recognize Newman says more about them than him. Deserving people are overlooked in other countries, too; in his estimable career as a journalist, R.W. Apple Jr. of *The New York Times* never won the Pulitzer Prize. Newman is a Companion of the Order of Canada and has received several honorary degrees as well as the Michener Award for Journalism, among others. He has also sold more than 2 million books. Sometimes this country has a way of compensating.

Among Newman's books is a biography of Conrad Black, the entrepreneur, historian, plutocrat, and phrasemaker. Newman and Black have had their differences but they share a view of the culture of envy in Canada. In *A Life in Progress*, his dense memoir, Black recalls a conversation with Pierre Trudeau in 1982 when one of Black's companies was under police investigation. An angry Black complained to Trudeau that "the destructive fixation of the envious English-Canadian mind required that the highest, happiest, most agile flyers be laid low, as a cat, faced with a garden of birds, pursued the most swiftly flying and brightly feathered, the one whose destruction would most frighten the others." Of course, he was the brightly feathered bird. His interpretation of the tall poppy syndrome is "a sadistic desire, corroded by soul-destroying envy, to intimidate all those who might aspire to anything in the slightest exceptional." He recalled that Trudeau said he was familiar with the phenomenon and what made Canada hard to govern was that French Canadians "like a winner and mercilessly boo a loser, and English Canadians indulge a loser and . . . lustily boo a winner." Envy is a recurring theme in Black's memoir, which was published in 1993, before he renounced his Canadian citizenship to accept the seat in the British House of Lords. He sees resentment in many places in Canada, especially in the media. "The vintage Canadian spirit of envy was at its most sulphurous with the young journalists," he sniffs, arguing that they could never accept that they were the "chroniclers rather than the chronicled." He described Canadians as "an envious, whingeing people" who had created a culture of victimhood, driving this native son away.

The tall poppy syndrome thrives in our political hothouse. We think politicians are venal, vapid, and vainglorious. When they want a raise, our instinct is to deny it; really, now, the nerve of you! Then we complain about the quality of our politicians. Our disdain for public service is spreading. The antipathy is magnified by governments seeking to be seen as squeaky-clean and a media eager to scrutinize expense accounts and travel budgets for extravagance or malfeasance. Newspapers think it is important enough to report that the prime minister's chef went to Egypt (at a cost of two thousand dollars!) "to share recipes" with the chefs of sixteen other nations "courtesy of the Canadian taxpayer." It is also important for the well-informed citizen to know, figuratively speaking, the bottle of wine the Ambassador to France served a visiting delegation of beekeepers or that the Minister of Justice took a government plane to attend the Rotary Club in Lethbridge. Or that the Conservatives use the government Challenger jets half as much as the Liberals did. We dine out on a minister's expense chits, airline tickets, and hotel bills, which now appear on the Web. No wonder restaurants in Ottawa are closing. The mandarins are afraid to be seen lunching with the wrong people – or perhaps lunching at all.

When Allan Gotlieb was Canada's ambassador to Washington, he arranged to have *The Globe and Mail* sent to his residence on Saturdays. An Ottawa columnist learned of this "extravagance" and howled as though our plenipotentiary had committed murder. "It makes me feel sick," Gotlieb groused to his diary, knowing that readers would wonder why he needed the newspaper at home on the weekend or why he didn't go to the airport and pick it up himself. "How long does one have to be in public life to get used to this shit?"

Money matters in Canada. Canadians look askance at public salaries, perquisites, and benefits, as if no politician or public servant could possibly deserve them. It may be why the governor general is paid $114,725, far less than a federal Cabinet minister. The spending of Brian Mulroney, the mellifluous glad-hander who was prime minister from 1984 to 1993, became an obsession. "Closets designed to hold hundreds of shoes, including dozens of pairs of loafers, are among the lavish furnishings of 24 Sussex Drive," the Canadian Press reported on April 16, 1987. "Brian Mulroney's closet was designed to accommodate 30 suits and 84 pairs of shoes, including at least 50 pairs of Gucci loafers . . ." This Emperor had too many clothes. Mulroney had reached a level of consumption "that would shock most Canadians," columnist John Ferguson observed. The reality was that Mulroney had invited this kind of scrutiny when he and his predecessors attacked Pierre Trudeau for a suede couch and fifty-dollar ashtrays in the waiting room of his office on Parliament Hill. Or, years earlier, when the Tories pilloried Trudeau for accepting an indoor swimming pool at 24 Sussex Drive from anonymous donors. In the blood sport of politics, the Liberals were soon asking Mulroney if taxpayers were paying for his children's food.

Whatever Mulroney's personal excesses, the interest here was odd, even unseemly; at root, it was about disparaging politicians. We like to do this. As Hugh Segal said, this *idée fixe* over Mulroney's spending "falls into the tradition of pettiness with which we treat people in public life . . ." Pierre Pettigrew, no friend of Mulroney, winced years later when he recalled this inquisition. As the minister of foreign affairs, who would face questions on his own spending in office, he said: "You know, we can be very petty, very mean in Canada." We can, we are, and it demeans us. Yet our appetite for this is large. *On the Take*, a self-described "exposé of greed and crime in the Mulroney years," was a publishing phenomenon in the mid-1990s. Written by investigative journalist Stevie Cameron, it topped bestseller lists for two years. Eventually, her tireless reporting about Mulroney would yield some startling revelations that he never fully explained. But the early reports of his extravagances were voyeurism. As William Thorsell wondered years later: "Who emerged wholly humiliated in that famous episode, if not the public scandalized by such banalities?"

Mulroney's imbroglio made it politically impossible to renovate 24 Sussex Drive for years after. When Jean Chrétien moved there in 1993, he wouldn't spend any money on the house; according to a frequent visitor, he proudly declared the curtains on the windows had been made from the tablecloths used at the G-7 summit in Halifax. When Paul Martin arrived ten years later, he wouldn't touch the house, either. Susan Delacourt of the *Toronto Star* wrote that Martin knew "that any move to fix up the home in a substantial way – with taxpayers' dollars – would be a public-relations disaster." By then the house – a Gothic revival pile built above the Ottawa River in 1866 – was in grave disrepair. It was cold and draughty in winter and oppressively hot in summer. The kitchen was small and dated, the windows filled with unsightly, dripping air conditioners, like those in a tropical tenement. The sunroom was so chilly in winter that it was wrapped in clear plastic, which seemed to be taking the federal energy conservation program a little far (though Jack Layton of the New Democrats advised installing solar panels). When Sheila Martin opened the house for a charitable event, visitors walked around and expressed "disappoint-ment, shock and embarrassment." No wonder. The prime minis-ter's residence looked like a tarpaper shack in Appalachia.

When Martin expressed his reservations, the leader of the Opposition pounced. Naturally. Stephen Harper said he was delighted with Stornoway, the official residence. It was the best place he'd ever lived; Martin should stop whining and worry less about his needs than those of Canadians. "We have a $9-billion surplus, and I'd like to see some money go to taxpayers rather than our obsession being our personal living accommodations," carped Harper. There it was, then. If we can make politicians live in genteel shabbiness, like a déclassé socialite forced into a home-less shelter, why not? It is as irresistible as soaking the rich. *Take 'em down a peg. That'll show 'em.* Before Harper lived there, Reform Party leader Preston Manning had wanted to sell Stornoway. Before him, Bloc Québécois leader Lucien Bouchard refused to move in. And so on. It was always about politics, never about ensuring proper official residences for the prime minister of Canada and the leader of the Opposition. Not that they should resemble the

Kremlin or the Elysée Palace. Just dignified, modest homes, befitting the leaders of a rich, resentful country.

A recent illustration of the tall poppy syndrome is the pillorying of Adrienne Clarkson, the broadcaster, publisher, diplomat, and writer who was Governor General of Canada from 1999 to 2005. When she left Ottawa after a feverish period at Rideau Hall, some called her the finest governor general since Roland Michener in the 1970s, or Georges-P. Vanier in the 1960s, or the finest in memory, or the finest in history. In six years, Clarkson reinvented a dusty, antiquated institution. With her husband, John Ralston Saul, the novelist, essayist, and philosopher, she arrived with an idea of herself and the office and brought it to life. Watching her installation in the Senate, a friend in the Visitor's Gallery whispered to another: "She's been preparing for this all her life." His response: "She didn't have to prepare."

Clarkson brought with her a record of professional and public service, a term as Ontario's agent general in Paris, a familiarity with every region of the country and its history, fluency in both languages, and intelligence, energy, and imagination. This is the depth and experience a governor general should have. Indeed, a reason that Clarkson was extraordinary in the role is that her four predecessors were pedestrian. Roméo LeBlanc, Ramon Hnatyshyn, Jeanne Sauvé, and Edward Schreyer were decent, honourable, successful politicians. But each was chosen to repay a debt, confer an honour, or set a precedent. It mattered little that Hnatyshyn couldn't speak French or that LeBlanc was phlegmatic, that Sauvé was aloof and that Schreyer was eccentric. To be the first Ukrainian, Acadian, woman, and Manitoban was enough to make the appointment. Clarkson was the first immigrant to become governor general, having fled Hong Kong as a child early in the Second World War. She was also the first governor general who had not been a professional politician or career diplomat. She was articulate, stylish, refined, attractive, opinionated, and self-confident. Very self-confident. Her husband was all that, too.

This was unsettling to Little Canadians. In the history of the office, no viceregal couple was as prominent. And none suffered as much criticism and calumny from the press and the politicians. The rain of brickbats from the travelling carnival of harpies and handwringers began before the couple arrived at Rideau Hall and continued until they left. In a column in *The Globe and Mail* before the new governor general took office, Jan Wong wondered why Clarkson made her feel uneasy. "She doesn't seem, well, like a Chinese refugee," Wong decided, as if Clarkson was not Chinese enough. Strange that; would she have asked if Clarkson were Jewish or Ukrainian enough? That was only the first of Wong's ninety-eight theses nailed to the door of Rideau Hall. The list of Clarkson's affronts included her early departure one year from a literary festival in British Columbia; a televised interview from her hospital bed after she had given birth; her long, painful alienation from her daughters; her marriage to Saul shortly before she became governor general; and her dispute with a neighbour over his expansion. "Sorry, Mom," sneered Wong. "She's Adrienne Clarkson, and I'm not."

When Clarkson got to Ottawa, nothing was too petty. Her clothes were too loud. Her friends were too elitist. Her tastes were too rich. Her indiscretions and offences were unending. Clarkson misses the funeral of the Lt. Governor of Alberta, a friend and confidant, and a columnist hisses that "the nation's Empress of Excess was merrily vacationing with haughty husband in Paris." She goes to the theatre in Ottawa accompanied by Richard Mahoney, who at the time is running for the Liberals in Ottawa, and is accused of "cozying up to Paul Martin's pals in the hope of being reappointed to her lavish life at Rideau Hall." She visits skid row in Vancouver, and she is "degrading" the homeless and "exploiting" their poverty. Even straight reportage has an edge: "The couple arrived – a little late – on foot, dressed casually, as if out for an autumn stroll," said *The Globe and Mail*. A whole book was given over to their foibles and contradictions, called *Mr. & Mrs. G.G.: The Media Princess & the Court Philosopher*. None of this prevented Clarkson and Saul from performing their duties – travelling, speaking, honouring, receiving, hosting, sponsoring – and a whole manner of other responsibilities that they carried off with aplomb.

The lowest blow came in a gossip column in the *National Post* on November 22, 2004. A three-sentence item written by Gillian Cosgrove attributed scurrilous behaviour to the governor general. Although Clarkson had always ignored such allegations, she could not let this one stand. Soon after, a *mea culpa* on page two of the newspaper conceded "a number of fundamental errors and intentional misrepresentations appeared. The editors regret this and apologize to all concerned." The wording came from Rideau Hall. The column was dropped from the website. The columnist was dropped from the newspaper.

The drumbeat of criticism ebbed and flowed but never went away. The detractors resented that the viceregal couple repainted and redecorated much of Rideau Hall and some of its outbuildings, displayed Canadian art and furniture from government warehouses, served fine vintages from the country's best wineries (promoting Canada's vintners is one of Saul's passions), and presented organic, creative food prepared by the country's best chefs. They clucked when she travelled some 150,000 kilometres a year, often to small communities in the North (among the four hundred villages, towns, and cities the couple visited over their six years). Most of all, though, they howled when she led a visit to Iceland, Finland, and Russia in 2003 accompanied by a delegation of 59 "Rosedale" associates. It cost $5.4 million. Having asked the governor general to make the trip, the government panicked when the critics started bleating. It cancelled the second half of the visit, to Norway, Denmark, and Sweden, which had been two years in the planning. A parliamentary committee even hastily summoned her principal secretary from Europe to testify, questioned her for an hour, then chastised her for having flown home business class.

Clarkson was rising above her station. This is a cardinal sin in a resentful country. The governor general should not fly to her cottage on Georgian Bay on a private plane (even though the RCMP insisted on it after September 11). Go commercial. The governor general should not attend the sixtieth anniversary of D-Day because Queen Elizabeth was attending too (even though the governor general is Canada's commander-in-chief). Stay home. "Of course, it's no secret that Mrs. Clarkson and Mr. Saul are elitists – they love the titles and the ceremony and the fine wines," sniped the *Ottawa Citizen*. "Their Sussex Drive address is not a regular stop on the pizza-and-chicken wings delivery routes." Well, let them eat rice cakes at Rideau Hall and take the bus to the cottage. Tim Wiebe of Calgary caught this smallness of spirit in a letter to the *National Post*: "Canadians tend to be an egalitarian lot, downplaying differences in income, ethnicity and other social variables as relatively unimportant, and funding the lifestyle of the over-the-top self-appointed ostentatious Louis XIV couple in Ottawa is a national embarrassment."

In 2004, after Clarkson had been in office five years, it all came to a bizarre climax. When the politicians learned that her budget had risen to $41 million from $17 million a year, they balked. That she was travelling and entertaining far more than her predecessors, including making annual visits to Canadian troops in Bosnia and Afghanistan, scarcely mattered. In one of those exquisite moments of our nationhood, the Parliament of Canada told the Governor General of Canada that she was spending too much. It would have to slap her wrist. So, in a fit of pique, it cut $417,000 from her budget. But when pinched parliamentarians learned that her office was planning to eliminate children's winter activities at Rideau Hall, they winced. Joe Preston, a Conservative MP, said that "it's always easy to point at the most glamorous things and say you're going to make people suffer because of this." His colleague, Peter MacKay, a future foreign minister, advised: "If they have to cut children's programming, I would suggest they maybe have to serve less caviar at the next cocktail party."

What was behind all this? Try a culture of resentment. One of Clarkson's loudest critics was Pat Martin of the New Democratic Party, a peppery populist from Winnipeg who wanted to reduce Clarkson's budget by the cost of her circumpolar visit. You might have thought that Martin would have approved of Clarkson and Saul publicizing the homeless or visiting rural Canada or making the office a *Canadian* institution. From dropping royal toasts at state dinners to rearranging (or removing) some of the royal portraits at Rideau Hall and ensuring ceremonial pipers played Canadian music, they always promoted the country. But Pat Martin and his ilk could not see Clarkson and Saul as reformers or exemplars (no one ever mentioned that not only did Saul not receive a salary or pension for his work at Rideau Hall, he also gave up lucrative speaking engagements to avoid any conflict of interest). Rather, Clarkson and Saul were effete, impudent snobs, high-hatted and snooty, kicking back on the plush sofas and rolling around in the thick oriental carpets. Said Martin: "Frankly, Canadians would like her even more if there was a little bit more of the common touch demonstrated here instead of an elitist role."

An elitist role. What does that mean? Probably, that the governor general and her husband were stuck up. They had gotten too big for their boots. They had highfalutin ideas and champagne tastes. They didn't shop at Winners or the Gap. (Actually, they did.) We live in an egalitarian society, as we remind ourselves, and we cannot have aristocrats or arrivistes rising above the rest. Perhaps this, rather than money, was what was behind the antagonism of Martin, John Reynolds, and other critics. Or the antagonisms of the Canadian Taxpayers Federation, which never saw a public penny that was not misspent. (This obsession did not end with Clarkson. When Michaëlle Jean visited Africa in November 2006, CTV News reported from her first stop that she would be on the continent for twenty-four days – an unprecedented journey. "But what's it going to cost?" asked the earnest reporter.)

Clarkson was not blameless. She should not have gone on the CBC to answer questions about her spending and said, "I am above the law." Rather, she might have said: "Constitutionally, my office is above the law and that is why I cannot discuss this." It was unwise of her to take the large delegation of artists, native leaders, entrepreneurs, and industry representatives on the circumpolar tour, but not because they were not legitimate. She and Saul should have anticipated the criticism. That the cost of her trip was about the same as a royal visit or the "Team Canada" missions, that she pioneered the strategic use of the state visit, that the trip was value for money in publicity and prestige (as Russian president Vladimir Putin told Stephen Harper years later) were sound points. But this was less about reason than resentment. Clarkson's critics weren't going to give her a break. They would never see her unpublicized acts of kindness, from making bedside visits to the dying to award them the Order of Canada to raising money for street kids in Thailand. Or small acts of protest, such as refusing to shake the hand of the Ambassador of Burma, a country notorious for its human rights abuses. They could never acknowledge how hard she worked, which may have contributed to the heart condition for which she had a pacemaker inserted in her last summer in office. They would not appreciate, among her other achievements, her establishing the Governor General's Northern Medal and the Clarkson Cup for excellence in women's hockey.

No, there remained a lingering feeling about Saul and Clarkson that she later ascribed to "malice, ignorance and a certain kind of tall-poppy syndrome." In societies where the holders of high office are respected, even revered, this kind of criticism would be *lèse majesté*. In others, it would have been unthinkable, even laughable. In Canada, deriding the couple was strangely acceptable, at least by the elite. In fact, it was lent legitimacy by a government that abandoned its own appointee. For myriad affronts – such as denying Clarkson the opportunity to open the Canadian War Museum on May 8, 2005, a role she had hoped to perform as commander-in-chief – Clarkson never forgave Paul Martin. She thought him unsophisticated and unwise, a prime minister who did not know the country. Some prim reviewers scolded her for telling tales in her memoir, *Heart Matters*. Michael Valpy of *The Globe and Mail* lamented that Clarkson had "trashed constitutional convention" and "may have irreparably destroyed the special relationship" between the governor general and the prime minister. He called her book "revenge," counselling Clarkson to take an oath of silence. Given her shabby treatment by the government, however, Clarkson actually showed more restraint than revenge. There was more she could have said – much more – and didn't.

What Clarkson broke at Rideau Hall was not confidentiality, which was Valpy's concern, but convention. She changed how we view the office. So successful was her appointment that the government chose as her successor neither a professional politician nor a diplomat but a woman, an immigrant and a broadcaster married to a lanky intellectual with an association with France, film, and philosophy. As Clarkson departed, editorialists paid tribute, the sweet encomiums flowing from even her harshest critics. Historians praised her, too. Despite the opprobrium directed at them, Clarkson and Saul were able to forge a relationship with ordinary Canadians, an emotional bond unseen in that office since it was filled by Georges-P. Vanier and his wife, Pauline. This was particularly evident in their visits to rural Canada, where few had gone before, and the warm reception they received in community halls and church basements. It was really no wonder, a year later, that Canadians would line up to buy her memoir and fill halls across the land to hear her speak. Adrienne Clarkson and John Ralston Saul had earned the warm applause of a grateful nation. And at the end of the day, in our shambling, shuffling way, we offered it.

Moderation, Caution, and Prudence

An observation among foreigners visiting Canada – and occasionally among Canadians themselves – is that it is boring, dull, lifeless. This has provided much material for many comedians. Years ago the *New Republic* famously held a "boring headline-writing contest." The winner was "Worthy Canadian Initiative." This is the stereotype, the cliché of Canada. It makes some Canadians uneasy, even defensive. Actually, it should make them proud.

In 1964, Senator Barry Goldwater stood at the Republican National Convention in San Francisco and accepted his party's presidential nomination. Goldwater was a conservative whose view of government and the role of the state was outside the mainstream, which is why he could oppose both civil rights legislation and the Tennessee Valley Authority. He was a libertarian who believed in small government. His memorable speech enthralled his baying co-religionists. "Extremism in the defence of liberty is no vice," he thundered. "And moderation in the pursuit of justice is no virtue." It is hard to imagine a politician in Canada making that kind of speech. It isn't us. We don't think that way. If we appear tepid in temperament, it may be because of a deep-seated attachment to stability and predictability. It helps to have an aversion to ideology – some would say, more bluntly, that we just don't like ideas – because that could lead to stridency, or even militancy. We dislike militancy. Much as it may make us a target of ridicule, moderation is our métier.

If we could list our seven greatest virtues, moderation would surely be among them. It is hard-wired in our genes. "Nothing is more characteristic of Canada than the inclination to be moderate," observed Vincent Massey in his book, *On Being Canadian*.

"We are not given to extremes in Canada." When we speak of extremes we speak of the nature of the land, which moves from mountain to lowland to farmland to tundra; the fluctuation of the temperature, from the cold of the Arctic to the heat of the Prairies; and the diversity of the population, among the most heterogeneous on earth. Extremes? They are not in politics or ideology. The Canadian is not the European, riven with ancient feuds and simmering hatreds, or the American, possessed of ambition and confidence that have brought great achievement and great affliction.

Our sense of moderation runs through our history, government, and politics. In 140 years of nationhood, Canada has had little civil unrest. Our rebellions, whether led by William Lyon Mackenzie, Louis-Joseph Papineau, or Louis Riel, have neither been long nor bloody. Our riots, in Montreal, Toronto, and Winnipeg, have been few. We have not had a revolution or a civil war, which gave birth and unity to the United States. As John Ralston Saul has noted, Canada has suffered only eighty-six deaths in civil strife in its history. While we had the Battle of the Plains of Abraham and the Battle of Queenston Heights, we had no Lexington, Concord, Antietam, or Gettysburg. The two wars fought at home were waged between bigger powers; in the wars abroad we have never fought for conquest or colonies and we have never fought alone. We have had no coup d'états and have had only two political assassinations (D'Arcy McGee in 1868 and Pierre Laporte in 1970). Our exposure to terrorism has been generally limited to the bombings and kidnappings of the Front de libération du Québec in the 1960s.

Our belief in the rule of law – as expressed in the oft-cited "peace, order and good government" of the British North America Act – meant there was no Wild West in Canada. There was a West that was settled. But it was rarely wild. The reason was the austerity, deference, and temperance of the people under the authority of the North-West Mounted Police. The Mounties exemplified rectitude across the West. Up North, when thousands of dreamy-eyed prospectors were flooding into the Klondike in 1898, the Mounties manning the Yukon–Alaska border post refused entry to anyone who did not have a year's provisions, which had to be hauled up the daunting Chilkoot Trail. It was prudent, even paternalistic, and it was Canada. Pierre Berton explains the Canadian sense of caution this way: "We are not an impetuous people. That's a fault in some ways, for we lack the panache that goes with impetuosity, the entrepreneurial buccaneering that sometimes builds nations (and sometimes destroys them). Like the Mounted Police, we prefer to ask questions first and shoot only as a last resort." Canadians are not those Irish lads rambling across the countryside recalled by Frank O'Connor, the writer. As he tells it, whenever they reached an orchard wall that seemed too high for them, they would throw their hats over. That way they had to follow them and continue their journey. Canadians might well scale the wall, but they would prudently keep their hats on their heads, lest it rain.

Politically, moderation is our credo. From the Quebec Act of 1774 to Confederation in 1867 to the conscription plebiscite in 1942 to the patriation of the Constitution in 1982, we have shown an extraordinary instinct for compromise. We have also had an instinct for continuity. Since 1867, our political system has changed little. There have been amendments to the Constitution, some realignment of powers between the provinces and the federal government, the evolution of Cabinet government, and the arrival of new provinces and territories, new departments, agencies, and offices. In 1982, most significantly, Canada brought home the British North America Act and entrenched the Charter of Rights and Freedoms. Beyond that, though, the nomenclature of the system of government has remained essentially the same. A constitutional monarchy. A governor general. The Supreme Court. A prime minister and cabinet. The House of Commons and the

Senate. Powers and roles have changed, but institutionally, Canada hasn't. Canadians wanted it that way. Because we have had no insurrection or revolution, we have not had to remake our government. We have not had two empires or five republics, like France, nor three Reichs, like Germany. We did not overthrow the monarchy, like Russia or throw out the British, like the Americans. In 2007, Canada remains much as it was in 1867. For a twenty-first-century country, a nineteenth-century constitution is both a comfort and a burden.

Stability is us. We dislike minority government because it is unpredictable. We are not Italy, which changes governments the way runway models change outfits. Historically, minorities are uncommon in Canadian politics; in thirty-nine general elections, Canadians have elected minority governments twelve times. Between 1974 and 2004, Canada had only nine months of minority government. Most of the time the country has favoured majority government. As long as the government is honest, competent, centrist, and progressive, Canadians are inclined to keep it around until they have reason to think otherwise. Once they gave a government five consecutive majorities; twice they have given governments four consecutive majorities. In a country without term limits, like those restraining the president of the United States, it isn't unusual in Canada for a prime minister – Macdonald, Laurier, King, St. Laurent, Trudeau, Mulroney, or Chrétien – to remain in office for nine, ten, or more years. This political inertia is especially true in the provinces, where British Columbia, Alberta, and Ontario have kept governments around for decades. Canadians like continuity more than they fear senility.

While there have been as many as five parties at one time in Parliament, only the Liberals and the Conservatives have held power. Indeed, the Liberals have governed Canada for most of its history. Both the Liberals and the Conservatives have evolved since their origins in the nineteenth century, but they share many of the same principles. Both have provided sound administration, more pragmatic than ideological. The Conservatives may tilt to the right and the Liberals may tilt to the left, but this movement is marginal; both have tried to hold the centre. This is where Canadians want their parties to be. "Why does a Canadian cross the street?" asks writer Allan Fotheringham. "To get to the middle." It isn't to say that Canadians have no taste for more ideological parties, such as the Co-operative Commonwealth Federation and its successor, the New Democratic Party, which is social democratic. Or the Social Credit Party and the Parti créditiste, which were committed to free enterprise. Or, in the 1990s, the Reform Party, which began as a populist movement in western Canada. Or, the Bloc Québécois, which is both secessionist and social democratic. But Canadians have never entrusted them with power.

If the Liberals are known as Canada's "Natural Governing Party," it is because they have governed Canada for eighty of the last 110 years. They are the most successful political organization in the democratic world. How have they done it? Shrewdness, agility, and opportunism. The Liberals have acted as conciliators between French and English; demonstrated prudent economic and fiscal management, by and large, coupled with inventive social welfare programs; appealed to the middle class of urban, central Canada with a moderate nationalism and state interventionism; co-opted the ideas of other parties, from pensions and unemployment insurance on the left to tax cuts and deficit reduction on the right; chosen eminent leaders, alternating strictly between French and English, a tradition they reaffirmed in 2006. In other words, they have given Canadians what they want.

Whenever the Liberals lose their managerial prowess, as they did in 1957, 1984, and 2006, they lose power. Each time they were replaced by the Conservatives singing the siren song of change. But as the Liberals were not always liberal in government, the

Conservatives were not always conservative. Whatever the campaign rhetoric or partisan demands, their fondness for the centre meant that no government of either political stripe had licence to arrive in Ottawa and undo what its predecessors had done. None would dismantle medicare, cancel official bilingualism, reverse privatization and deregulation, withdraw from peacekeeping, renege on foreign aid, quit NATO or NORAD. The Liberals were not going to rescind the free trade agreement in 1993 any more than the Conservatives were going to return the British North America Act to London in 1984. Much as they may have opposed free trade and patriation in opposition, they accepted them in power because that is what Canadians wanted. This doesn't mean they had no flexibility. Tax cuts and budget cuts, yes. Higher spending and fewer entitlements, yes. Creating or selling Crown corporations, yes. But a fundamental change of philosophy, like Franklin Roosevelt's in 1933 or Margaret Thatcher's in 1979? Rarely, and more likely among voters who elected the Parti Québécois in Quebec and the CCF in Saskatchewan. Governments could certainly be bold, such as the Liberals on the Constitution and the Conservatives on free trade. But it is hard to find a government in Ottawa, even those swept into office like the Conservatives in 1958 or the Liberals in 1993, that was ever so different in principle that it meant a radical change in practice. Governments know that to be doctrinaire is to be un-Canadian. This country prefers gradualism.

So it was the last time that Canadians chose a new national government. The election of January 23, 2006, marked the end of a long, cold campaign that was expected to be shallow, nasty, unnecessary, and inconsequential. Actually, it was substantive, surprising, urgent, and decisive. The election was a crystalline reflection of character as politics. It gave Canadians almost exactly what they ordered: a new government, a new prime minister, a realignment of the opposition, a shift in power to the West. If the election suggested change, this was managed change. The outcome was so shaded that it seemed a highly contested, carefully crafted compromise. And what could be more typical of Canada than that?

In the election less than two years earlier, on June 28, 2004, Canadians had denied the Liberals a fourth consecutive majority. Unpersuaded by Paul Martin, the former finance minister who had succeeded Jean Chrétien as prime minister six months earlier, they gave the Liberals 135 of 308 seats in the House of Commons. This was 20 seats short of the majority of 155, creating the country's first hung Parliament in twenty-five years. Like most minority governments, this one was short-lived. Only nineteen months later, Canadians went to the polls again and elected the Conservatives with a minority. The electoral system is an imprecise instrument of public will, but this time it offered a change of government more than a change of direction. Call it liberalism without Liberals or Conservatives without conservatism. Canadians rejected Liberals more than they embraced Conservatives; they knew they were enjoying the fruits of the strongest economy in a generation and the management that brought it, but they disliked the corruption in Quebec. It was time for a change. When the saturnine Stephen Harper came calling with a middle-of-the-road platform, they were reassured that he did not have hooves, horns, and a tail. Their big fear? That he was too conservative. Harper wisely saw this, softened his social conservatism, and fashioned a platform so bland that Conservatives could be seen as Liberals without the ethical baggage. Trying to distinguish between them, wrote Peter C. Newman, was like "watching synchronized swimming." So, after several weeks of product demonstration, Canadians decided they would buy the vacuum cleaner Harper was selling as long as they could take out an extended warranty. Which is what they did.

Ten days before the election, the polls showed Canadians were ready to give the Conservatives a majority. Then, having listened to Harper again and reconsidered, they retreated; they had buyer's regret before the sale was made. So they elected the Conservatives but withheld enough support to keep them to a minority. This would compel the Conservatives to seek allies, make deals, modify their program, and, most importantly, ask for another mandate in some two years rather than four. Judicious and measured, Canadians were sending the Conservatives a message: you're in power but you're on probation.

In constructing their thirty-ninth Parliament, the electors of Canada addressed a few other matters, too. Worried that the new government would have no representation in Quebec (the Conservatives began the campaign with no seats in French Canada), they elected ten Conservatives, one of the election's most surprising outcomes. Worried about western alienation, they elected a prime minister from the West with a majority of his caucus from the West, which was unprecedented. Worried that there would be no effective opposition if the government won in a landslide, voters ensured the Liberals won more seats than the Conservatives had had in 2004. They had decided to discipline the Liberal Party rather than destroy it. A spell in opposition would give the Liberals a chance to change leaders, review policy, and rebuild their organization. If the Conservatives were in power, the Liberals were in purgatory, and neither was necessarily a permanent state of being. If the Conservatives succeeded in office, they would be rewarded with a majority; if they failed, the country's "Natural Governing Party" would return from exile. Two other ways a prudent public acted randomly to keep this fractious country together: voters took seats away from the secessionist Bloc Québécois, denying them half the votes they boldly predicted in Quebec; and they gave seats to the New Democratic Party, creating a progressive counterweight to check any drift to the right under the Conservatives, an influence the NDP tried to use in 2007 to prod the government to write stronger environmental legislation.

So there it was, then. Canadians wanted change and got it. They wanted Paul Martin out and Stephen Harper in, and they got that. They wanted the secessionists weakened and the federalists strengthened and the social democrats invigorated, and they got that. Their measured electoral engineering brought a change in Parliament, step by step, wrapped in conditions and caveats. In Canadian politics, this is called moderation.

Ambiguity, or the Value of Vagueness

"Sweet are the uses of adversity," declares Duke Senior in Shakespeare's *As You Like It*. Surveying our own national experience, a Canadian might say: "Sound are the uses of ambiguity." For ambiguity has served Canada well. Historically, the lack of clarity in our identity (who are we?) and in our destiny (where are we going?) has helped us to avoid the big questions that might undermine our unlikely enterprise in a harsh land next to the greatest power on earth. Looking at other peoples in the twentieth century, we know what divisions can do. Ambiguity, which we have raised to a fine art in our political life, has allowed us to broker the differences of region, religion, race, and language that have always threatened our survival. As a people, ambiguity has kept us undefined. It has also kept us together.

Canada, it has been said, is less a country than a question. What is it, anyway? What does it stand for? What is its *raison d'être*? Is it French, English, or both? Is it a multicultural mosaic? American or European? Free market or social democracy? The canniest of our politicians have always understood the power of ambiguity. Certainly Mackenzie King, who was prime minister for more than twenty-one years, never took a position if he could avoid one. Bruce Hutchison called his portrait of King *The Incredible Canadian*. He might have called it *The Ambiguous Canadian*. King was the apotheosis of ambiguity. F.R. Scott, the poet, law professor, and social activist, paid tribute to him in verse:

. . . . . .
He blunted us.

We had no shape
Because he never took sides,
And no sides
Because he never allowed them to take shape.

He skilfully avoided what was wrong
Without saying what was right,
And never let his on the one hand
Know what his on the other hand was doing.

The height of his ambition
Was to pile a Parliamentary Committee on a Royal
    Commission,
To have "conscription if necessary
But not necessarily conscription,"
To let Parliament decide – ·
Later.

Postpone, postpone, abstain.

Only one thread was certain:
After World War I
Business as usual,
After World War II
Orderly decontrol.
Always he led us back to where we were before.

He seemed to be in the centre
Because we had no centre,
No vision
To pierce the smoke-screen of his politics.

Truly he will be remembered
Wherever men honour ingenuity,
Ambiguity, inactivity, and political longevity.

Let us raise up a temple
To the cult of mediocrity,
Do nothing by halves
Which can be done by quarters.

As Scott notes, it was the conscription crisis of 1944 that allowed King to use ambiguity most adeptly. King knew the dangers to Canada of drafting French Canadians to fight overseas. Although he had promised not to introduce conscription in 1940, he realized its necessity as the war went on. So he advanced the notion slowly, cautiously, and even consulted the people in a national plebiscite in 1942. Even there, memorably, he said that the outcome would not necessarily lead to conscription. Conscription if necessary, he promised, but not necessarily conscription. That gave him latitude. Scott was scalding in his assessment of King, but history less so. Ambiguity was a strategy. As historian Michael Bliss writes in *Right Honourable Men*: "In fact the words were precise, the policy was clear, and the approach sensible. Conscription would divide Canada. King would do it if he found it necessary, but he would not do it unless he found it was absolutely necessary. . . ."

Ambiguity has had other uses in national politics, particularly in the minefield of constitutional reform. In the Quebec referendum of 1980, for example, Pierre Trudeau made three decisive interventions that rallied the flagging federalist forces, reversed the polls, and defeated the secessionists led by René Lévesque. Trudeau offered renewed federalism by promising to amend the British North America Act to satisfy Quebec's long-standing demands. "I know that I can make a most solemn commitment that following a No vote, we will immediately take action to renew the constitution and we will not stop until we have done that." He went on to say that he and his colleagues from Quebec, where the Liberals held all but one seat in the House of Commons, would lay their seats on the line for change. After the referendum was won, and the government introduced a plan to patriate the Constitution with a Charter of Rights and Freedoms, some Quebeckers said they were betrayed by Trudeau's version of renewed federalism. Some accused him of trickery, even fraud. More gently, some called it ambiguity. Asked columnist Marcel Adam of *La Presse*: "Is it conceivable that, being the fine politician he was, he decided, in the circumstances, an ambiguous commitment to reformed federalism might be interpreted in such a way as to turn a vast number of Quebeckers away from the temptation of voting 'yes.'" Adam said "by choosing to be vague," Quebeckers had to interpret what he was saying. Trudeau strongly denied that, arguing that anyone who knew his thoughts on federalism – which were no secret after years as a social critic in Quebec – understood where he was going, even though he had not campaigned for re-election in 1980 on the Constitution (as he had in his losing campaign in 1979). What he might have called ambiguity, others called equivocation.

Of course, constitutions of nations are full of ambiguity because they must stand for years and judges of another time must interpret their meaning far removed from the circumstances that informed the original drafters. One of the reasons the United States Constitution has lasted since 1789 is that it is written with room for interpretation. As a student of the law, Trudeau knew the uses of ambiguity and turned them to his advantage. But when it came to ambiguity in the Meech Lake Accord – the set of constitutional proposals approved by the provinces and the federal government at a lakeside retreat in 1987 – Trudeau was unforgiving. In analyzing the accord, he reserved his harshest judgment for the contentious clause that would recognize Quebec as a "distinct society" within Canada. The big question was what that meant and how it would be manifested. If Quebec were considered a distinct society, would that give the provincial government the right to establish its own regulatory broadcasting commission, for example, or its own foreign policy? Or to encroach upon minority rights? Or, on the other hand, would it mean nothing at all, mere "window-dressing," as the premier of Alberta called it? When the supporters of the Accord argued that it was more symbolic than interpretative – that it was paying deference to a distinctiveness in language and culture, but that the courts would not allow Quebec to expand its authority – Trudeau would have none of it. This kind of legal shading was deadly here, he protested. Either the clause meant something, in which case a separatist government could use it to demand new powers for itself, or it did not, in which case the secessionists would say they had been duped at Meech Lake. In the end, its nuances no longer subtle, its promises no longer ambiguous, the Accord collapsed under Trudeau's relentless, clarifying logic.

Of course, the secessionists who derided Trudeau for his ambiguity in 1980 were not above using ambiguity themselves. Actually, it was less ambiguity than deception. So nebulous were the referendum questions of 1980 and 1995, when the secessionists came within a half point of winning, that the federal government was determined to prevent Quebec from leaving Canada on a trick question. It wanted to ensure that the next time the government of Quebec asked Quebeckers about their future in Canada, there would be a clear question that would have to win the support of a clear majority. Their response was the Clarity Act, which was passed by Parliament in 2000.

But even the Clarity Act, seemingly a foreign agent in our

culture of ambiguity, isn't necessarily clear. While it allows the federal government to refuse to recognize the result of a vote on an unclear question, it doesn't spell out the size of the "clear majority" that would have to support it. Is 50 per cent plus one enough? Is 55 per cent enough, as it was when Montenegro voted to leave Serbia in 2006? Two-thirds, the benchmark for a treaty to be ratified by the United States Senate? Three-quarters, the number of states needed to approve an amendment to the United States Constitution? The bill doesn't say. Joe Clark, then leader of the Progressive Conservative Party, thought that other than that element, the Clarity Act was far too clear. He warned that being too clear would foreclose options for a government in the event the sovereigntists won a referendum. Without such a law, he said, "a government of Canada could consult, delay, negotiate, hold its own referendum, and employ all the other instruments of ingenuity and ambiguity by which previous governments, in previous crises, have kept our country whole." Joe Clark could have been Mackenzie King. So could Stephen Harper. When his government passed a resolution in the House of Commons in late 2006 recognizing that Quebeckers form "a nation," Harper knew that it would mean different things in Quebec and the rest of Canada. He knew that as long as it was not written into law in the Constitution, it would appease nationalists, hearten federalists, and cheer separatists. That is the value of vagueness.

Civility, Generosity, Altruism

It may well be that Canadians are as polite, tolerant, and civil as the stereotype suggests. Certainly they *think* they are; hence the enduring image of "the nice Canadian." Anna (O. Douglas) Buchan, the wife of Governor General John Buchan, found the gentility of Canadians striking. "I maintain, what is the simple truth, that nicer people than the Canadians I never met," she wrote in her memoir, *Unforgettable, Unforgotten* in 1945. "They are forthcoming without being gushing, generous almost to a fault, and the most loyal of friends." This high level of civility in Canadians is something that foreigners from poet Rupert Brooke to writers Alistair Horne and Andrew Malcolm note. Generally speaking, Canada's civic culture confirms it. As we hear *ad nauseam*, Canada is a compassionate society that blunts the hard edges of life. Canada decided a generation or two ago that it would insulate its people from the ravages of the free market by establishing universal health care, old age pensions, a minimum wage, family allowances, unemployment insurance. This is a choice. Universal health care, for example, is one that Americans have rejected, though the programs of the New Deal in the 1930s softened the impact of the Depression. The Canadian social welfare system reflects a philosophy in Canada, which is why it is a better country for the poor than the rich. Indeed, it has become so important that it is now part of our self-image. In an extraordinary sense, empathy has become an emblem. We worship our social programs. It is as if we stand up and say, as a people: "I am Medicare, I am a Canadian." It can be tiresome and self-aggrandizing, and ultimately destructive if it is the end of your ambition. It is the same instinct, though, that allowed Canadians to adopt official bilingualism and liberal immigration. The first showed the evolution of a society that had been insensitive to French Canadians and saw a need to accommodate the language rights of minorities. The second showed the evolution of a society that was at times anti-Semitic, anti-Catholic, and anti-French. It restricted Jews from clubs and schools, put Japanese Canadians in jail, and taxed Chinese immigrants. Canada was small, parochial, prejudiced. It was white and Anglo-Saxon. But it changed, as progressive peoples do, and that spoke to the decency of Canadians.

Yet, in many ways, the nice Canadian isn't always nice. The most proper of peoples loves the most violent of sports; indeed, he sees hockey as a form of self-expression and isn't scandalized by hitting or fighting. His humour is often condescending, biting, and mocking. He allows unacceptable levels of homelessness and child poverty, especially among aboriginal people. In civic culture, decency is often missing. The decorum in the House of Commons is often far from civil; indeed, it can be malicious. In the early 1980s, John Crosbie, the provocative Newfoundlander, called his fellow Atlantic Canadian Allan MacEachen "the gay deceiver." When Crosbie was confronted by a reporter afterwards he affected innocence, though his intention was not lost on MacEachen, who denounced "personal references" in the House. In the fall of 2006, Peter MacKay appeared to refer to his former lover Belinda Stronach, who had left him and his party for the Liberals, as "a dog." It set off ten days of recrimination that sullied the institution. MacKay denied he had actually said "dog" and refused to apologize. No better is the Senate, where the members of a standing committee accused the staff of a senator of spying on them; it was a new low in incivility, said one senator. Neither the Senate of Canada nor the House of Commons is the Legislature of Taiwan, where members have been known to punch one another, but Parliament is not a seat of civility, either.

One measure of incivility is the way former leaders treat each other. Unlike former presidents of the United States – whose respect for the office leavens personal antagonisms toward each other – former prime ministers know no such constraint. They are not former heads of state, with the dignity and pageantry that that confers. They do not retain their title when their service is over. The prime ministry isn't the presidency; the office isn't greater than the man. Indeed, the prime ministry imposes no such inhibitions on those who have held it. Which may be why Canada has a sordid history of hostility between former prime ministers, even those of the same party. Their relations over the last generation or so, while different in tone and intensity, have not been tempered by a code of conduct, let alone respect.

John Diefenbaker and Lester Pearson, for example, despised each other. They glared at each other across the floor of the House of Commons for almost ten years as leaders (switching sides in 1963 when Pearson became prime minister and Diefenbaker became Opposition leader). This is the prime reason prime ministers develop mutual antipathy; invariably they have a history in the Commons. Diefenbaker, for his part, was petty and pompous. He resented Pearson's fame, his urbanity, and his politics. That Pearson could pass Diefenbaker a note of thanks in 1957 for defending the honour of E.H. Norman, the diplomat who had jumped to his death in Cairo amid harsh allegations from Washington that he was a Communist ("John – I have been deeply touched by your words – and I want to thank you very sincerely for them . . .") cut no ice with Diefenbaker. For his part, Pearson could be determined, even ruthless, though historian J.L. Granatstein thinks Pearson was "a much more decent and honourable man than John Diefenbaker." When Pearson died in 1972, Peter C. Newman recalls that Diefenbaker seemed to dance on Pearson's grave. Learning that Pearson had suffered from jaundice before his death, Diefenbaker telephoned his wife and exclaimed, nonsensically: "Olive, he's as *green as a beet.*"

Despite their political differences, Brian Mulroney came to office in 1984 with a favourable impression of Pierre Trudeau, with whom he had clashed in his few months facing the prime minister across the floor. It was said that Trudeau saw Mulroney, not John Turner, as his natural successor; he believed that Mulroney was a stronger federalist. Turner felt betrayed by Trudeau, who had left Turner to make a number of contentious political and diplomatic appointments that gave Mulroney ammunition to bombard him on patronage during the election campaign that summer. Mulroney, for his part, was sanguine about Trudeau. "You've got to hand it to the old Trude," he said, "he's really got style." At first Mulroney wanted to use Trudeau in a public way on international questions, but Trudeau was uninterested. Whatever goodwill there was between them was destroyed by the Meech Lake Accord, which Trudeau savaged in an essay in French and English newspapers in May 1987. "What a magician this Mr. Mulroney is," he railed, "and what a sly fox!" His pen dripping with sarcasm, he called Mulroney "this clever negotiator" who had sold out the country. "Alas, only one eventuality had not been foreseen: that one day the government of Canada might fall into the hands of a wimp. It has now happened." Later, he would call Mulroney "a sniveller" and "a constitutional pyromaniac." For Trudeau, Mulroney would develop a burning antipathy. He took his attack very personally. He had a list of grievances against Trudeau he generously shared with Peter C. Newman, who was gathering material for a biography he never wrote. Trudeau was "a coward and a weakling" whose fiscal irresponsibility "left the single worst record of any country in the history of an industrialized nation." Or, he was "that son of a bitch Trudeau" who personally vetoed the idea of a royal commission on war criminals. "The damage that he did in his last term may turn out to be irreparable." When Newman asked if they ever saw each other, Mulroney said: "I ran into him once – he was having lunch with (Senator Michael) Pitfield. As a former prime minister you have to be civil, that's all . . ."

Mulroney's view of his predecessors and his successors was scathing. He was angry that Joe Clark, whom he had unseated as leader in 1983, had never invited him to dinner at Stornoway during Clark's seven years as Opposition leader. "I always treated Joe Clark with the greatest of respect," he said, though in private he was telling Newman that he considered Clark inept and weak. "His greatest success was in persuading the Ottawa press gallery that he's a humble, modest guy," said Mulroney. "He's anything but." Mulroney called John Turner "a poor bugger" who had "more bitterness and malice in him than I have ever seen in anybody." That was generous given what Mulroney had to say of Jean Chrétien, his successor: "I have never in my whole life seen anybody less well equipped to lead a great national party or to become prime minister of Canada than this guy." Mulroney told Newman that he was astounded that Chrétien could renounce his promise to repeal the Goods and Services Tax and the North American Free Trade Agreement: "Only a mean, dirty bastard would do something like that, or a fucking stupid one. And you know what? He's both. And he's sucking in this bunch of assholes in the press gallery in Ottawa." It was apparent the antipathy was mutual when Chrétien showed no great concern that the RCMP investigated Mulroney's alleged role in the Airbus affair but brought no charges.

Turner and Chrétien didn't like each other, either. Former Newfoundland premier Frank Moores went fishing with Chrétien not long after he had lost the leadership to Turner in 1984 and reported that "he really hates Turner with a passion." Chrétien left Parliament and undermined Turner, who put down a revolt in the leadership review in 1986 and then resigned the leadership in 1990 after losing two elections. When Chrétien said nice things about Turner at the leadership convention in Calgary, there was so much bad blood that Turner's wife, Geills, could be heard hissing from her seat, "Oh, shut up, Jean!"

Though Liberals both, the tradition of hostility between prime ministers reached new heights with Jean Chrétien and Paul Martin. Although Chrétien had made Martin his finance minister in 1993, Martin was always uneasy and mounted a *coup d'état* that pushed out Chrétien. The former prime minister could not forgive him. It ignited a civil war in the Liberal Party that stained Martin's two feckless years in office. Their personal relations were so bad that when both men attended the funeral of former cabinet minister Mitchell Sharp, they could not look at each other. Their smouldering antagonism pitted Liberal against Liberal and contributed to Martin's defeat in 2006, which ended his political career. His flameout would make him the Anthony Eden of Canadian politics.

It may not always have been this way among all prime ministers. Joe Clark always said that Pierre Trudeau treated him with respect, and Clark responded in kind. Diefenbaker was contemptuous of Trudeau, but Trudeau admired Diefenbaker. He cried at his funeral. "I love that old man," he said. There is some kindness among prime ministers, but not much.

Is this antipathy between leaders peculiarly Canadian? Probably not. But it is entirely foreign to politics as practised by the Americans, to whom Canadians like to contrast themselves. It is encouraging, for example, to watch Bill Clinton and George H. Bush, whom Clinton defeated after one term in 1992, travelling together to raise money for AIDS or for the victims of the Asian Tsunami. Harry Truman asked Herbert Hoover to lead a commission on hunger after the Second World War. John F. Kennedy called Dwight Eisenhower and Harry Truman for advice. So did Lyndon Johnson. Ronald Reagan praised the leadership of Kennedy. Clinton invited all his predecessors to the White House. Jimmy Carter gave the eulogy at Gerald Ford's funeral. It isn't to say that presidents always like each other or don't see an advantage in maintaining good relations. But it is telling how the nation's highest office imposes a civility upon those who have held it. In Canada, it does not.

And if former prime ministers do not treat each other well, it may because Canadians don't treat them well, either. By and large we consider former politicians losers. We don't value their public service. Many of them struggle to re-establish careers in private life after they leave politics, and many, if not most, would have been better off financially had they never entered politics. Former prime ministers come in for a benign disdain. Joe Clark, who served for nine months in 1979 and 1980, said that we have denigrated public life beyond anything he could have imagined. "It's almost as if you are being penalized for your service," he told Roy MacGregor of *The Globe and Mail* in 2007. Kim Campbell, who served for a few months before her crushing defeat in 1993, said public service is respected in other countries but "it's not honoured in this country." Brian Mulroney, who won two consecutive majorities in the 1980s, said "in Canada, if you lose anything, you become a pariah." They are not wrong. It doesn't mean that former leaders become lepers or paupers; Mulroney has become wealthy out of office. But Campbell, who was not rich, was happy to accept an appointment as Consul General to Los Angeles when Jean Chrétien graciously offered it in 1994, and Joe Clark was happy to serve Mulroney when he made him foreign minister in 1984. But the idea that the country would value their counsel, seek their expertise, or put them to work – well, in Canada, we just don't do that.

Are Canadians generous, in terms of charity? If foreign aid is one measure, the answer is no. At least not today. A generation ago Canada was one of the world's top ten nations in international assistance. In the last decade or so, however, the country has fallen into the bottom ranks of the world's leading donors. In 2002, its nadir, Canada was nineteenth of the world's twenty-three leading nations in terms of international giving. While Canada was committing as little as 0.22 per cent of its gross domestic product to foreign aid a few years ago, today Canada gives about 0.32 per cent. But it is still below the average of leading donors. Worse, it is only slightly more than half the level in 1975–76 and well below the international standard of 0.7 per cent set by Lester Pearson and an international blue-ribbon commission created by the World Bank in 1969. Ever since, governments of both stripes have promised to reach 0.7. Canada never has. Ironically, one of the biggest supporters of aid was Paul Martin, who even solicited the support of Bono, the outspoken rock star. In 2005, in an audacious betrayal,

Martin announced that Canada would not make a commitment to reach 0.7 per cent. It was a surprising reversal that was reversed in turn by the Conservatives when they came to power in 2006. They recommitted Canada to reach 0.7 but set no date. Riding the strongest economy in recent years, throwing off billions of dollars in budgetary surpluses, Canada could still set no timetable to reach the goal that Norway, Sweden, Denmark, Luxembourg, and the Netherlands had reached or surpassed. Or the figure that six countries (Belgium, Britain, France, Finland, Ireland, and Spain) have committed to reach by 2015. Instead, Canada preferred to talk about its generosity. Our refusal to embrace 0.7 is a moral failure.

Individually, Canadians are said to be "extremely generous," as the head of a major Canadian charity put it. No doubt many are, especially in a crisis. The biggest donors are the working poor, who give the largest percentage of their wealth, 1.7 per cent. As a nation, Canada's response to the famine in Ethiopia in 1984 (particularly the Inuit, who gave a disproportionate amount) or to the Asian Tsunami in 2004 was magnanimous. When floods, fires, or natural disasters happen, Canadians respond. Statistically, figures from 2004 suggest that more Canadians (5.6 million in 2003) are giving, and in absolute terms, their total contributions ($6.5 billion) are rising. More wealthy Canadians are establishing foundations and endowing cultural, scientific, and medical institutions, some bearing their names. There is an aristocracy of philanthropy. In 2006, Peter Munk gave $37 million to Toronto General Hospital, the largest donation ever to a Canadian hospital; he also gave $6 million to the Munk Centre for International Studies at the University of Toronto. Richard Li, the son of Li Ka-shing, attended a gala for the National Arts Centre Foundation in Ottawa in the fall of 2006 and agreed to match what the gala had raised with his own contribution of $1 million. Lawrence Tanenbaum donated $50 million to the United Jewish Appeal and $25 million to Mount Sinai Hospital in Toronto. Michael Audain of Vancouver gave

$2 million to the National Gallery of Canada. Jean Coutu, the entrepreneur and pharmacist, spends millions fighting poverty and illiteracy in the Third World, among other causes. There are others.

Generous as they are, these do not represent a benevolent elite in Canada. (In fact, the percentage of giving falls as income rises. Those earning over $60,000 give only 0.5 per cent of their income.) There is a lot of wealth in Canada and not enough goes to charity. According to *Canadian Business*, Canada has about forty-six billionaires. The collective wealth of the one hundred richest Canadians was $153.7 billion, in 2006. The five richest men in the country are Galen Weston ($9.2 billion); James, Arthur, and John Irving ($5.3 billion); Jeff Skoll ($5 billion); Jim Pattison ($4.5 billion); and Paul Desmarais ($4.2 billion). Do they and others worth less make charitable donations commensurate with their wealth? We know that some give away some money, but how much?

The question came into sharp focus upon the death of Kenneth Thomson on June 12, 2006. The richest man in Canada, the ninth richest in the world, Thomson had a personal fortune of around $19 billion. The obituaries hailed the nice, quiet, bland, self-effacing, "fundamentally decent man," as Peter C. Newman remembered him. Thomson was sharp, shrewd, and vulpine in business. His eccentricities were tearfully recounted, his walks with his dog, his love of family. It was all very polite, because we don't speak ill of the dead, less so of the wealthy dead. One of the notices recalled, two years earlier, Thomson's "breathtaking act of generosity" in giving his art collection to the Art Gallery of Ontario. It was valued at $320 million and it came with $70 million for a new building to house it. Conrad Black could write of Thomson's "philanthropic scale" as if it were beyond measure. Actually, that wasn't so.

Two weeks later, Warren Buffett announced that he was giving away US$31 billion, about 85 per cent of his fortune. Here was one of the world's richest men, the genius of Omaha, Nebraska, no less unassuming and homespun than Kenneth Thomson. And here was an entirely new order of philanthropy. We didn't need Warren Buffett to show us what generosity is, but it helped. Buffett had what Thomson lacked – a social conscience, a sense of obligation, an understanding of the wages of wealth. No one would say that in Canada when he died. *The Globe and Mail* dutifully turned over an entire section to his memory, running grandiloquent tributes from its publisher and editor. This is what a newspaper does when its proprietor dies. His competitors, though, were equally deferential. About how he ran his string of papers, about how small and poor they were in quality, there was nothing. And his legendary parsimony? Well, when it was mentioned, it was just an amiable eccentricity.

We expect hosannas from the editors of *The Globe and Mail* and curator of the Art Gallery of Ontario; to speak ill of your boss and benefactor would be foolish, as well as impolite. But it was typical of the deference of the media in Canada to lionize Thomson as it did. And it brought to mind something else: when Bill Gates was worth some US$50 billion or so in the giddy 1990s and announced that he would give away half of his wealth, a full-throated chorus of naysayers in the United States told him that no, it wasn't enough. He would have to do more. And Gates was persuaded to be even more generous. Now his foundation will give away all but millions of his money. It is a wonderful thing to see Gates talking about what he hopes to do to battle AIDS in Africa after he steps down as chair of Microsoft and turns full-time to philanthropy. He and others face social rebuke if they don't give; it's part of the culture. Not in Canada. Thomson never talked of philanthropy, at least in a real way, or giving away 85 per cent of his money. In fact, when congratulated for his gift to the AGO, he denied that he was a philanthropist and told a petitioner not to use that term in describing him. Actually, he said he was just looking for a place to keep his paintings. It was frank – and sad. He never talked publicly of giving away 50 per cent of his wealth. Or 25 per cent. Or 5 per cent. Or 1 per cent. And when he didn't, there was no one of stature in Canada to challenge him. There was no one to ask if he had any understanding of the obligations of money, that strange octogenarian in the cardigan sweater walking his dog around the neighbourhood and buying hot dogs buns on sale at the corner store. But, oh, when he gave away his art collection – for which he presumably got a tax receipt – he was the Deity of Charity. The applause spoke of the nature of philanthropy in Canada, which is still seen more as beneficence than duty.

Newman called Thomson "the quintessential Canadian." If charity is the criterion, let's hope not. In philanthropy, Canadians are not Thomson, but they aren't Americans, either, who donate two and a half to three times more of their time and money to charity. According to one study, Americans donate 1.67 per cent of their aggregate income, Canadians donate 0.72 per cent. Skeptics will say it is not a fair comparison and to a degree they are right. The generational accumulation of wealth, the size of the economy, and the incentives of the taxation system have created a culture of giving in the United States. It doesn't really exist in Canada, "a nation of hit-and-run millionaires," as business tycoon and philanthropist Christopher Ondaatje describes them. One of our problems is our reticence. Like the fourth son of the Jewish Haggadah, who does not know how to ask, we are reluctant to appeal for money and when we do, we are too ready to take no for an answer. We are poorer for it.

Our civility is not without its dangers. It makes us blissfully detached. We are not given to anger about much of anything. No one got mad at Kenneth Thomson. No one shook his fist in his face and attacked his miserliness or how he treated the employees of his newspapers. We are easy on people here. We don't ask much and we don't hold them responsible. The allegations and charges of fraud against Alan Eagleson, the former head of the NHL Players' Association, originated in the United States. He was initially indicted there, as was Conrad Black, who was still warmly applauded in the fall of 2006, when he addressed the Empire Club of Canada and was invited often to share his thoughts in the country's newspapers. Indeed, in 2007, the *Literary Review of Canada* asked him to review Margaret MacMillan's fine new book on Richard Nixon's visit to China, and was obviously unconcerned when he declared at the outset that his long friendship with the author would make him incapable of speaking ill of the book; it was as if, in the face of wealth and power, we are too ready to defer, retreat, and suspend the rules (friends don't review books of friends). Brian Mulroney has never satisfactorily explained why he accepted three hundred thousand dollars in cash, in hotel rooms, in meetings with Karlheinz Schreiber only months after he left office in 1993. More troubling, we have never forced him to explain; Canadians were more agitated over the mountain of shoes in his closet than the notion that a former prime minister had received cash from a man from whom he had been accused of taking bribes while he was prime minister. When WestJet admitted to stealing corporate information from Air Canada in 2006, which looked and smelled like a criminal act, it agreed to apologize and make a charitable contribution. That was all. Are we too civil for our own good? Do we take moderation to extremes?

The contributors to Irvin Studin's anthology could not cover the many splendours of the Canadian personality, much as they tried. They understood, all did, that what it means to be a Canadian is the existential question of Canada. It is the search for ourselves, relentless, endless, Sisyphean. Even in the country's 140th year, Canadians take strange comfort knowing that the question will always give a self-absorbed people something to discuss, should they ever exhaust the Constitution, the United States, medicare, hockey, and winter. It is the way of the Chameleon Canadian.

Chapter 8

The Future Canadian

In the autumn of 2005, John Ibbitson sent a valentine to Canada. He put it in a red-and-white envelope called *The Polite Revolution: Perfecting the Canadian Dream* and sealed it with a Maple Leaf. Ibbitson, a journalist, novelist, and playwright, asked Canadians to look beyond the distemper of their politics and recognize themselves as a great people. His book rested on an eloquent argument that resonates from his opening sentence: "Sometime, not too long ago, while no one was watching, Canada became the world's most successful country." To Ibbitson, the purveyor of superlatives, Canadians are the successful people.

In the spring of 2006, Michael Ignatieff announced his candidacy for the leadership of the Liberal Party of Canada. "Sometimes you only see your country when you are far away," he said, referring to his twenty-eight years living in Britain and the United States. After a life travelling the world exploring nationalism, democracy, and human rights, he found Canada "a serious country," an adjective he repeated six times in his address. To Ignatieff, the chronicler of nations, Canadians are the serious people.

Here, then, is the land of the successful and the serious and unafraid to say it. "The world needs more Canada," declares a leading national bookseller, belying any traditional claim to modesty and inhibition. We are no longer "the unknown country" of journalist Bruce Hutchison in the 1940s or "the voiceless country" of poet Douglas LePan in the 1960s. Today, more Canadians wave the Maple Leaf at hockey games and wear it on backpacks and bikinis. Cloying politicians enthuse about "the Canadian Way," as Paul Martin did in coming to the aid of the victims of the Asian Tsunami in 2004, reminding everyone of our generosity and compassion. On Canada Day, 2005, a visiting Dutchman winced at the orgy of tub-thumping and chest-beating on Parliament Hill; it reminded him of torch-lit nationalist rallies in Europe. Often falsely, Canadians have come to see themselves as a country of international stature – a leading economy, a leading peacekeeper, a leading donor. When, for several years in the 1990s, the annual surveys of the United Nations found Canada the world's most desirable place to live (we have now slipped to fifth), Canadians and their leaders seized upon it with a self-confidence and pride once unimaginable.

Historically, Canada is a *parvenu* among nations. For most of our existence we have lived in contented isolation – "alive, but not kicking," as Rupert Brooke put it. Let the United States, Great Britain, France, Russia, Italy, China, and Japan shape the modern world, not us. Up to not that long ago the impact of Canada on art, music, literature, science, philosophy, and diplomacy was modest. We didn't map the polar regions, like the Norwegians and the British, or explore space, like the Russians and the Americans, or circumnavigate the globe, like the Spanish and the Portuguese, or unlock the secrets of mathematics, like the Germans. We didn't write like the French or the Irish. The French coined the term *japonisme* to describe the influence of the Japanese on the West in the nineteenth century and *le tumulte noir* in the twentieth century to describe the impact of black culture on France. As Brian Moore tells us, no one, not even Canadians themselves, were speaking of Canadianism, let alone *le tumulte Canadien*.

We were too busy striving and surviving. This country was big but small, a cultural and intellectual backwater. "I wondered why I felt so bitter about Canada," mused Norman Levine, the expatriate who visited Canada in 1956 after leaving it to live in England a few years earlier. He chronicled his cross-country odyssey in a savage account called *Canada Made Me*. "After all, it was part of a dream, an experiment that could not come off. It was foolish to believe that you can take the throwouts, the rejects, the human kickabouts from Europe and tell them: Here you have a second chance. Here you can start a new life. But no one ever mentioned the price one had to pay; how much of oneself you had to betray." In 1978, Robert Fulford, the esteemed editor of *Saturday Night*, discovered that Canadian culture was unknown beyond Canada. It lived in a vacuum above the forty-ninth parallel. "We think we are in history, but history doesn't think we are in it," he wrote.

So much is Canada an exemplar today, we like to think, that if it did not exist we would have to invent it. That wasn't always so. Until the mid-twentieth century, Canada was the world's wall-flower. We had no influence as a conduit of ideas or an instrument of innovation. We had no *mission civilisatrice* like France and no Manifest Destiny like America. We were a dominion, earnest and modest, not an empire.

As Alistair Horne remarked, a demagogue of the ilk of the red-baiting Joe McCarthy (the misguided Wisconsin senator of the 1950s), or the wealth-sharing Huey Long (the corrupt Louisiana governor of the 1930s), is unlikely to spring from our midst. That isn't to say that we haven't had our demons. If Horne had looked more closely while he was visiting Canada in 1958, he would have seen the authoritarian regime of Maurice Duplessis, the head-strong premier of Quebec, and the soft anti-Semitism that created the "Jewish quota" at McGill University. A quarter century later, in 1981, Horne would have heard Bharati Mukherjee, the elegant Indian writer, lament the quiet racism in the 1960s and 1970s that drove her to the United States. Horne hailed "the good sense and goodness" of a people that would never produce a Hitler or a Stalin; it isn't us. Will we produce a Churchill or a Roosevelt? Not likely. That isn't us, either.

So let's be honest with ourselves. This country is bigger than we are. Ralph Waldo Emerson once called nineteenth-century America a poem in search of a poet. Canada is still a promise in search of a people. Successful, serious, and self-congratulatory that we are, we have still not created a spirit worthy of this blessed place. At the end of the day, with ruthless frankness and exquisite truthfulness, we can look into our soul and say this of ourselves: Canada isn't a great country but it is a *good* country. And good isn't bad when it becomes better.

Better. We have always tried to be better. Once upon a time Canada was mostly rural, agrarian, white, Christian, French and English. Once we harboured prejudices toward those of different faith, colour, and region, though never as deep as those of other peoples. Once we had no citizenship, no flag, no anthem, no high court of last resort, no citizens' honours, no charter of rights. Once we hid in our "fireproof house," as Senator Raoul Dandurand called Canada in the 1920s, we went to war when others went to war, we were invisible in the councils of the world.

Countries change. Character changes. Canada has always been comfortable with change. So it is today. We do not live unwashed by the currents of contemporary thought. We're not the nomads of old, lost in the folds of the African desert. Today we are in the slipstream of the modern world; some would say that we *are* the slipstream. It is why the face of Canada is black and white, living in cities, speaking many tongues, worshipping many gods – or none at all. What André Siegfried saw in 1908 and Andrew Malcolm saw in 1985 is a world away. Our much-vaunted deference to authority, for example, has faded; our deep-seated attachment to the land has diminished. We are now the urban Canadian and the defiant Canadian. Yet our fondness for compromise, ambiguity, and moderation endures. So does self-doubt, whatever our declarations. The beliefs of Robert Baldwin and Louis-Hippolyte Lafontaine and their commitment to democracy and responsible government 175 years ago find an echo among us today. We still do not covet colonies or fight wars of conquest. We still value peace and order and we hope (but do not expect) that contentment flows from it. We still dislike public malfeasance. The extremism of gnarled, old prejudices – excluding the Jews, taxing the Chinese, interning the Italians and Ukrainians – is gone today.

The Unconscious Canadian, the American Canadian, the Casual Canadian, the Capital Canadian, and the Chameleon Canadian are the people we are. But none is necessarily the Future Canadian. No law decrees that we ignore our past, devalue our citizenship, begrudge success, or accept mediocrity. Nowhere is it written that commercial Ottawa must look like the Valley of Ashes or that citizens must denigrate their politicians. There is nothing in our genetic code that says Canada's wealthy must be miserly or that we must abjure heroes or thrive on *schadenfreude*.

How to become a more self-confident, more accomplished people? How to fashion ourselves to make a new claim on the twenty-first century – or to ensure that we survive it? Dear Canadians, there are ways. There are always ways.

We can begin by rediscovering our past. We can no longer afford to be ahistorical. It is time for the serious country to get serious about teaching its history. We can do this in a progressive way, introducing Canada's past to students in primary school and carrying it through secondary school. A solid grounding in history and civics would expose young Canadians to their rich national experience. As J.L. Granatstein and others have recommended, we should have national standards for teaching history across the country – a clear expression of what any student, anywhere, should know by the time he or she graduates from high school. Having taught the basics, let a hundred stories flower, be they regional history, immigrant history, women's history, or labour history. Introducing national standards in history should be part of transferring education to federal jurisdiction, as it is in other leading industrialized states. Those who have grown up here and those who arrive here must understand our foundational beliefs.

Outside the classroom, there are encouraging signs. Among them are the restoration of Pier 21 in Halifax, where immigrants arrived between 1928 and 1971, and the success in English Canada of the *Heritage Minutes*, the sixty-second television mini-films illuminating our past commissioned by the Historica Foundation. The work of Historica, under the leadership of Colin Robertson, a spirited former diplomat, has been superb. So has that of the Dominion Institute. Its "Memory Project" has preserved the stories of Canada's war veterans. Because of the institute's lobbying, the federal government will bury the last veteran of the Great War (assuming his family agrees) with a state funeral. Let's not stop there. We should hold a state funeral for the last veteran of the Second World War, too, and make a national holiday of April 12, the anniversary of the Battle of Vimy Ridge, where 3,598 Canadians died. Call it Vimy Day, which means something to Canadians, and drop Victoria Day, which no longer does. At the same time, on December 11, we should mark the passage of the Statute of Westminster in 1931.

Saving Canada's forts, churches, ancestral homes, and factories, as the auditor general has recommended, should be another priority. It is gratifying that the government has committed money to repair the National Arts Centre, the National Gallery, and other institutions. But the aware nation needs to observe as much as conserve. One way is to establish a program to identify the graves of *all* Canadians of stature. A place to start, for example, is those of three luminous diplomats – Hume Wrong, Norman Robertson, Escott Reid – who lie beside Lester Pearson, their friend and colleague, at

MacLaren's Cemetery, above the village of Wakefield, Quebec. Another imperative is to save jewels such as the dignified Alma College for Ladies in St. Thomas, Ontario. Why not create the National Trust of Canada, modelled on the venerable British charity independent of government, which preserves parkland, gardens, homes, and other properties of historical or cultural significance? The cost of losing them is too high for a country with too little physical history. We must learn to become custodians of the national heritage. We can be very good at this; the recent restoration of the Library of Parliament is resplendent. It is the most beautiful room in Canada.

With restoring old things comes creating new ones. There is some hope here. While the Canadian History Centre is dead, the Canadian War Museum lives, rising triumphantly from a grassy escarpment in the shadow of the Parliament Buildings. Meanwhile, the Canadian Museum of Civilization is planning to open a permanent gallery in 2007 to celebrate the achievements of twenty-five great Canadians. The creation of a new museum and the enhancement of an old one are a step forward. Another would be to abolish admission fees for all our major museums, especially those in the national capital. (In Britain, attendance at national museums has risen an average of 83 per cent since fees were lifted in 2001. In Washington, none of the museums and galleries of the Smithsonian charge admission.) At the same time, we must support the smaller museums around the country. Wherever they are, visiting museums and galleries should be part of the educational curriculum for all schoolchildren. A national portrait gallery is also fundamental to telling our story. Its place is in the national capital, not in Calgary, however welcoming that kicking city. To establish the gallery outside Ottawa, in the headquarters of a corporation, diminishes its purpose. With a national portrait gallery, a renewed Canadian Museum of Civilization, a new museum policy, the elimination of museum admission fees, the establishment of national standards for teaching history, and the preservation and identification of our physical past, Canada might begin to remember again.

How to have a more mature relationship with the United States? It begins with understanding. A poll in November 2006 found that almost a quarter of Canadians think that we are fighting in Afghanistan to please the Americans. George W. Bush is an easy mark, and Canadians have reason to distrust him. But Bush will not be president forever (the next president, from either party, may well come from the Midwest or Northeast, which know us better). That antipathy colours our view of Americans. "Canada has a prime minister who thinks the United States is not only our ally, but also our model," Stéphane Dion told the Liberal Party on December 1, 2006. His remark illustrates the immaturity of our attitude toward the United States. Promoting a greater awareness among Canadians of Americans, through a more vigorous commitment to social and educational exchanges, would help. Persuaded that we know America, universities have been slow to establish programs and courses on the United States. The University of Western Ontario and the University of Alberta have established new centres of American studies. The Foundation for Educational Exchange between Canada and the United States of America has also tried to promote a dialogue.

In our distaste for the misadventure in Iraq and the ineptitude of the president, Canadians forget the America of Franklin D. Roosevelt and Harry S. Truman, who introduced the Marshall Plan and helped create the institutional architecture of the postwar era, in which Canada played a part. We forget that Eleanor Roosevelt chaired the committee at the United Nations that crafted the Universal Declaration of Human Rights. It was drafted by her colleague, John Humphrey, a former professor of law at McGill University. In December 2008, the sixtieth anniversary of this seminal document, let us honour the contribution of both

Mrs. Roosevelt and Professor Humphrey, especially their commitment to democracy and human rights. A small way is to establish a museum to them in the binational Roosevelt Park on Campobello Island in New Brunswick, where Professor Humphrey was born and Mrs. Roosevelt summered. When we convince ourselves about our diverging values, let us remember the values we share, too.

Ultimately, Canadians will become less wary of Americans – and less vulnerable to the narcissism of small differences – when we become more confident of ourselves. Dion was half right: the United States *is* our ally, and it isn't solely because of geography and history. Canada is blessed to have America as a neighbour. And in many ways it *is* our model. We can learn much from its ambition, its genius, its enterprise and its excellence, some of which it is now demonstrating in innovative ways on the environment. The challenge is knowing what to take and what to leave, recognizing that the bed we share with the Americans is the one we ourselves have made.

A mature people understands their dependence and either tries to diminish it or comes to accept it. The latter surely doesn't mean embracing Pax Americana or taking out dual citizenship, as did Alanis Morissette, the singer from Ottawa who now happily calls herself a "Canadian-American." It means understanding that sovereignty means never having to say you're sorry. As Canadians, we can say no to the Americans, whether it is to the deportation of Maher Arar or the folly of Iraq. And we should, vigorously. Or, we can say yes to the Americans, whether it is Afghanistan or the border. America is the land of the superlative and Canada is the land of the comparative, and we understand the difference. A self-aware people understands that no two peoples in the world are as alike as Canadians and Americans and says of their insecurity: *get over it*. One day the American Canadian will.

Restoring meaning to our citizenship may be easier than trying to reverse our Ameri-skepticism. If we do believe that there is a problem with our citizenship – that we offer too much for too little – then it is time to re-examine it. To begin, we should make citizenship harder to acquire, less a right than a privilege. Extend the waiting period from three to six years; ensure applicants absorb the principles of this country and speak one of the official languages; strengthen the knowledge and language test; rewrite the oath to reflect real obligation. With a Charter of Rights should come a Charter of Responsibilities (a proposal explored creatively by Randolph Gherson, a former Canadian diplomat). We are not alone in revisiting this. The United States is revamping its citizenship tests to make them less about dates and facts and more about the country's fundamental principles. Britain has recently added language and citizenship tests. Australia is considering tougher language requirements and a harder quiz on history and culture to create what John Howard, its prime minister, calls "a strong and compelling national identity." Canada should follow suit.

As for dual citizenship, we need to know more about its costs and benefits. Abolishing it would be problematic as long as other countries allow it. In addition, landed immigrants might be discouraged from becoming Canadians, fostering a permanent community of exiles here. Imposing tougher requirements on residency or making citizens living abroad pay taxes may be an option. Charging them more for passports would offset the cost of the benefits of citizenship, such as the consular services citizens expect in foreign countries. Much of the challenge here is taking citizenship seriously. That means deepening and enhancing our commitment to Canada, so that holding dual citizenship is not even a consideration for those holding high office, especially the governor general and the prime minister.

Making citizenship more difficult to attain does not mean that we have any less responsibility to those who acquire it. Our challenge is making new Canadians feel at home in Canada and aware of the nature of their adopted country. Too many are left on their own and fail. Robert Putnam, the respected American sociologist and author of *Bowling Alone*, finds that growing immigration and large-scale diversity are leading people to "hunker down" and "act like turtles." Society is fragmenting. Celebrating Bollywood in Toronto or a television series like *Little Mosque on the Prairie* is wonderful as long as it promotes understanding, not segregation. The answer to alienation is public education and the celebration of civic culture. One instrument is the Institute for Canadian Citizenship, in Toronto, founded by Adrienne Clarkson and John Ralston Saul, which promotes the values and principles of the country. Theirs and other organizations help immigrants find a place in our society. And find a place they should – bringing with them their spirit, energy, and idealism. It also means leaving behind their hatreds and prejudices. We do not want those here, and we should be unafraid to say so, clearly and forcefully.

Too many new Canadians are staying too long in Yann Martel's Hotel Canada, reluctant to leave their comfortable, well-appointed rooms. We risk becoming a nation of agoraphobics, living in fear of venturing out into a national commons. We must create more public space. Our imperative isn't to restrict immigration but to manage it. This may mean directing immigrants to settle in places other than Metropolitan Toronto, which is attracting most of them. It may mean asking tougher questions and demanding longer residency. If the road to Canada's New Jerusalem lies through Little India and Chinatown, let us understand that it may be long, rough, steep, and narrow. And if living in Canada is winning the lottery, as Jan Morris says, why not charge more for a ticket?

There are other ways to foster a new patriotism. One is mandatory public service. Sometime in their adult lives, Canadians should serve in the military or in the Canada Corps, which was established with high hopes in 2004. Or they should work in a hospital, a hospice, a women's or homeless shelter. The point is to serve the country and understand the country. Community service, which is now demanded in some high schools, is the way. Isn't this the time to do this? Other ways to deepen loyalty to Canada is to make July 1 Dominion Day again and to declare a national holiday on February 15, the day the Maple Leaf flag was first flown in 1965. Heritage Day, as it might be called, would fall between New Year's Day and Good Friday, in the dead of the Canadian winter. All this would comprise a new civic liturgy.

It is important, as well, to foster pride in our national capital. It is one thing to fix cultural institutions. It is another to build new ones. There is much to be done. Develop the historic character of Victoria Island, and other parts of the glorious Ottawa River, as educational and recreational venues. Declare a moratorium on unsightly office buildings and pedestrian apartment houses downtown and invite architects to imagine a grander Ottawa. Invest in beauty, a useful credo for all those Canadian cities that we have assaulted with ugly bridges, underpasses, expressways, and towers. Ensure that embassies are not built helter-skelter and that our best friends have pride of place. Mark the homes of former prime ministers and other notables with explanatory plaques and create neighbourhood walking tours around them. Display the country's founding documents – the British North America Act and the Charter of Rights and Freedoms – in Library and Archives Canada on Wellington Street. Make it possible for every child to come to Ottawa during their school years and pay for part of their trip by raising money in their communities. All this would help Canadians see Ottawa as theirs, as proud, conscious citizens.

You cannot tell a people to be less envious and suspicious of success, or more generous in praise and encouragement. But we can make civic life more civil. Politicians can be shown more respect, particularly when it comes to their salaries and their expense accounts, which they should not have to post on the Web. The media does not have to report every misspent penny as if it were our last, making the auditor general's annual report an orgy of recrimination. For their part, politicians do not have to make a virtue of criticizing every repair to official residences, which are now getting some of the work they need. They do not have to insult each other in the House of Commons and they should learn to apologize. There are civilized ways of doing things. We are a rich country. We can afford generosity.

A compassionate Canada has created a society of universal health care, social welfare, and regional equalization. It is a choice this country made. But generosity doesn't end there. It is time that Canada had the most imaginative foreign aid program in the world. While we are increasing international assistance at 8 per cent a year, we have set no target for reaching 0.7 per cent of gross domestic product, the international standard. It is unconscionable – immoral, really – that we have not. We are a trillion-dollar economy, wealthier than we have ever been. Before we erase the budgetary surplus through lower taxes, let us remember our obligations to others. At the same time, we can be more generous at home. As the number of billionaires grows in Canada, so do their obligations. It will take a sea change to alter the ethos of giving in Canada, where we are afraid to ask for money. More tax incentives are a way to begin, yes, but start with the idea that great wealth should be shared. Many of our wealthy realize this and have been magnanimous; too many have not. We should accost them, implore them, shame them. We criticize many things in Canada, but we rarely give our reluctant rich a hard time. We should.

Let us do better, as well, in celebrating excellence and using talent. It is time that we inscribe the names of the greatest of our men and women in the Hall of Honour of Parliament, distinguishing between the bona fide Canadian hero and the ersatz Canadian Idol. After all, that was its purpose. The governor general should establish an annual award for Canadians who do exemplary work abroad. The government, as an institution, should form an advisory body to draw upon the expertise of former prime ministers in all manner of ways; the same could be done for senior public servants. The government should look for ways to restore the lustre of the civil service. The members of the Order of Canada, one of the country's sterling institutions, should choose the governor general (who should become Canada's *de jure* head of state when the Queen dies). This would confer credibility on the appointee and avoid the taint of politics.

As we learn generosity, we can relearn ambition. After all, ambition built Canada. The Canadian Pacific Railway, the St. Lawrence Seaway, and the Trans-Canada Highway were great national projects. There is the microwave network, the CN Tower, the subways of Montreal and Toronto, and Churchill Falls and James Bay, those massive hydroelectric dams in Newfoundland and Quebec. In the 1980s and 1990s, we took on other kinds of nation-building: freeing the British North America Act from British trusteeship; entrenching a Charter of Rights and Freedoms; forging free trade with the United States and Mexico. It is time to build again. Our cities need infrastructure, particularly transportation, and a new emphasis on great cultural institutions, such as the construction of the Canadian Museum for Human Rights in Winnipeg and the renewal of the Royal Ontario Museum in Toronto. The border needs more crossings, especially between Windsor and Detroit. Canada needs better roads and faster trains between Montreal, Ottawa, and Toronto, linking Kingston, London, and Windsor. The same goes for Edmonton and Calgary in burgeoning Alberta. It is time to build a national power grid. Most important, it is time to turn our imagination to energy conservation and environmental protection. There is no reason that Canada cannot become the world's greenest country and Ottawa its greenest city. The environment is the foremost issue of our time and we are poised to lead here, if we have the desire. Other audacious acts? Creating a true common market, freeing the movement of goods, services, labour, and capital within Canada. Establishing a national securities regulatory commission. Narrowing the urban-rural divide. Celebrating the possibilities of the North and reasserting our claim to the Arctic as the ice cap melts. Offering more opportunity to aboriginals and immigrants. This should be our agenda of ambition.

Here, then, are the questions facing Canadians. Do we have the will to reclaim our past? Can we overcome our inferiority/superiority complex regarding America? Can we make our citizenship meaningful? Can we turn Ottawa into a great capital? Can we restore civility to our politics, salute success in our lives, do good at home and around the world?

For all that we have done on the upper half of North America, survival may well be our greatest success. Those countries of wealth and stature with which we compare ourselves – the United States, Britain, Italy, France, Spain, Germany, Japan, Australia – do not live in fear of falling apart. None of their leaders worry, the way ours do, about tomorrow. This never goes away in Canada. In the last generation or so, every decade or so, our agents of division have tested our angels of unity. In the 1960s, it was the FLQ bombings and Charles de Gaulle's "*Vive le Québec libre!*" In the 1970s, it was the October Crisis and the election of the Parti Québécois. In the 1980s and the 1990s, it was the sovereignty referendums and the collapse of constitutional renewal. Like the much-expected pandemic, Canada is overdue for a great reckoning; the return of the Parti Québécois in Quebec City, sooner or later, will surely bring one. We are used to it by now. We are also used to finding a way out. When Pierre Trudeau was asked to name his greatest achievement in almost sixteen years in office, he replied: "I survived." So has Canada, in strange and wondrous ways, for 140 years.

Skeptics might say that Canada's survival isn't as extraordinary as it seems, given the security of our borders and the endowment of our resources. Some might even say that, like the British in the Battle of Britain, we have had more advantages than our mythology allows us to admit. Maybe so. But that should not understate Canada's uncanny sense of self-preservation. In the face of climate and distance, depression and drought, war and rebellion, responsible and irresponsible government, the country endures. Many have doubted that it would. Naturally, the bond-traders, the currency speculators, and the shiver sisters have always bet against us and they have always been wrong. The reason is that there is more to Canada, and its character, than there seems, and it deceives people. George Grant, the philosopher, lamented that we would fall into the arms of the Americans in the 1960s. René Lévesque, the secessionist, promised the independence of Quebec in the 1970s. Ed Broadbent, the social democrat, said that we were through if free trade succeeded in the 1980s. Brian Mulroney, the alarmist, said the same if constitutional reform failed. We are still here. For fourteen decades, Canada has found a way to get by. We often forget that Canada isn't a young country, as our untutored leaders tend to call it. In fact, as a constituted entity, we are old; few nations have been around in their present form as long as Canada.

The reason we have lasted? Canada usually does the sensible thing. When we wanted to settle the hinterland, we invited immigrants. When we threatened to divide over conscription in the 1940s, we equivocated. When we thought the country was "passing through the greatest crisis in its history," as a royal commission warned in 1965, we embraced official bilingualism. When war threatened in the Suez Crisis, we mediated. When we thought Vietnam and Iraq a disaster, we balked. To prevent a permanent underclass, we created a social safety net. To avoid insolvency, we erased the deficit. There was no vision here, just instinct, impulse, and an unspoken sense of the quotidian work of preserving a country. It makes our enterprise fitful and fragile, yes, but not one that will easily disappear. In the language of nations, let it be said, Canada isn't a question mark; it is a colon. We believe that there is more to come. That our story will continue. That others will follow. That our best years lie ahead.

Still, we must realize that there is nothing immortal about Canada. The Soviet Union and Yugoslavia have collapsed. Korea and Cyprus remain divided. China, Indonesia, Malaysia, Nigeria, and other heterogeneous states worry about survival. Other nations worry about solvency. In 1900, Canada and Argentina were both seen as nations of the future. Over the next century, Canada succeeded and Argentina failed. The difference was that Canada enjoyed honest, democratic leadership while Argentina endured corrupt, repressive rule. Argentina is more lively and stylish than Canada, and thinks highly of itself. It is also broke and broken.

A modest prediction: the greatest threat to Canada in the next half century will come not from the United States, which won't absorb Canada, or Quebec, which won't leave Canada (the *indépendantistes* will not win a referendum with a clear majority on a clear question). More likely, the threats to Canada will come from immigration and decentralization. The first will be the great migration. In the next fifty years, the fraying environment and poverty will force millions to leave Africa and Asia, and Canada will face pressure to increase its immigration. Much as they will enrich Canada, immigrants will challenge it. The strains of multiculturalism are already emerging. The second threat will be the quiet devolution. The provinces will continue to demand more powers from the centre and will get them. The Conservatives believe in a smaller federal government. Instinctively, Stephen Harper is a devolutionist; given a majority, he will reduce the authority of the dominion government. After he is gone, his successors will face the same demands for more autonomy from the regions.

The resolution passed by Parliament in 2006 recognizing *les Québécois* as a nation is a body blow to the idea of one Canada, accelerating the prospect of a hollow central authority that speaks for no one. If unchecked, devolution will balkanize Canada, transferring powers to the provinces and turning the Parliament Buildings into a tourist attraction. The failure of the centre to hold, and the division of Canada into fiefdoms held by swaggering sultans, will be exacerbated by the elements of our character: the failure of memory, the weakness of citizenship, the tolerance of ethnic nationalism, the willingness to compromise one too many times. This is a weakness at our core.

The great migration and the quiet devolution will test our capacity for innovation, our sense of moderation, our fondness for ambiguity, and our instinct for survival. Once again, Canada will have to find a way to muddle through, whatever its endless existential questions. Every generation has had to face down the forces of disintegration and every one has. In the years ahead, Canada will have to summon the strength to imagine a country with a clearer idea of itself, a reason to exist at home and abroad, a *projet de société*. A country. Not a cliché, as some would have it. One that believes in itself and has a purpose for itself. A country in more than name.

Canada gave the world basketball, the zipper, Pablum, the paint roller, and, yes, the telephone. If Britain is Burberry – brilliant, durable, and recognizable – Canada is BlackBerry – reliable, modern, and practical. This is the country of three seas, unnamed lakes, romantic rivers, trackless tundra, thick forests, young mountains, and deep valleys. This is the country of the smoked meat sandwich, the Beaver Tail, and the fiddlehead. This is the country of peacekeepers on the ten-dollar bill and reformers on the fifty-dollar bill, making Canada's banknotes its grace notes. Finally, it is the country of ice and skates.

We glide on ponds, lakes, and rivers, and in schoolyards and backyards, too. In Canada, skating is a pastime; skating with a stick is a purpose; skating with others with sticks is a passion. We call that hockey. And hockey, oh hockey, is our high church. For this is the country of the Trail Smokeaters, the Edmonton Oilers, the Toronto Maple Leafs – and the Olympic women's hockey team. Most famously, it is the country of the Montreal Canadiens. Even their name says something about us. Up to the late 1800s, *les Canadiens* were the real Canadians, those who spoke French and lived in Quebec. It is fitting that the name of the greatest team in hockey should marry Montreal, once the foremost city of Canada, and *les Canadiens*, the first Canadians. They have come to represent not just the city and Quebec but something greater than that, the country itself.

For *les Canadiens* are what we were, what we are, and what we may be. For years, they were French and English in perfect balance, one of those few national institutions that brought us together. They were Harvey, Harris, Worsley, and Moore. They were Savard, Rousseau, Tremblay, and Plante. They were the country itself, winning and losing, but mostly winning. In the history of the sport, no team has won more professional championships. Twenty-four pennants hang from the rafters of the Bell Centre in Montreal. And how they won! They were élan itself. The fire of Maurice Richard, the moxie of Doug Harvey, the tenacity of Henri Richard, the power of Bernie Geoffrion, the wings of Yvan Cournoyer, the tentacles of Ken Dryden. Most of all, there was Jean Béliveau, the quintessence of class itself, floating above the maelstrom, his stick a paintbrush sweeping across an incandescent white and blue canvas. Their retired numbers hang from the rafters, too. This is our national portrait gallery.

Their language was not so much English and French, but success. They were what we were. Today, the Canadiens are not just English and French; in fact, they are hardly either, any more. Today they are the world – Swiss, Finns, Russians, Americans, French, Czechs, Kazakhstans. They have no identity crisis. They have no resentment or jealousy or ambiguity and show moderation in everything but the pursuit of excellence. They do not ask who they are and no one asks them. Their temple is cloaked in history – the championships they have won, the torches they have passed. They know where they are from and who came before them. They do not agonize over divided loyalties or different nationalities. They know instinctively where they belong, in the Dominion of Success. These are *les Canadiens*, and these are the Canadians of imagination.

Now, marching to the end of the first decade of the twenty-first century, we are buoyed by our prospects. We have much of what the world wants: space, land, resources, stability, security, tolerance. It is safe to say that we will not disappear, though there will always be those who predict it, wish it, or fear it. It is also safe to say that we will not be what we were; indeed, few of us will remember what we were. But we who live here believe – we must believe – that there will be a country called Canada and that it will exist as more than a virtual country. It will be more than an area code, a postal code, an email address. And we will find, much as it may appear lacking today, the courage, the will and the wisdom to survive. One nation or two, one government or many, one voice or none; we believe in the promise of Canada and struggle to be worthy of it. To deny that is to betray our past and our birthright. We must persevere. We have come too far. We have built too well. We have seen too much. We have fought too hard. We have too much to do. We are favoured and we are unfinished.

Selected Bibliography

Adams, Michael. *Fire and Ice: The United States, Canada and the Myth of Converging Values.* Toronto: Penguin Group, 2003.

Bernstein, Richard. *Fragile Glory: A Portrait of France and the French.* New York: Alfred A. Knopf, 1990.

Black, Conrad. *A Life in Progress.* Toronto: Key Porter Books Limited, 1993.

Brooke, Rupert. *Letters from America.* London: Sidgwick & Jackson Limited, 1931.

Bryce, James. *The American Commonwealth.* London: The Macmillan Company Ltd., 1914.

Bryson, Bill. *Notes from a Small Island.* New York: Avon Books Inc., 1995.

Buchan (O. Douglas), Anna. *Unforgettable, Unforgotten.* London: Hodder and Stoughton Limited, 1945.

Cameron, Stevie. *On the Take: Crime, Corruption and Greed in the Mulroney Years.* Toronto: Seal, 1995.

Clarkson, Adrienne. *Heart Matters.* Toronto: Penguin Group, 2006.

Cohen, Andrew. *While Canada Slept: How We Lost Our Place in the World.* Toronto: McClelland & Stewart Ltd., 2003.

Conway, Jill Ker. *True North: A Memoir.* Toronto: Alfred A. Knopf Canada, 1994.

Cooper, John. *Great Britons: The Great Debate.* London: National Portrait Gallery Publications, 2002.

Dilks, David. *The Great Dominion: Winston Churchill in Canada 1900–1954.* Toronto: Thomas Allen Publishers, 2005.

Fenby, Jonathan. *France on the Brink: A Great Civilization Faces the New Century*. New York: Arcade Publishing Inc., 1998.

Fotheringham, Allan. *Birds of a Feather: The Press and the Politicians*. Toronto: Key Porter Books Limited, 1989.

Gallant, Mavis. *Home Truths: Selected Canadian Stories*. Toronto: Macmillan of Canada, 1981.

Gannon, Martin J. *Understanding Global Cultures: Metaphorical Journeys Through 23 Nations*. London: Sage Publications Inc., 2001.

Gatenby, Greg. *The Wild Is Always There: Canada Through the Eyes of Foreign Writers*. Toronto: Alfred A. Knopf Canada, 1993.

———. *The Very Richness of That Past: Canada Through the Eyes of Foreign Writers Volume II*. Toronto: Alfred A. Knopf Canada, 1995.

Gotlieb, Allan. *The Washington Diaries 1981–1989*, Toronto: McClelland & Stewart Ltd., 2006.

Granatstein, J.L. *Who Killed Canadian History?* Toronto: HarperCollins Publishers Ltd., 1998.

Griffiths, Rudyard, ed. *Great Questions of Canada*. Toronto: Stoddart Publishing Co., 2000.

Hillmer, Norman and Granatstein, J.L. *The Land Newly Found: Eyewitness Accounts of the Canadian Immigrant Experience*. Toronto: Thomas Allen Publishers, 2006.

Horne, Alistair. *Canada and the Canadians: Profile of a Modern Nation*. Toronto: Macmillan Company of Canada, 1961.

Hutchison, Bruce. *The Unknown Country: Canada and Her People*. Toronto: Longmans, Green & Company, 1943.

Ibbitson, John. *The Polite Revolution: Perfecting the Canadian Dream*. Toronto: McClelland & Stewart Ltd., 2005.

Iyer, Pico. *The Global Soul: Jet Lag, Shopping Malls, and the Search for Home*. New York: Alfred A. Knopf, 2000.

Kaplan, William. *Belonging: The Meaning and Future of Canadian Citizenship*. Montreal & Kingston: McGill-Queen's University Press, 1993.

Karnow, Stanley. *Paris in the Fifties*. New York: Times Books, 1999.

Kilbourn, William. *Canada: A Guide to the Peaceable Kingdom*. Toronto: Macmillan Company of Canada, 1970.

Leacock, Stephen. *Canada: The Foundations of its Future*. Montreal: Gazette Printing Company Ltd., 1941.

———. *Sunshine Sketches of a Little Town*. McClelland & Stewart Ltd., 1931.

Levine, Norman. *Canada Made Me*. Ottawa: Deneau & Greenberg, 1979.

Malcolm, Andrew H. *The Canadians: A Probing Yet Affectionate Look at the Land and the People*. Markham: Fitzhenry & Whiteside Ltd., 1985.

Martin, Paul. *A Very Public Life: Volume I, Far From Home*. Ottawa: Deneau Publishers, 1983.

Massey, Vincent. *On Being Canadian*. Toronto: J.M. Dent & Sons (Canada) Ltd., 1948.

Moore, Brian. *Canada*. New York: Time-Life Books, 1963.

Morris, Jan. *Journeys*. Oxford: Oxford University Press, 1984.

Newman, Peter C. *Here Be Dragons: Telling Tales of People, Passion and Power*. Toronto: Douglas Gibson Books, 2004.

———. *The Secret Mulroney Tapes*. Toronto: Random House of Canada, 2005.

Paxman, Jeremy. *The English: A Portrait of a People*. London: Penguin Group, 1999.

Resnick, Philip. *The European Roots of Canadian Identity*. Toronto: Broadview Press Ltd., 2005.

Robins, John D. *A Pocketful of Canada*. Toronto: W.M. Collins Sons & Co., 1946.

Siegfried, André. *Canada: An International Power, New and Revised Edition*. London: Jonathan Cape, 1949.

———. *The Race Question in Canada*. Toronto: McClelland & Stewart Ltd., 1966.

Simpson, Jeffrey. *Star-Spangled Canadians: Canadians Living the American Dream*. Toronto: HarperCollins Publishers Ltd., 2000.

Studin, Irvin. *What Is a Canadian? Forty-Three Thought-Provoking Responses*. Toronto: McClelland & Stewart Ltd., 2006.

Tocqueville, Alexis de. *Democracy in America, Volume I*. New York: Schocken Books, 1972.

———. *Democracy in America, Volume II*. New York: Schocken Books, 1972.

Vance, F. Jonathan. *Building Canada: People and Projects That Shaped the Nation*. Toronto: Penguin Group, 2006.

Wells, Paul. *Right Side Up: The Fall of Paul Martin and the Rise of Stephen Harper's New Conservatism*. Toronto: McClelland & Stewart Ltd., 2006.

Acknowledgements

No book is the work of the author alone. While one name may appear on its cover, a statement of this length is a collective enterprise drawing on a small army of contributors. So it is with *The Unfinished Canadian*.

When I raised the subject of this book with Douglas Pepper, the president of McClelland & Stewart, he immediately wanted to publish it. He has been encouraging, attentive, and convivial, as has the managing editor, Elizabeth Kribs.

This work would have been more difficult and less agreeable without the help of Kristina Roic, a journalist in Ottawa. Kristina made nocturnal visits to the public library and into cyberspace, where she found mountains of material on subjects as esoteric as the sales of sports utility vehicles in Canada, the origins of the tall poppy syndrome, and the size of Hispanic America. She brought organization, enthusiasm, and humour to this enterprise. Lauren Grainger gathered superb material on the United States and Canada while Jordan Smith examined how foreign visitors have viewed Canada. Alexander Cohen, who has a keen interest in history and current events, unearthed forgotten books, including Brian Moore's *Canada*.

Editor Laurie Coulter was clear and meticulous. She caught errors, pruned prose, rearranged sections, and always saw the forest through the trees when I had lost my way. Her instincts were unfailingly sound and her manner consistently generous. She was ably assisted by Jenny Bradshaw, who is blessed with a sharp eye and a deft ear as a copy editor. Jenny was energetic and imaginative. It was a pleasure to work with both of them.

Victor Rabinovitch, the director of the Canadian Museum of Civilization, graciously explained the history, content, and mandate of the biggest museum in the country. J.L. Granatstein, the country's premier historian, reflected on his time at the Canadian War Museum and provided sound thematic advice. Rudyard Griffiths of the Dominion Institute shared his considered view of the country and its history, as did Colin Robertson of the Historica Foundation, who read the manuscript diligently. Ronald Cohen, the superb bibliographer of Winston Churchill, graciously referred me to sources and addressed fine points. Peter Boehm, an assistant deputy minister at Foreign Affairs Canada, generously elaborated on the highly successful evacuation of Canadians from Lebanon in 2006, in which he played a key role.

I want to express my particular gratitude to Norman Hillmer, professor of history and international affairs at Carleton University. Professor Hillmer introduced me to obscure sources, gave parts of the manuscript a careful and constructive reading, and suggested the title of the book. He is a colleague and a friend of great kindness.

Most of all, let me thank my wife, Mary Gooderham, a journalist, author, and editor. She cheerfully read the manuscript, line by line, word by word, with a skeptical, unsparing eye. If her name is not on the cover of this book, her fingerprints surely are. For this and more, I owe her much.

Andrew Cohen
Ottawa
February 22, 2007

Index

DATE DUE

20. 10 30			

DEMCO 38-296

Please remember that this is a library book,
and that it belongs only temporarily to each
person who uses it. Be considerate. Do
not write in this, or any, library book.